SITE-BASED MANAGEMENT IN EDUCATION

HOW TO ORDER THIS BOOK

BY PHONE: 800-233-9936 or 717-291-5609, 8AM–5PM Eastern Time

BY FAX: 717-295-4538

BY MAIL: Order Department
Technomic Publishing Company, Inc.
851 New Holland Avenue, Box 3535
Lancaster, PA 17604, U.S.A.

BY CREDIT CARD: American Express, VISA, MasterCard

PERMISSION TO PHOTOCOPY–POLICY STATEMENT

Authorization to photocopy items for internal or personal use, or the internal or personal use of specific clients, is granted by Technomic Publishing Co., Inc. provided that the base fee of US $3.00 per copy, plus US $ .25 per page is paid directly to Copyright Clearance Center, 222 Rosewood Drive, Danvers, MA 01923, USA. For those organizations that have been granted a photocopy license by CCC, a separate system of payment has been arranged. The fee code for users of the Transactional Reporting Service is 1-56676/95 $5.00 + $ .25.

SITE-BASED MANAGEMENT IN EDUCATION
HOW TO MAKE IT WORK IN YOUR SCHOOL

I. Carl Candoli, Ph.D.

LANCASTER · BASEL

Site-Based Management in Education
a TECHNOMIC publication

Published in the Western Hemisphere by
Technomic Publishing Company, Inc.
851 New Holland Avenue, Box 3535
Lancaster, Pennsylvania 17604 U.S.A.

Distributed in the Rest of the World by
Technomic Publishing AG
Missionsstrasse 44
CH-4055 Basel, Switzerland

Copyright © 1995 by Technomic Publishing Company, Inc.
All rights reserved

No part of this publication may be reproduced, stored in a
retrieval system, or transmitted, in any form or by any means,
electronic, mechanical, photocopying, recording, or otherwise,
without the prior written permission of the publisher.

Printed in the United States of America
10 9 8 7 6 5 4 3 2 1

Main entry under title:
 Site-Based Management in Education: How to Make it Work in Your School

A Technomic Publishing Company book
Bibliography: p.

Library of Congress Catalog Card No. 94-62043
ISBN No. 1-56676-223-5

To my helpmate of over forty years, my wife Joan, without whose assistance and support none of my career successes would have been possible. She has provided quiet support and counsel at every point in a forty-year career in education and has been the inspiration for any accomplishments attained during that time. Joan has been and continues to be the anchor for the family, and we all appreciate her so much.

To our daughter, Julie, who has faced adversity and illness over the past four years, my very best wishes for a complete and timely recovery. Her timely reactions and editing immensely helped speed the writing process and provided a sounding board for ideas and concepts. She brought her attorney's skills to bear and made the manuscript much tidier and focused.

Contents

Introduction ix

1. **DEFINITIONS, PARTICIPANTS, AND GOALS OF SITE-BASED MANAGEMENT**   1

    Definitions 1
    Participants 11
    Strategic Goals (Positive and Negative) 25
    Questions Often Asked About SBM 31
    Vignette #1 34
    Vignette #2 36

2. **SITE-BASED MANAGEMENT—HOW DOES IT AFFECT THE VARIOUS PARTICIPANTS?**   39

    State Department Of Education 41
    Central Office—Superintendent and Support Staff 54
    School Principals 71
    Teachers 83
    Parents and Community 95
    Vignette #1 102
    Vignette #2 105
    Vignette #3 107

3. **PITFALLS, HURDLES, AND OPPORTUNITIES UNDER SITE-BASED MANAGEMENT**   111

    Legal Issues 112

Union/Contract Issues 129
Governance Issues 147
Vignette #1 161
Vignette #2 163

4. A PLANNING/EVALUATION/ DECISION-MAKING MODEL FOR SITE-BASED MANAGEMENT   167

The CIPP (Context, Input, Process, Product) Model 168
School/District/Program Evaluations 182
Urban Elementary School Simulation 189
Personnel Evaluations As A Derivative 197
Questions Arising From the Use of the CIPP Model
   for Evaluation 203
Vignette #1 205
Vignette #2 209
Endnotes 211

Glossary 213

Introduction

American education has always been under attack for not meeting the promise of universal education that American democracy advocates. The educational system has constantly dealt with the need to organize to better meet the needs of the students of the country. Regardless of the millions of students who have been well served, the system continues to strive to meet those difficult needs presented by the students who are not succeeding in the current system.

As American education has struggled through a number of attempts at restructuring/reorganizing over the past several decades, one concept seems to have caught on as a real opportunity for schools and school systems to really reorganize with students foremost in the process. With the focal point being the adaptation of the school/system to serving the students first and foremost, the emerging Site-Based or School-Based Management concept is becoming a tool for those who wish to return the American school to its original mode of serving children as its only objective.

Each decade and its specific concerns seem to bring a new attempt to reorganize the schools of the country—starting with the Conant studies of the 1930s and 1940s, continuing with the Sputnik era concerns over the teaching of science, and on to the concerns over the teaching of hard-to-educate children, the teaching of children with a different primary language, the teaching of urban children, the teaching of rural children, and, finally, the teaching of children of different cultures and melding them into the American dream; many attempts to resolve the issue of the quality of American education have been initiated. More recently, the question of the role of education in the teaching of values and of prayer in the schools has become a most visible and demanding issue for the schools of the country.

As more and more of the nation's resources have been allocated to education, each unit of government has deemed it necessary to place demands on the system. Because of this, the schools have become almost paranoid in their attempt to meet the various demands, some of which are quite contradictory and self-defeating. The organization of the nation's schools has become very specialized in their composition. As each level of government has added its own priorities to the system's tasks, the need for specialized personnel to oversee the particular tasks has become paramount. Thus, we see that there are specialists for every task undertaken by the school system, ranging from specialists for bilingual education to specialists for serving the poor children to specialists for foreign languages and mathematics and extending to specialists for every subject in the curriculum. Additionally, there are specialists for decentralization, for business, for transportation, for security, for food service, for administration, for instruction, for public relations, and for everything that is encompassed by the system.

The highly centralized bureaucracy, which developed along the lines of the huge, highly centralized corporate and governmental organizations, has tended to use much of the resources originally intended to serve the children of the system to, instead, support the centralized organization. Much the way business has learned that the day of the huge centralized bureaucracy can no longer be justified, so, too, schools and school systems have learned that the huge central office, with specialists of every stripe and description, can no longer be able to be justified and supported. Heightened awareness on the part of the public and its demand for increased accountability on the part of the educational system have also contributed to the need for a complete restructuring of the schools and how they deliver educational services. Indeed, in most large school systems, almost 50% of the per pupil expenditure goes to support the infrastructure of the school organization and, therefore, does not go toward the direct support of the child's education.

An anomaly in all of this is that, while many, many changes have taken place in the organizational structure of education and while huge growth in terms of specialists and the central bureaucracy have occurred, little change has come to the classroom or even the campus. Typically, school campuses are organized the same way today as they were several decades ago. Oh, there have been some superficial changes, and the classrooms are much more pleasant and flexible, but the basic structure of the individual classroom is still the same today as it was in the early days of the American school system. The concept of Site-Based Management is seen as an attempt to return to the days when the campus, or school site, made every decision concerning the student and was held responsible for those decisions.

The emerging definition of the Site-Based Management concept is that it is a way of forcing individual schools to take responsibility for what happens to the children under their jurisdiction and attending their school. The concept suggests that, when individual schools are charged with the total development of educational programs aimed at serving the needs of the children in attendance at the particular school, the school personnel will develop more cogent programs because they know the students and their needs.

It is also expected that the need for huge central bureaucracies will diminish as local schools take more of the planning and delivery burden from them. In light of the emerging demand for accountability for student outcomes on the part of educators and the system, this development makes the school site the focal point of such evaluation and places the burden to do something about meeting the educational needs of the students at that site. Teachers, principals, and communities know their students best and can better plan the specific programs needed by their students.

As each wave of reform hit, various states mandated certain developments on the part of the schools of that individual state. In the 1970s, it was state testing and minimum competency, a movement spearheaded by such states as Michigan, California, and New York. In the 1980s, as the reforms of the 1970s proved inadequate, the emphasis became a state-directed curriculum and mandated evaluation of personnel. This was spearheaded by such states as Texas, Kentucky, Connecticut, and Pennsylvania. As this reform also proved to be inadequate for changing the way students performed, state legislatures began to realize that education reform could not be mandated from above and that the huge centralized bureaucracies needed to monitor the reform were not appropriate to the needs of the local school and its students. Thus, we see that, in the decade of the 1990s, the pendulum has shifted from the state level to the district level and, more importantly, to the school-site level. True, the state still insists on the setting of broad goals for the educational system in the form of objectives for achievement and student accomplishment, but the movement is toward the local school system developing specific objectives with which to meet those broad state goals. As awareness that the campus, or site, is the local unit that has the most impact on the student heightens, systems are increasingly moving toward the establishment of some sort of Site-Based Management concept in order to better deliver educational services to the children. Other districts are more rigidly centralizing their organization in order to more firmly monitor the delivery of education to the students of the district. This handbook will best serve those who wish to decentralize their operation so that the site, or campus, level has flexibility in making decisions that affect the students at their location.

This book is written in four major sections, each devoted to a particular area of concern under the Site-Based Management (SBM) concept: The first chapter attempts to define the various terms used in the concept and describes the various participants involved, giving a thumbnail sketch of their obligations under SBM. In addition, Chapter 1 defines the goals and objectives, both positive and negative, that are ascribed to the SBM concept of school organization.

Chapter 2 is devoted to an in-depth look at how the SBM concept affects the various actors in the process and develops their various roles and activities that must be performed if the concept is to succeed. As part of this chapter, questions that arise and must be dealt with and a range of possible responses are discussed.

The third chapter of this handbook deals with the pitfalls, the hurdles, and the opportunities that accompany the move into a Site-Based Management type of operation. This section considers the legal issues involved. Certain union/contract issues are analyzed, and a variety of governance issues are explored in order to make the reader aware of the problems that could present themselves and of the opportunities that are encompassed in SBM development.

Chapter 4 presents a planning/accountability/decision model for use under the SBM mode of operation. The SBM development is an appropriate vehicle for utilizing the Context, Input, Process, Product (CIPP) model of planning/evaluation/decision making, and the model is presented as a mechanism for keeping the SBM mode on target and intact.

Chapter 1

DEFINITIONS, PARTICIPANTS, AND GOALS OF SITE-BASED MANAGEMENT

DEFINITIONS

Site-Based Management

This is sometimes referred to as School-Based Management, School-Based Leadership, or School-Based Decision Making. The concept is that local parents and teachers know their students best and that, through cooperative efforts, they can develop the appropriate programs needed by their children. The concept suggests that certain decisions are the purview of the local site and, thus, have precedence over the central office on these decisions. Typically, the decisions that are decentralized are those that directly affect the student, i.e., program decisions, curriculum decisions, time allocation decisions, and instructional decisions.

While some districts have gone all the way in extending the right of schools to make these decisions, others have restricted the decentralization flexibility to those decisions regarding pedagogy and style of teaching, rather than turning over the whole strategic planning effort to the individual schools. Thus, while the method of delivery of programs is up to the individual school, the meeting of the strategic objectives directly influences the program at the local site. Each building of the school system develops an improvement plan, which is based on the strategic plan of the system, and, through negotiations with the central office, the improvement plan is agreed to and time lines are set for the improvement(s) to begin. This campus improvement plan (CIP) becomes the document against which the school is evaluated over the coming academic year.

Several states (Michigan, Connecticut, Colorado, Kentucky, and Pennsylvania, among others) have introduced the concept of charter schools, which is another offshoot of the Site-Based Management (SBM) concept. Under this provision, a group (teachers, community, private corporation, etc.) develops a proposal for educating a student body. This proposal is submitted to either the state department of education or the governing board of the school system. If approved, the charter is initiated and the group is given the time specified in the proposal to establish the school that they envision for the children under their jurisdiction. Included in the charter are student expectations as to achievement and growth that the charter school must meet.

This, of course, is the extreme application of the SBM principle and provides a complete break from the system. The charter usually mandates complete flexibility for planning and delivery of services and specifies that the students will be served at a cost no higher than the per pupil cost of the district. However, when considering how much of the per pupil costs of the district are allocated to the site, roughly 50%, this is really an opportunity to make a nice profit for the private body or for providing extra resources for the community body initiating the charter. The charter school opportunity has attracted the attention of many private corporations, including Whittle and others. They hope that, through prudent management, they can make a profit while still serving the students of a community.

We shall focus primarily on those SBM schools established through the cooperative efforts of the school system and permitted through board of education policies or state laws. This handbook will attempt to answer some of the more pressing questions and address some unanticipated issues that arise when such a dramatic step is taken.

Centralized Decision Making

Centralized decision making is the typical process in most school systems. Strict procedures and/or processes are established for making almost every decision concerning the operation of the district and the schools/classrooms of the district. Procedures are established for every emerging condition, and, as new situations arise, they are responded to with a new policy governing the issue. Every situation, ranging from grades to instruction to time allocated to discipline, is governed by a specific policy. The building principal and the teachers are almost automatons in their performance.

This type of system usually operates very well but cannot respond well or quickly to emergencies and/or differences. The procedures book is well developed, and the system usually has a fine reputation for being a good school system. This type of school organization is often top heavy with administrative personnel and is a traditionally oriented district. It is best suited to relatively homogeneous systems where the students are largely from similar backgrounds and economic status.

Decentralized Decision Making

Large organizations concerned with the slowness of decisions and how ineffective these decisions were becoming began to establish certain parameters for making these decisions on a more decentralized basis. These large school districts provided their mid-management administrators the opportunity to react to emerging situations and to make those decisions locally as the need arose. The need to present a more humane and human face to the community also led to some of the decentralization efforts. As early as the 1960s, New York City and Chicago underwent efforts to decentralize their school systems. While these efforts were largely rudimentary and merely involved the decentralization of the huge central staffs to a more regional location, they were, nonetheless, efforts to make the system more responsible to its constituents. However, the established procedure was the guiding light in making decisions and woe be to the administrator who ignored the procedures that had been established for a particular situation. More recently, some decentralization efforts have attempted to permit the local staff and administrator flexibility in making certain decisions. Site-Based Management permits great flexibility in making decisions concerning students and how they are to be educated.

State Department of Education

Each state has the power to establish and govern all education systems in the state. Local boards of education are really agents of the state elected locally, and they must govern the local schools in accordance with state laws on education. Every state has a state department of education-type of organization, except for Hawaii, which has only one school district for the entire state and, thus, the state department is also the local school system organization. The state department of education serves at the pleasure of the legislature and the state board of education and exists, mainly, to monitor the state laws pertaining to education and providing leadership for those in the educational systems of the state. Each state has the power to establish and govern all education systems in the state.

During the 1970s and 1980s, state departments of education became much more centralized than ever before, with almost every state mandating certain programs and procedures from the local districts. While state departments are not involved in the direct education process with students, they do have enormous power to influence the education of public school students in the state.

State Board of Education

Most state boards of education have policy-setting and enforcement power. State boards of education, along with the state legislature, set the expectations for the public schools of the state, establish strategic educational plans for the state, monitor the schools of the state, and distribute the monies that the state provides local districts. The state board of education is usually elected, but some are appointed by the legislature and/or the governor. State superintendents are, likewise, either appointed and/or elected. State legislative bodies expend much energy in passing laws governing the local education system and mandating certain programs and curricula. State boards of education have the duty to enforce the educational laws and to set education policy for the schools of the state. Furthermore, the state board is charged with monitoring the state education laws and how well the local school districts meet the intent of those laws.

Local Board of Education

The principle of local control by a lay board of education is a most important principle of the American school system. Democratic principles require that agencies such as school districts are to be governed by lay citizens of the state and community. Members of the local board of education are state officials elected or appointed locally. They serve, usually for no pay, for a specified term and are charged with the setting of educational policy consistent with state law.

Many boards do not recognize the fact that they are state officers and think that they can develop any type of system that they wish; however, they are soon indoctrinated into the realities of the state education laws. Most boards accept the premise that they are to establish education policy and to hire a good superintendent who shall perform the duties of chief executive officer of the board. Some, however, do not accept this pattern and insist on participating in every decision made in the school system. This often leads to difficulty in the system, with the state sometimes entering the debate and taking action against the board. Sometimes, this behavior is reflected in the resignation of the superintendent and/or the recall of certain board members by the electorate. The principle of local control by a lay board is a most important principle of the American school system.

Superintendent of Schools

The superintendent position is unique to the United States and Canada and is that of chief executive officer of the board of education. The person serves at the pleasure of the board of education, usually holding a contract for a specified number of years. As chief executive officer of the board of education, the superintendent is charged with the implementation of all policies of the board and state and federal laws governing education and must provide leadership to the system. Most superintendents have served as teachers and principals during their career and have gained certification for the position by attending classes and completing certain certification requirements. Typically, the requirements include several years of service as a teacher, attainment of mid-level management positions, and additional certification work completed at a local and/or state university. Many states have initiated a testing procedure as a final requirement for attaining the superintendent's certificate.

Principal

The principal is the administrator responsible for the activities and program conducted at the school where he/she is the principal. Usually, the principal has served as a teacher and has, through advanced education and meeting certification requirements, become licensed to be considered for the principalship. He/she provides the leadership to the school staff and community in the delivery of the instructional program of the school. In the traditional organization, the principal implements board policy and follows procedures as established and monitored by the central office. In the emerging Site-Based Management school, the principal becomes the lightning rod for every change and program that is implemented at the school and assumes a much more important role in the scheme of things. He/she must work well with such diverse groups as those in the faculty, staff, and community. More than just following policy, the position requires that the person be a planner, a leader, and a conciliator in order to be successful. The principal under the SBM concept is, in fact, a mini-superintendent and serves the community/school as the chief executive officer.

Support Staff—School

The people involved at the school level, either professionally or in a nonprofessional capacity, are known as the support staff. They may include such personnel as cooks, secretaries, custodians, teacher's aides, and other nonprofessionals or such certified personnel as psychologists, counselors, and other specialized personnel. They perform their specialty at the site level. They have full rights as members of the staff and are expected to participate in the decisions made under the SBM proviso.

Support Staff—System

These are the folks who provide the multitude of services ranging from transportation to maintenance to food services to security in the noninstructional area. They also includes the many specialists who develop the instructional program, the curriculum of the district, the business office personnel, and others who are certificated and provide services that are so important to the local site, but who are quartered away from the actual site. These personnel are often referred to as being part of the "bureaucracy" and are often in charge of one facet or other of the school system. Under SBM, this staff must move from a "directing" staff to a true support staff and be available to the school for the resolution of any problem that it has. This requires a different set of skills and a vastly different mind-set.

Community Member

Community members are those who live in the school attendance area. They are primarily the parents of the children who attend the school but can also include any citizen living in the attendance area who desires to participate in the affairs of the school. Community members are often the source of substantial resources in the form of donated services, volunteer assistance, and special techniques and/or knowledge about specific topics. The community is often the source of support and sustenance for the school and its personnel.

Participatory Governance

Under the SBM concept, participatory governance is the rule, rather than the exception. Each element of the campus organization, school staff, principal, students, parents, and community are provided the opportunity to participate in the decisions to be made at the school. Usually, a site governance committee is selected with representation from each element of the school community. This committee is charged with making certain decisions affecting the school and its students.

Strategic Plan

The strategic plan is the document that the school system utilizes to delineate the activities and programs of the school system for a specified period of time. The plan covers all aspects of the school district and specifies the resources needed to implement the plan. The strategic plan usually answers the questions, ''what, where, when, why, and how'' and is the guiding light for the members of the school system staff. The strategic plan is usually assembled through the cooperative efforts of staff, students, community, and board of education. It is updated annually as a result of the annual evaluation, at which time the objectives are revised and/or new objectives are highlighted for the coming year.

The strategic plan forces the board to make priority decisions as to where they allocate the resources available.

Campus Improvement Plan

The campus improvement plan (CIP) is assembled by the local school unit after the strategic plan is adopted by the board of education. It is developed as a site response to the strategic plan but also incorporates the local nuances needed to make the strategic plan a reality for the local school. In other words, the strategic plan sets the mode for the CIP, but the CIP is the local interpretation of the strategic plan into site-based objectives that reflect the needs and strengths of the local staff, student body, and community. The CIP is developed locally by the staff, principal, and community and is presented to the board. The board and local community then negotiate the plan as the mechanism for implementing the program at the local school for the coming year.

Organization of the School District

When projecting the structure of the school district under the SBM type of organization, several changes come quickly to the fore. These changes are best shown through the use of sample organizational charts (see Table 1.1 and Table 1.2). Table 1.1 is a typical organizational chart utilizing a traditional organizational structure, while Table 1.2 shows the organization under an SBM structure.

As Table 1.1 shows, the structure of the traditional organization is strictly a top-down decision-making, directive-issuing organizational pattern, while Table 1.2 shows the participatory nature of the organization.

Table 1.1 indicates the many layers of management that must be appeased in order to arrive at a decision and is a pyramid, with power flowing from the top and, finally, down to the school-site levels. Each layer of the organization has certain prerogatives and decision-making authority, all of which affect the school.

Under Table 1.2, the school has a straight line reporting relationship to the chief executive officer (superintendent), and all of the other central office personnel are support staff, on call at the request of the school. This allocates the decision power in a vastly different manner than does the traditional organizational pattern.

TABLE 1.1 Traditional Organizational Chart.

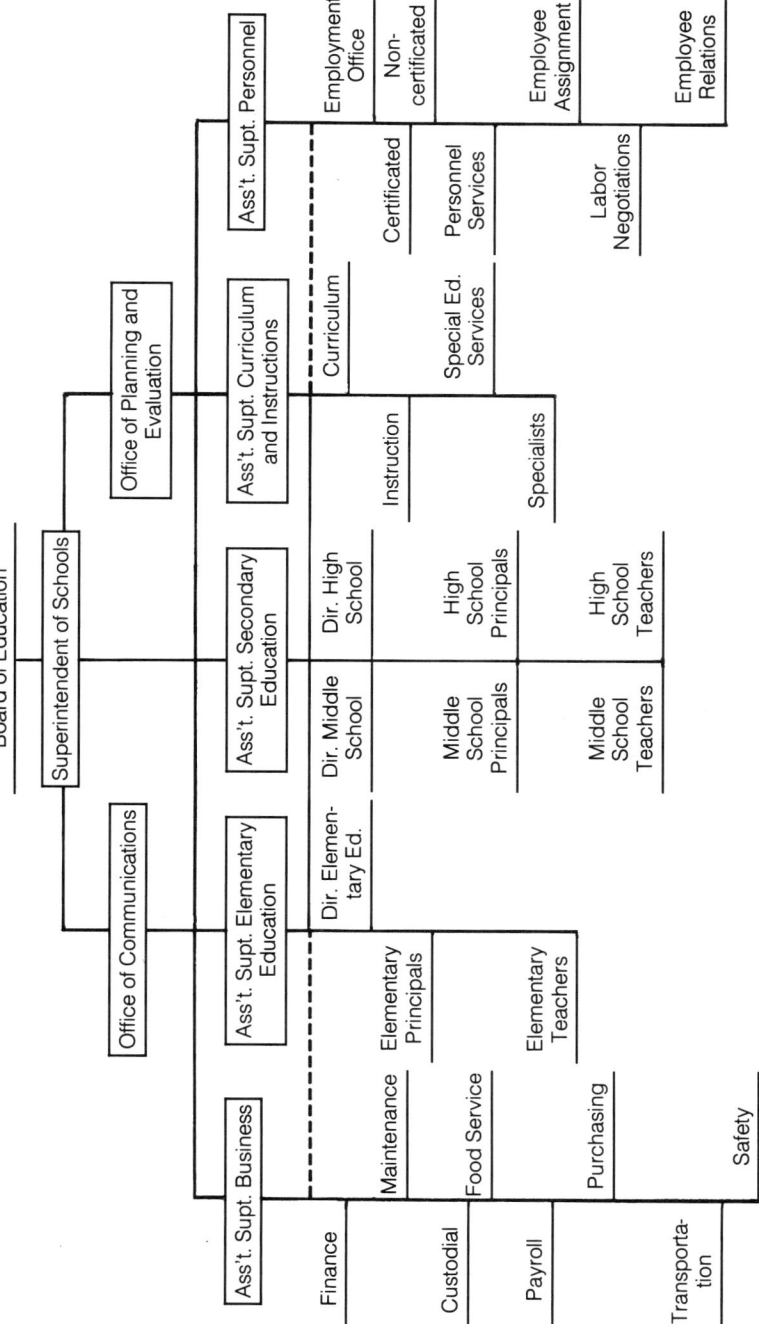

9

TABLE 1.2 *District Organization under SBM.*

Community — Board of Education — Office of Superintendent — CIC — Principals — Teachers — Students

Planning and Evaluation | Communications | C and I | H. I. Services | Human Resources | Finance | I. S. Services

As Table 1.2 also indicates, the number of central office staff members could be vastly reduced under the SBM type of organization and those resources allocated to the school to assist in the planning and delivery of needed programs directly to the students. Table 1.3 is provided to indicate the organization of the local campus under the SBM type of organization.

PARTICIPANTS

While SBM is easy to define and identify, the number of individuals and groups that must participate in the process in order for it to be successful is quite extended. This section of the handbook will identify those particular elements and attempt to define their contribution to the effort.

School Staff—Teacher

The total staff of the school, including teachers, principal, nonteaching staff, and support staff, must become familiar with the concept and accept their roles in the execution of the SBM mandate for it to be successful. The basic premise of SBM is that the staff of a school are the most knowledgeable and understanding about the educational needs of a student body and can, through careful and focused planning, develop the appropriate programs to enable the students to achieve in the manner that they should and can.

Because the teaching staff has the most to gain and/or lose from movement into the SBM arena, they must, first and foremost, be committed to the notion that they can and will develop appropriate programs for the children in their charge. This means that they must have the ability to conceptualize and develop different approaches to instruction if that is what is needed to enable the students to succeed.

The move from a traditional program and organization to SBM demands a change in the traditional role of the teacher: from a conventional role of dispenser of facts and data to a role as manager of the learning system. This learning system is predicated on the particular learning style of each student, and the teacher must manage each of the students' learning styles and prepare instruction according to those learning styles. This is, of course, a difficult and vastly different process than has ever been attempted before in American classrooms.

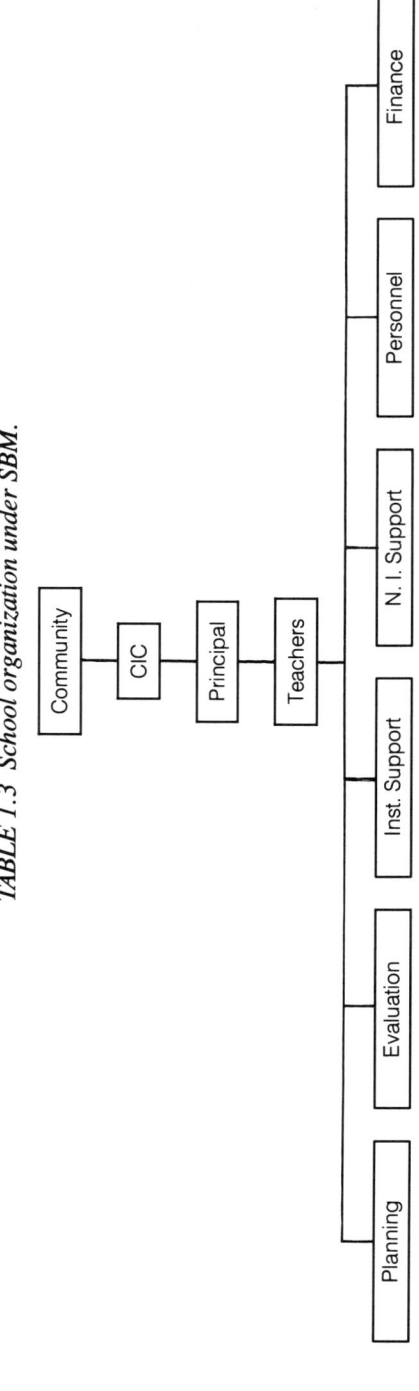

TABLE 1.3 School organization under SBM.

Among the increased demands that this places upon the teacher are the ability to diagnose the learning styles of each child in the class and, further, the capacity to develop an instructional process that meets the learning styles included in the total class. The teacher must gather the appropriate responses to reach each child from whereever he/she can and direct them to the child in the appropriate milieu and time. This is a most rigorous and demanding professional task for the teacher. The teacher can no longer shut the door to the classroom and do her/his thing while all others are excluded from the room. The needs of the student take precedence over everything, and cooperative planning is called for between the various teachers on the staff. SBM strongly suggests a requirement for individual education plans (IEPs) for every student in the class.

Teachers must accept the notion that the development of IEPs for every student takes many staff members working cooperatively in order to bring the best resources and talents to bear on the needs of the particular student. This, of course, means that teachers must learn to work together, must develop the capacity and talent to plan for each student, must learn to diagnose and prescribe programs to meet the needs of every student, and must match students to teachers who can best help the student. The day of the teacher as the individual performer is gone, replaced with a team effort geared to assisting every student in meeting his/her potential.

The teacher must also participate in the development of the school plan for improvement, as well as assist the principal and community in developing the policies that shall govern the school in all of its efforts. While not every teacher has the time or inclination to participate in all of the activities of the school, teachers must choose those from among them who are willing and able to contribute to the development of a total school effort to implement Site-Based Management.

With the advent of the personal computer and through the magic of technology, the classroom teacher has enormous assistance in the development and manipulation of a constant data pool on which to base decisions concerning the applicability and appropriateness of certain programs. The tracking of student achievement is made so much easier through the use of the computer. Teachers can quickly accomplish a series of chores needed before individual programs can be developed.

The teacher is the primary professional charged with the responsibility for developing all facets of the program for the student in his/her classroom. The talents and skills needed to successfully involve other staff members and parents in the decision-making process must be developed and honed for the process to work as it is intended. Thus, the teacher must form alliances with significant others in the student's life, i.e., parents, advisors, etc., to gather sufficient data on which to base program efforts. The more that the teacher knows about the student, the better the program will meet the needs of the student. Diagnoses based on data lead to successful prescription for appropriate programs to serve the student.

The teaching staff must learn to accommodate every contingency that might arise under the organizational pattern. First, they must do away with prescribed time sequences for each subject since the amount of time will vary with how much time each student needs to master the topic. This means that class sizes and groupings will vary from the norm, and the teaching staff must become comfortable with this kind of shifting arrangement in order to serve the students. It is also important to suggest here that peer teaching and learning are extremely appropriate under an SBM arrangement. It is not possible to anticipate all of the various kinds of groupings that might prove effective under the SBM approach to instruction, but it is safe to say that the teacher must be very flexible in her/his approach.

School Staff—Nonteaching or Support

While not directly engaged in the teaching act, the non-teaching or support staff of the school has a vital role to play under the SBM concept. Each of the nonteaching staff member provides key support services to enable the classroom teacher perform his/her duties. Whether the services be direct services such as guidance, psychological support, health services, or other, the direct support staff is a part of the group that must diagnose and develop appropriate program efforts to meet the students' learning needs.

The professional support staff assists the teacher by participating in the diagnostic process and advising in the prescriptive process. Each of the specialists can and do make significant contribution to the final plan by providing the expertise needed to develop an appropriate diagnosis of the child. Each support staff member can call attention to certain facts and data about the child and interpret these data to assist in the final IEP. In many instances, the psychological personnel are charged with the translation of certain tests and other data so as to make the classroom teacher aware of specific needs and/or idiosyncrasies the student brings to the school. The psychologist serves as an excellent sounding board for the teaching staff as they develop the final IEP for the student.

Each professional support staff member brings with him/her certain strengths and professional capacities that should be utilized in the development of IEPs for each student. The nurse or health member of the team has health data that could influence the type of instructional program that is appropriate for that student, while the counselor has certain personal facts and data needed to ascertain what specific types of instructional approaches are most proper for that student. By providing their professional expertise and specific talents, these professionals can contribute much to the final IEP as it affects the student.

The noncertified members of the team are equally important because they provide the indirect support services that are so important to the successful implementation of programs under the SBM concept. These paraprofessionals do the many tasks that are so critical to school functions and without which the school and the students cannot be served. Such "mundane" tasks as cleaning the school, maintaining the equipment and classrooms, providing for the utilities needed to make the school comfortable for the students and staff, preparing the food for the students and staff, and keeping track of the many records that are so crucial to the welfare of each student and staff member are all noteworthy tasks that must be performed in a timely and appropriate manner. These people must also be considered valuable support team members, and, as such, they must be included in all of the planning efforts and decisions made at the campus. Often, in our experience, these personnel make valuable contributions because they possess certain talents and skills that are not present in the professional component of the staff.

Principal

The principal of the school is the most important element of the school in terms of implementation of SBM and all that it implies. This professional educator must be a most flexible and accommodating individual who has a set of values and an unshakable resolve to serve the students of the school. His/her primary role is to be the advocate for the students of the school and to make sure that all of the activities at the school are directed toward the development of appropriate programs to serve those students.

Being the successful principal in the traditional school is much easier and less demanding than being the successful school leader under the SBM concept of operation. In the traditional organization, the principal utilizes the procedures manual before making a decision and has the central office to call on in those cases where the procedures manual does not address the issue. Under SBM, the principal must make decisions, often cooperatively, that reflect what is best for the individual student. While the central office is on call, its advice and counsel are just that, and the principal must make the final decision and take the responsibility for that decision.

Principal certification programs do not prepare individuals for assuming this new kind of role. Indeed, most certification programs ignore the instructional leadership component of the principal's role entirely and focus instead on business management, personnel, and other activities of the principalship. As the instructional leader of the school, the principal must exercise the vision to make the staff and community aware of the school's potential and the path toward achieving the projected gains.

Under SBM, the principal must become the chief planner for the building and learn to utilize the many strengths of the staff and community in the planning effort. The principal must be skilled in all areas of school administration in order to perform the tasks of the principalship under Site Based Management. This includes such disparate areas as finance, instruction, personnel, support services, and every other area that impacts the local school effort to bring an appropriate educational program to the students. While the principal is only one person among many professionals, he/she sets the stage for professional involvement and cooperative development of programs and activities to serve the students and community of the school. The capacity of the principal to engender cooperative involvement of the entire staff and community is the extent to which the school can meet its role in the education of the students in the attendance area.

The emerging role of the principalship is one that demands the capacity to be both a manager and a visionary—to be able to develop a grand plan for meeting educational objectives, as well as managing the scarce resources allocated the school. The principal must be able to meld the total staff and community into a cohesive force directed toward the implementation of a well-planned and well thought out education program to serve the students of the school.

Therefore, the position of principal is becoming among the most important positions in the school hierarchy and demands that the very best personnel of the school system aspire to these positions. University programs for certification of principals must change to reflect the emerging roles and responsibilities being assumed by (allocated) principals. This means that the position's value and status must reflect the new and emerging definition of the position. The salary and status accorded the position of principal should be, at least, at the level of recognition of those who fill directors' positions and, perhaps, equal to those at the assistant superintendent level. While remuneration and recognition are not the most important things to consider for principals, they are important to the totality of the situation and must be provided for if the district is to become a true SBM district.

Superintendent

As the chief executive officer of the school system, the superintendent must also change many behaviors and previously held responsibilities in order for the SBM concept to be effectively implemented. First and foremost, the superintendent must set the stage for a dramatic change in the entire role and concept of the central office staff: from one of directing the system and programs to one of supporting the local units as they develop plans to meet the needs of the students in their charge. This is probably the single most important and difficult task the superintendent faces when the system commits to developing the SBM approach to the delivery of services. Second, the superintendent must recognize that he/she must share the development of a vision with all of the principals of the school system and assist the principals in their participation in the effort. Third, as the local board develops policies to permit the development of the SBM concept, the superintendent must assist the board in recognizing the changes needed in their behaviors so that the SBM concept can proceed.

The planning role of the superintendent becomes even more important under the SBM concept because his/her office now initiates the development of a series of plans at the school level to implement those strategic goals and objectives that have been adopted as the school system objectives. As individual schools develop their CIP to meet the district's strategic goals, the superintendent must evaluate those plans against the system's strategic plan and negotiate the appropriate CIP to implement.

This requires much greater planning expertise and the ability to interpret the school plans as they apply to the master plan for the district.

In the area of school operation, the superintendent must also change his/her position from one of unilateral control and complete authority to one of shared control and support activity. As the schools develop their plans, the superintendent must become the advocate for the schools and provide them the necessary support in order for them to implement their plans. The superintendent must become a committed evaluator, as well as an exemplary planner. Evaluation becomes a most important activity for the central office. The superintendent must lead in the development of the capacity to gather and interpret the data necessary to the evaluation process.

With staff and community at the local school level becoming much more involved in the planning/evaluation/decision-making process, the office of superintendent must become the appellate body, which mitigates disputes and disagreements that arise from time to time. This means that the superintendent must develop listening skills and become much more tolerant of differences. His/her office must also learn to develop consensus and to apply the skills needed in order to negotiate successfully the plans for each school.

The role and responsibilities for the office of superintendent must change. New and different skills will be important for the person who fills the position of superintendent of schools. While still assuming the responsibility for the education of all students in the system, the emerging role is more one of collaboration, of support activity, of consensus building, and of providing vision and leadership to a most disparate set of schools and staff in order to provide the best possible program of education for the students of the system.

Central Office Staff

The central office staff of the school district has the most to lose and/or gain from the implementation of the SBM organizational pattern. Obviously, the central office loses authority in terms of the power to dictate and direct program activities to the various schools. In addition, some may perceive that the central office suffers a reduction in status among the hierarchy and patrons of the school system.

It is true that the central office personnel must markedly change their mode of behavior and their own perceptions of the tasks that are assigned them. For example, the personnel located at the central office must become accomplished planners/evaluators and support personnel. Because this role is so different from the traditional role that they have performed, some doubt that this can be accomplished without major implications for the district as a whole. If the central staff does not or cannot accept this new role, the SBM process is doomed to failure, because the central staff can and will subvert the entire process and make sure it is not given a chance to succeed.

The typical central office staff member is a specialist in one of the many disciplines that comprise the total program of the district. This person has the most knowledge about the particular area of his/her expertise and is employed to develop the district's expertise in that particular area. Site-Based Management suggests that all of these experts become generalists in the planning/evaluation arena, while continuing to provide the special expertise that the district originally employed them for. Since the local school is charged with developing specific improvement plans and since the school must develop responses to every curricular area, through their Campus Improvement Plans (CIPs), the central staff's contribution to this effort is to be available for consultative participation in the development of the CIP at the request of the school. The central staff must also be available and ready to evaluate CIPs and to negotiate the final CIP for implementation.

The introduction of the SBM concept must be predicated on the system's needs and should spring from a long and careful discussion of how the district can make student program offerings more appropriate to the needs of the student. This discussion should set the stage for an exploratory move to consider the various options available to the school district and for more extended discussions about these various options. In larger districts, it is soon apparent that more flexibility is needed to respond to unique and particular student needs.

Once the central staff decides that there are better ways to organize the delivery of education services and that, perhaps, the flexibility inherent in SBM is appropriate for district consideration, the mechanism for dramatic change is in place. It is always best to allow the SBM concept to emerge from such discussions because, if the process is started through a local initiative, it will have a greater chance for survival and successful implementation.

One district known to the author decided to train every one of its curriculum specialists as planners/evaluators and also decided to take two years to make the transition of the major role changes in the organization. To the everlasting credit of the central staff involved, approximately twenty-five persons, this approach worked very well. The central staff embraced the new and emerging concept by participating in defining and trying their new role over the two years. As a result, this district is now into its third year under the SBM concept, and the central staff is fully involved in the development and testing of the model they are using.

In many districts known to the author, where state law has mandated the move to SBM, the central staff has deliberately and carefully subverted the effort by placing roadblocks and obstacles in the way of implementation. In these cases, the central staff view the process as a threat to their job security and do their utmost to destroy the concept. This is very shortsighted and delays the move to SBM for a long period of time.

The central staff has an important role and a significant responsibility for the introduction of SBM and its successful implementation by changing their own perceptions of the role that they must play in the process. As the central staff starts to consider the changes in their behavior patterns that must accompany the move to SBM, they soon realize that they are moving from a directing position to a supporting position and that those skills needed are much different from those previously used skills. The central staff of the district must have a participatory role in the development of the concept as it applies to the district and must "buy" in to the concept and be comfortable with it.

Parents and Community

The community, too, is an essential component of the SBM process because they must be full partners in making the process work for the betterment of the students' instructional program. By community, we mean the parents of the students at the school, as well as the other community members, including the business community, who have so much invested in the educational system and who support it through the taxes they pay.

The community really owns the school and, because they own the institution, they have a participatory right to be a part of the governance structure. Typically, the community does not directly participate in the governance of the education system but, rather, participates through the members of the board of education that they have elected. Under the SBM concept, the community is directly involved through membership on the site council and its efforts. This is not a PTA type of activity but a much more demanding and explicit role for the community.

The parents and community participate directly in the planning process and in the development of the CIP which provides the direction for the school as they strive to improve the students' performance. The community also must participate directly in the evaluation effort because the school judges its efforts at implementing the CIP for the year.

Parents and community have great insights as to the effectiveness of the program and can, through their assistance and support, make the program even better and more effective.

Parents have much to contribute to the educational effort through a number of support activities. These activities include volunteering at the school, providing assistance to teachers at the school, providing expertise in topics in which they have knowledge, giving support and assistance to those directly involved in the evaluation effort, and providing general support activity for the program of the school. Many parents have special skills and attributes that could make the program much more effective and focused. Other parents and community members have the talents needed to make the program much more effective in dealing with the special differing needs of each student. For example, some parents can tutor students in mathematics or science or other curriculum areas, thereby providing "one-to-one" assistance.

Most community involvement committees generate community participation by developing the strengths of the various elements that the community provides and matching these strengths with the specific needs that the school identifies. In this way, the community is able to offer its assistance to the school while not wasting the effort and energy of its members in meaningless activities.

Through active recruitment and encouragement of persons with specific skills to join the effort, a community involvement committee can generate almost all of the expertise necessary to meet the various and diverse needs of the student body. By carefully planning and identifying student needs, the community involvement committee can determine those skills needed by the students and staff that must be generated from outside the community and initiate a search for these particular strengths in the broader community. In one district known to the author, the site governance committee chooses the community involvement committee through the use of those volunteering their time and efforts and by encouraging those who have something to contribute to get involved with the process. This particular district encouraged the adoption of all of the schools within the district by outside groups such as businesses, church groups, service clubs, and/or other community minded groups and, thus, provides for those areas that the local community could not meet. In this way, a much broader and more comprehensive effort can be mounted to meet the diverse needs of the student population.

State Department of Education

For an SBM concept to succeed, the state department of education must be involved to the extent necessary for them to ignore deviations from the state mandates that may be irrelevant because of the different focus of the SBM concept. For example, SBM demands much more flexibility and capacity to respond to particular situations without consulting a manual of policies and procedures. If a school were to make a response to a situation that is not in accordance with state policies, the state department could conceivably veto the approach of the school and destroy the SBM concept. Some exemption for those schools that choose to implement the SBM style of operation is in order, so that the schools choosing to embark on this type of organizational pattern can do so without fear of retribution.

While certain rules and regulations are needed to protect the students of the state, many of these become a restrictive mandate on the implementation of SBM at the school level. For example, the rules and regulations governing the pupil/teacher ratio that is in effect in some states could destroy the staffing pattern and adult/student ratios that are a part of certain SBM plans. Where the state may place a 22/1 student teacher ratio as an absolute, the school may wish to implement a 10/1 adult/student ratio, and, in order to accomplish that, they may have to go with a 30/1 student/certified teacher ratio, with the rest of the staff being made up of paraprofessionals. If the state department were to strictly enforce the student/certified teacher ratio, the district or school that wanted to provide a student/adult ratio of 10/1 could not do so. Some sort of exemption policy should be developed so that schools who wished to deviate from certain state laws and policies could get the exemption for a specified number of years or until the evaluations could be accomplished. These evaluations could be used to certify the concept and/or deviation and permit the deviation to continue.

In some states, the department of education initiates the movement toward SBM because the state law requires that it be implemented and charges the Department of Public Instruction (DPI) with its execution. In these instances, the DPI encourages the local districts to initiate planning for the implementation of an SBM concept. As was indicated earlier in this handbook, this is not the best way to get into the development of such a concept and should be looked at with great care and doubt. If the local district has the desire to explore and develop the concept, the task becomes one that is so much easier and more likely to succeed. At any rate, the DPI must be alerted to the need for exemptions whenever the local district embarks on such an enormous change, and the DPI must agree that they will observe and not secondguess the effort for a prescribed period of time.

State departments can and should develop the capacity to assist and encourage local districts to move toward SBM by providing consultative planning and evaluation assistance and by offering staff development activities that provide the local staff with training in the alternative types of behavior necessary to the successful implementation of SBM. This is not an easy task and one that some, of the bureaucratic persuasion, might consider below their dignity. However, when one considers that the previous, top-down directed reforms in education were complete failures, the change in duties for the state department is also in order. State officials must consider that their roles will change from one of complete control and direction to one of planning and evaluation through support activity and staff development in order for the needed changes to occur.

State officials must accept the new and changed roles that are mandated in order for new and emerging organizational patterns to reach fruition. It is important for the state to define what education should do, in broad strokes, and then assist the local districts in developing their strategic plans, under which CIP's can be formed and direct student learning programs can be delivered. The state must assume a monitoring role and an evaluative role in which the local district is examined and its strategic plan is approved for implementation. Then the state should assist the local district in providing the assistance to the school as it determines the priorities and parameters of the CIP.

State departments of education have much to contribute in the form of developmental efforts and planning and evaluation. They can and must assist the local district as it develops its planning expertise and its evaluation capacity by offering its knowledge and talent in the training of local personnel.

Teacher Training Institutions

The universities and institutions of higher education must also recognize and understand their changed role under the SBM concept. Change is not only for the school staff and community under SBM. It also is implied for those who assist the local school by providing personnel and certified teachers. Because the definition of teacher is being modified from the person who dispenses factual knowledge to the person who is charged with the management of the learning systems that serve the student, the production of teachers requires massive change. This will mandate that teacher training institutions rethink their current programs and redefine their efforts in order to provide prospective educators with the necessary skills and techniques to serve the students of the school that is organized under the SBM concept.

Traditional teacher training programs are unable to assist the educator in developing the skills needed under an SBM type of organization in which the teacher is part of the governance and decision-making structure. The presentation of certain factual information is a far cry from the management of the learning system that provides the basis for the instructional program for the student. Such a learning system is predicated upon educational needs determined by the diagnoses of the student's learning capacities and needs. From these determinations, the program is derived and implemented. The capacity to perform such discrete and highly technical activities, in addition to knowing the subject matter involved with the particular grade and/or curriculum specialty, suggests that the prospective teacher must be educated at a much higher level than ever before.

Given the new role for the teacher as that of a participant in the total organization of the school, including the financial decision making, as well as the many other focal points of the institution, is it any wonder that the university must change its methods for preparing teachers for assuming their roles in the emerging SBM concept?

STRATEGIC GOALS (POSITIVE AND NEGATIVE)

Student Learning

One of the strongest rationales for moving toward the SBM mode of operation is the capacity to make the school more responsive to student needs. The basic premise of SBM is developing appropriate student learning goals and the flexibility needed to reach these goals.

As a district develops its particular strategic plan and prioritizes the goals and objectives for student learning, the probability of meeting those student learning goals must enter the picture and be recognized as an important consideration for the staff and board. If, under existing organizational patterns, the probability of success in achieving the student goals and objectives as developed for the district is not forthcoming, the district must consider other delivery systems for achieving the important student learning goals and objectives. Among the alternatives to be considered is the SBM type of organization.

The most compelling attribute of the SBM structure is the capacity for the school to quickly develop appropriate responses to emerging learning needs. The staff can and must develop IEPs for each student, and, in the development of these, many alternative approaches are in order. The school has the ability to grasp any of the alternatives in order to serve the learning needs of any student without going through the long and tedious process ordinarily needed before implementation of new and different programs.

Another significant attribute of SBM is that it forces complete attention on the needs of the students and minimizes the staff and adult needs for attention and power. While staff must focus on student needs, they can also be provided relief from bureaucratic directives and rules. Instead, the school, under SBM, can develop its own responses to the needs of the students under its jurisdiction and control.

For example, if the district's strategic plan calls for a priority to be given to the development of writing skills of students and the school has formulated an approach to the development of student writing skills through the use of newsletters produced by students and through the use of other similar approaches, the central office cannot force the use of their particular curriculum recommendation as the only approach to teaching writing skills. The school is free to use its own approach until the annual evaluation determines the validity and effectiveness of the approach.

Similarly, student instructional goals developed as priority strategic goals at the district level can be interpreted at the school level with a variety of differing approaches, as developed by the staff at the schools. Given the difference between schools and the variations among students and staffs, it is appropriate that every school develop responses aimed at the particular needs of the students at that site, taking into account the strengths of that staff. Such differences, while not always major or unique, are to be considered when developing appropriate responses to student learning needs. It is that flexibility that makes SBM the emerging structure to be considered in the coming decades.

A danger inherent in the SBM process is that the schools set their expectations too low and, thereby, cheat the students, by assuming such low expectations, which are far below the capacity of their students. That is why the Site Improvement Plan (SIP), or Campus Improvement Plan (CIP), must be the result of negotiations between the school and the central office, to determine the applicability of the plan to the strategic plan of the district. During the negotiations, the staff has ample opportunity to defend its plan and the level of expectations they have established for their students. At this time, the central staff has the obligation of making sure that the school plan is a realistic and appropriate activity to engage in. Such concerns as the level of difficulty of the program and the appropriateness of various responses to student needs must be considered at this time. School staff must, as they plan, consider the strategic plan of the district as the overarching parameter for the SIP. The strategic plan sets the limits and defines the particular goals for the school. The plan must reflect the school interpretation of the district's goals for student achievement.

Flexibility of Operations

The beauty of the SBM concept is its flexibility and ease of implementation. The school becomes the focal point of all instructional planning and delivery, and everything else is support for those activities. Thus, the student is recognized as the main concern for the staff of the school where the student is located and where he/she is to be served. Strategic goals for the district must encompass school flexibility to derive its student learning goals and objectives from the district's goals. These district goals must offer the needed flexibility to maximize the ability of the school to focus on the student needs deemed the most important for the school to serve. The district must develop policies directed at making the school the final authority in the development of programs of instruction for direct delivery to the student at that school. In summary, the district develops the overarching goals and objectives, while the school develops the specific student based goals and objectives.

In one district known to the author, the strategic plan of the district notes the major learning goals of the district in broad terms and also acknowledges the responsibility of the school to develop specific learning goals and objectives based on the actual data derived from that school. In this way, the district is assured that the school or site will follow the appropriate needs assessment for the students located on that site before arriving at specific instructional goals and objectives.

The setting of strategic goals at the district level is, appropriately, a policy issue and must be exercised by the elected board of the district. However, the board can, by policy, elect to shift the primary responsibility for the development of specific instructional delivery objectives to the school. This has been done in the district noted above, so that each school must develop their own CIP, which identifies the appropriate delivery system to be used at their site. This particular strategic plan acknowledges that the central staff is responsible for the planning process and for the negotiation of a final CIP for each school. Further, the strategic plan assigns to the central staff the duty of evaluating the school against the CIP, so that the board is assured that the various schools meet their obligations to the students at their site. This particular district has adopted the Context, Input, Process, Product (CIPP) model of evaluation and all reports are couched in CIPP terms so that the system has a common language on which to base its evaluation efforts.

In those states where SBM is a state mandate, the state law directing the move toward SBM supersedes any other law regarding the organization of local school districts. In one such state, Texas, where the state law mandates that school-level plans be developed for the delivery of programs, there is also a state mandate on pupil teacher ratio in grades K−4. This, in and of itself, is contradictory since one of the premises of SBM is the capacity of the school to develop its own staffing patterns to meet the needs at that site as they have been identified. The state response here is that each school can apply for an exemption from that particular law and have it approved in order to staff at a different ratio. Because teacher/pupil ratio is an important political item for teachers' unions and organizations everywhere, school districts are reluctant to ask for waivers on this item, and, thus, many good ideas for differentiated staffing patterns are lost.

In the aforementioned district, the local school is guaranteed the equivalent amount of dollars, based on average teacher salary, that student enrollment indicates. Therefore, when the school opts for a different type of staffing pattern, they are guaranteed the same amount of dollars that they would receive if they were to staff in the traditional way. Thus, with the budget generated through a differentiated staffing pattern, the school can fund the special needs they identify as being important to the students of that school. Again, flexibility is the name of the game, with a recognition that no two schools and no two student bodies are the same.

When a district embarks on this pattern of organization, one of the first lessons learned is developing a tolerance for ambiguity and differences. This is because each school will eventually come up with a slightly different way to meet student needs. Each may have an appropriate fix on how to serve the students at the school because of different strengths and weaknesses inherent at that site. The district strategic plan must permit this variance from the norm if the process is to be an emerging and dynamic process and not a fixed notion driven from above. Again, flexibility must become the norm and not the exception.

Those districts opting to organize along the SBM path must first define the SBM concept for themselves so that they are familiar with how they want the concept to evolve in their district. Most districts develop their SBM organizational pattern along the ways mentioned earlier in this document. That is, the district develops a strategic plan based on state education goals and mandates. Once this is done, the various schools develop their SIPs as an adjunct to the district strategic plan. These SIPs specify the particular programs that will be implemented at the site. These are intended to permit the school to meet the educational goals and objectives that have been adopted as board policy. After every school has developed their own SIP, the central staff and the schools negotiate and compromise about areas found in the SIP that may deviate from the strategic plan of the district. Once an agreement is finalized, the SIP becomes the vehicle against which the school is evaluated during the next academic year.

Reduction of System Structure and Bureaucracy

One of the quickly discerned outcomes of a move toward SBM is the reduction in complexity of system structure and a real savings in total expenditure for central staff. This reduction of staff or bureaucracy is attributable to the shift in responsibility for student learning from the central staff (those in directors' positions) to the site level where the students are located. This shift in responsibility makes extraneous many of the positions that were located at the central office.

One large urban district where the author served as superintendent eliminated some 400 professional educators from the central staff during the transition period. These personnel were not fired but were allowed to retire and/or transfer from the central staff to school-level staff positions. As might be expected, one of the outcomes of this type of personnel reduction is that those in the central bureaucracy will resist the effort with all of their capacity.

Another outcome of personnel reduction is that the general level of staff morale will increase, particularly at the school level, because of the increased allocation of resources made possible by the reduction. In another urban district known to the author, 250 central staff positions were eliminated because of this type of reorganization. This enabled the district to place its highest priorities on the improvement of teacher salaries and provided a salary structure that is among the finest in the country. A teaching staff of approximately 2,000, dividing the savings from the elimination of 250 positions at an average salary of $40,000, resulted in the ability to provide an average raise of $5,000 for each teacher in the district. In this manner, this district was able to develop one of the highest salary structures in the country.

While many central office positions can and should be eliminated, many support service positions remain important to the SBM concept. As was mentioned earlier, the role of the central office becomes one of support rather than direction. Implied in this shift is the notion that the central office personnel can and will become able to provide these activities that are important to the SBM concept. Since planning and evaluation are the functions allocated to the central office, these are two of the most important skills that must be encompassed at the central staff level. The remaining staff at the central office must learn to be advocates for the schools and assist those schools in the development of plans and objectives for delivery to the students.

Recently, while working with a large urban district in the Midwest, the author urged the district to assign central staff members to the various schools in the district (approximately sixty). These staff members were to function as advocates for the schools, to assist the schools as they developed their CIP, to act as the liaison as the CIP was negotiated with the central office, to provide planning expertise and support as the school attempted to implement the plan, and, finally, to be the primary evaluator of the CIP as implemented. One of the first things we discovered was that many of the central staff had to learn how to be support personnel. Many of the central staff members had become so used to giving orders and to having them followed, that they were simply not prepared to function as a support resource. Several central staff development sessions were quickly convened to provide techniques needed to allow them to function as support personnel, and extended discussions were held about the changed role for the central staff. Additional sessions were developed for planning and evaluation duties.

The process of changing the role of the central staff took place over a two-year period. This time was utilized by the system to implement SBM in six schools who volunteered to be the first to move toward the concept. As a result, when the total system moved into implementation of SBM, the staff was already indoctrinated as to the basic premises of the concept. It is now some five years into the plan, and the results are almost too good to be true. Student growth has exceeded expectations, and the staff is solid in its support of the SBM concept.

The Power Game

Unfortunately, many educators and board members love to play the power game of political machinations and intrigue. The SBM concept has no place for those individuals because SBM is predicated on the notion that local staffs and communities know their students best and can, given proper support, provide exemplary programs at the site.

Because education is so important, so visible, and so naive in its knowledge about the political process, politicians often make pronouncements about the system and how it should function. This lack of ability to defend themselves against such pronouncements by the spokespersons for the education system permits the politicians to make disparaging remarks about educators and the education system at will. Consequently, persons desiring a quick way to meet their political goals often stand for election as board of education members. This, of course, does the system little good and often makes the system a scapegoat for the political machinations of the member. More importantly, the person has little to contribute to the system and uses the platform to make a run at the political office of his/her ambition.

Boards of education do have tremendous power, but only as a total board can they exercise that power. Individual board members cannot take any unilateral action in the name of the board of education. It is only through action taken at a convened board meeting that policies are implemented and adopted. Abuse of the collective power of the board is sometimes attempted by certain members. If the abuse is serious enough, the state can intercede and take over the functions of the elected board until they either conform or are replaced. Most states have provisions for elected officials—recall for abuse of the elected office, and, in those states that don't have the recall provision (Texas and Oklahoma to name two), the state department can intervene on behalf of the students.

A local board that desires to make every call and set every policy and rule is well advised to forgo this type of organizational pattern. SBM requires a very understanding and supportive board. The board must be totally committed to servicing the students of the system and, further, must be able to accommodate ambiguity and differences among the various schools.

For those individuals who need power as a means of expressing their contribution, the SBM concept is inappropriate. Rather than power, the SBM concept calls for the development of a trusting and supporting relationship between the staff, the administration, and the governing board.

QUESTIONS OFTEN ASKED ABOUT SBM

The Question and Answer sections of the handbook were culled from the hundreds of questions asked of the author during the implementation of SBM in districts with which he has worked. These include those districts of which he was the superintendent (Lansing, Michigan, and Fort Worth, Texas), those districts who underwent SBM development by virtue of legislation passed during the time the author was Deputy Commissioner of Education (Texas), and the many districts with which he has worked as a consultant, including districts in the following states:

Texas, Indiana, Michigan, New York, Illinois, Ohio, Washington, Oregon, and California.

Q-1: Does SBM mean that the school must go it alone without support services from the district office?

A-1: No, the district office continues to provide support activity, but now the support is at the request of the school and not a mandate to provide programs in a certain way.

Q-2: Does SBM signify that the school can do whatever it deems best for the students, regardless of district policy and state and federal law?

A-2: Not at all. SBM means that the particular methods of delivering educational services are to be designated by the school staff. The learning goals are still set by the board in the form of the strategic plan of the district.

Q-3: Does the school involvement committee have the right to set the budget for the campus?

A-3: Within limits. The school involvement committee allocates the final amounts to the various budget items, but the budget allocation totals are governed by the board procedures that make sure that all schools are treated fairly and equally. After total allocations are made, then it sets the budget allocations for the various line items on the school budget.

Q-4: If the school wishes to really separate from the rest of the district, how can this be accomplished?

A-4: By developing a charter proposal, which, in several states, permits groups to develop proposals for the provision of educational services to the students enrolled at the site. After concurrence is arrived at, the charter is issued, giving the school a certain length of time to produce the expected outcomes for the students.

Q-5: SBM suggests a much more lengthy process of making decisions and delivering programs to students. How is the staff of a school going to find the time to do all of the developmental work necessary to implement SBM?

A-5: By a reexamination of the priorities and activities of the school. The move from a data and factual dispensing role for the teacher to a manager of learning systems is a massive change and requires a large amount of staff development. Also, the move from a single provider of facts to a cooperative approach to teaching the students the adopted educational objectives will free some resources to allocate to the planning and decision process.

Q-6: What if the school invites the community to participate in the process and no one chooses to get involved?

A-6: This is a real concern. Most school districts that get involved in the SBM approach do so because they feel that their community does want to get involved and wishes to have the opportunity to participate in the educational decisions affecting their children. Before a serious effort toward SBM is attempted, the community should be appraised of the process and should be invited to participate in the final definition of SBM for their district.

Q-7: With each school setting its own objectives, isn't there a danger that each school will go its own way and that there will be little common education offered the students?

A-7: Remember that each school sets its goals and objectives after the district has adopted its strategic plan for the district. Thus, the school must adhere to the district's strategic plan when developing its CIP, and, after this development is done, it must negotiate the final version with staff from the central office.

Q-8: What are the advantages of SBM?

A-8: There are many. First, this approach to delivering educational services permits the services to be tailored to the specific needs of the students receiving the service. Second, those that know the student best, i.e., the staff at the school where the student is enrolled, develop the particular program suited to that students' needs. Third, the staff and programs are evaluated according to the CIP they develop at the school, so that the evaluation is a fair and objective evaluation. Fourth, during the cycle of implementation, the staff can adjust the program as it is implemented to accommodate certain unforeseen needs and changes that occur. Finally, the SBM approach provides the opportunity for the staff and community to be truly involved in the decisions affecting their children and their site.

Q-9: What are the disadvantages of SBM?

A-9: There are also many disadvantages. First, it *is* more time-consuming than the traditional approach. SBM calls for the staff and community to get involved in every phase of the program, and this is a time-consuming process. Second, SBM places more responsibility for accountability on the teacher and the rest of the staff. Because the staff develops the program and the delivery system, they are to be held accountable for the results. Third, SBM requires the development of new skills and techniques on the part of the staff. The capacity to plan and evaluate is a new skill needed, as well as the capacity to work with fellow staff members cooperatively. These skills must be learned if the SBM process is to be successful.

Q-10: Is there danger of having the school drift as they develop their educational plan?

A-10: Not if the strategic plan for the district is in place. Then, the school must adhere to the priorities as set forth in the strategic plan and must plan to meet these strategic objectives at the school level. What is flexible is the particular methodology and pedagogy the school chooses to implement in meeting the strategic objective as set forth in the district plan.

Q-11: If the district strategic plan sets the parameters, where is all of the flexibility you talk about?

A-11: The flexibility is in the particular delivery system used to provide the program to the students. There is flexibility in terms of time allocations, in methodology selected to serve the students, in the allocation of resources to meet specific school needs, and in other decisions that are now made at the school.

VIGNETTE #1

Restructuring

The positions saved as a result of the move toward SBM can be and often are the basis for dramatic improvement in educator salaries across the board. For example, the reduction of the central office staff of a major Michigan school district during the first eight years of the SBM organizational scheme enabled the increase of the percentage of the budget allocated toward the teachers' salary component from just over 50% to a figure approaching 66%.

Vignette #1

The administration budget for the year in which SBM was initiated in this urban Michigan school district was almost 10% of the total budget, while the amount allocated to teachers' salaries was just about 50% of the total budget. After the SBM concept was introduced and the individual schools took the responsibility for many of the services originally provided through the central office, the need for such extensive services from the central staff was curtailed dramatically, with a resulting reduction of the central staff of almost 150 administrative and support positions at an average salary of almost $40,000. This translates into a savings of over $6,000,000 for redistribution to a teaching staff of approximately 1,800.

While this Michigan district did not fire any of its personnel, it did reassign those who wished to accept reassignment to positions for which they qualified at the school level and encouraged others to accept early retirement by providing perks for that purpose.

Today, this district is doing most of its curriculum development at the school level by providing stipends to select groups of teachers to develop specific programs for particular students. They also provide staff development in that particular program and field test the program with live students so that adjustments can be made as the need arises. Thus, the need for a highly sophisticated, large curriculum division is negated, and those positions can be eliminated from the central office.

This particular district made the decision to train its support staff in the planning/evaluation process and to make them available to the schools for the development of school expertise in these areas. These "advocates" for the school became the spokespersons or liaison persons for the school at the central level.

Today, the district has a salary structure that is among the highest in the state and nation, and its student achievement rate is much higher than an examination of the district's demography and economic status would project. This is because the SBM organizational pattern is well established and the total staff is committed to its maintenance and expansion. The strategic plan for the district is examined annually, with annual "work plans" being developed for the district and each school, as a result. These place a high degree of confidence on the prior year's results and evaluations and become the basis for the ensuing work plan.

There have been several superintendents since the inception of the SBM principles, and each has made important contributions to the concept as it has evolved in this district. Each has, in his/her own way, strengthened the concept and assisted in the institutionalization of the concept until, today, any hint of departing from the SBM mode would be tantamount to calling for a revolution. Teachers, principals, parents, community, and students are all comfortable with the processes and really like the flexibility the concept provides.

VIGNETTE #2

Restructuring

In a district in Oklahoma, where the author worked as a consultant for the past four years and where the district has made the decision to embark on a SBM pattern of organization, the decision was made to reorganize the central staff to provide for the planning and evaluation functions through the re-deployment of staff made obsolete as a result of the decentralization move. In 1990–91, there were over twenty-five central staff members serving in the curriculum and instruction division. With the move to SBM, the instruction division was curtailed to five persons, and the remaining twenty staff members were given the option of returning to a school for assignment or applying for the ten positions that were created to serve the planning/evaluation functions. All applied and were screened for the available positions, and the rest were reassigned to various schools. (Five as principals or assistant principals).

The author was charged with the staff development of the ten chosen for the planning/evaluation functions, as well as the remaining central office staff from the business and related divisions. Additionally, the principals were involved with the staff development effort, and, after the first year, the staffs of the various schools were also involved.

The first year, much time was spent in developing the service role for the central staff as a prelude to learning the planning and evaluation techniques. Once the group was comfortable with the changed nature of the central staff role, from directing to serving and supporting, the learning curve for the techniques needed for planning and evaluation rose dramatically, and real progress was made in developing the personnel as agents of the various schools.

The staff agreed that they wanted to learn the operating techniques for utilizing the CIPP model for planning/evaluation/decision making and, further, that they wished to develop the planning mode from the perspective of the schools to which they were assigned as the liaison person. Thus, they all developed the school strategic and work plans from the context analysis of the particular school and with the principal, parents, and staff as participants.

Once the district's strategic plan was operationalized and a district work plan developed, the central staff, who had actively participated in the development and operationalizing of the plans, had the district's strategic and work plans as a parameter for the development of the school plans.

During the second year, 1991−92, the central liaison staff members worked with the schools to which they were assigned to develop the school work plans or improvement plans for initiation during the 1992−93 academic year.

During this time (two years), the superintendent's committee on SBM developed operational definitions for the SBM process and for the district. They worked from an understanding that, while the board wanted the local schools to have maximum autonomy from the central office, they still had to conform to several board expectations for each school. The objectives held as priority for the district were the priorities the local schools had to serve, the school strategic plan had to honor the district's strategic plan, the local budgets had to balance and were limited to the budget allocation process, equal employment policies had to be maintained and honored, annual evaluations were required for every school and program, and every school had to develop a community advisory committee, which included parents and community members, as well as teachers and staff.

During year three (1992−93), the first efforts at implementation of the plans developed through the efforts of the school personnel, the central liaison staff were assigned to the school, and the members of the community advisory committee were initiated. It was decided that the first evaluation of these efforts would be delayed until the fourth year (1993−94) to give the program(s) a chance to become established before summative evaluations were attempted. It was later decided that the annual evaluation would be formative, as well as summative, in the sense that if the program held some promise, it would be adjusted and continued. Only if the program showed no promise and was not in sinc with the total thrust of the school would the summative evaluation recommend that the program be discontinued and the resources reallocated to other priorities.

It is interesting to note that, as the staff development effort has progressed, so has the risk-taking capacity of the various schools. As a result, each school is taking risks that ordinarily would not be attempted, and each school is actually evaluating the various programs on an ongoing basis so they can quickly redirect the program to make it more effective and focused on the appropriate audience.

The process, which takes at least five years to implement adequately, is proving to be a most effective and desired process for this district. Not only have they restructured the district, but they have provided the schools with planning/evaluation/decision-making assistance while saving at least ten central office positions and redirecting the other central staff positions to the task at hand. The author has noted, with great interest, the growing pride and emphasis on student growth and learning on the part of every school. The board, too, is pleased with the evolution of the SBM process and have taken steps to institutionalize the process by making it congruent with the modified policies of the district. As difficulties arise with existing policies, the board and superintendent make every effort to develop a modification of the policy causing the difficulty, such that it will become a supportive policy in the future. In this way, the board and superintendent are making every effort to provide support, through policy, of the SBM processes.

Chapter 2

SITE-BASED MANAGEMENT – HOW DOES IT AFFECT THE VARIOUS PARTICIPANTS?

Because the concept of Site-Based Management is so dramatically different from the traditional organizational pattern in education, the effect of SBM on the various participants deserves some mention. Upon reviewing the traditional organization, one finds that all or most of the decisions are made at the top of the hierarchy and handed down for implementation. Like military organizations and/or government organizations, the educational organization found it easier and more efficient to make the decisions centrally and at the top of the organization. As educational organizations grew and as the type and number of decisions to be made multiplied, it continued to be more effective and efficient to make these decisions centrally. During the latter half of the 20th century, the education organization grew because of specialization, and control remained central for the sake of expediency and ease of operation; however, as certain communities began to realize that their children were not being served, the demand for participation in the affairs of the school emerged as an important concept.

Parents of special needs students were among the first to demand that the system better serve their students. Other special interest groups followed. Those who had children with special learning needs were able to make a strong case for special treatment for their children because they were being left out of the educational process. Thus, the federal education acts were promulgated, mainly to provide for those children who had been overlooked and neglected by the system. Federal laws also began to protect those children, who, by virtue of poverty, race, or origin had also been neglected by the educational system. The intent of the federal laws was to correct a wrong.

As we now know, these federal laws, while enacted with the best intentions, did little to correct systemic flaws in American society, which were caused by factors other than those found in the educational system. The schools could not correct the flawed housing patterns of the country or the systematic "red lining" in real estate that has gone on historically throughout the nation. The schools had little influence on the wages paid employees of the nation, which really led to the discrepancy in family incomes throughout the country. The American school systems did a remarkable job of implementing a desegregation mandate that was not supported by the vast majority of the public and that finally led to further segregation of the people whom it was intended to bring into the mainstream. This was largely a result of the "white flight" from the cities of the country.

Finally, realizing that the schools alone cannot bring order to such impossible conditions as are generated by numerous social factors, the various states began to consider the notion that, if central decisions could not guarantee that all students could and would learn, then perhaps the capacity to make decisions affecting the children of a particular area at the location of the children was in order. We mention the various states because the state is the single most important governing body of the educational organization. This is because the federal constitution does not mention education and, therefore, the responsibility for providing education to its citizens is passed on to the states. Each state constitution does provide for offering education services to the citizens of the state and, usually, provides for the naming of locally elected boards to serve as the governing bodies for the local education systems. What is not often recognized is the fact that the local board of education is an extension of the state and is created to govern the educational system at the local level. Thus, local boards are really state officials elected and/or appointed locally to implement the state laws and regulations concerning education.

As the demands on the educational system grew and multiplied, especially during the latter years of the 20th century, the notion that local schools could and should have the power to accommodate local nuances and needs began to gain favor and strength. Site-Based Management (SBM) is one manifestation of such an idea. Because the nation is so dependent on the educational system to provide the essential elements of our society and to enable the "right of passage" for our citizens, the federal government has exercised its participatory obligations with the acceptance of the national norms for the educational system. These national norms, born of the governors' conferences on education during the 1980s and 1990s, have established the national expectations for the educational system, particularly in the basic subjects like mathematics, reading, science, and social sciences. From those national norms, each state has established state expectations and prerogatives for the local school systems to follow and emulate. Most states, Hawaii being the exception, provide the local districts the option of translating the state goals and objectives into locally acceptable language as the basis for the local strategic plans. However, the states insist on local districts meeting the state goals and objectives. To ignore these goals is to court disaster.

The following are short descriptions of the various participating bodies and their roles in the development of an SBM approach to the governance of education. Understanding the impact of SBM on these various bodies and groups is important to the implementation of the concept and should be understood by all participants in the process.

STATE DEPARTMENT OF EDUCATION

As was stated earlier, the state, as the unit of government responsible for education, has the ultimate say in the way education is delivered to its citizens. For this reason, the concept of SBM must be understood by those in the state department of education and must be supported as a viable alternative organizational pattern for the state's schools.

Most state departments of education are being forced into a posture of supporting SBM by the various state legislative bodies, which, as representatives of local communities, are being pressured by their constituencies into permitting SBM. State legislators react strongly to the pressures of the local electorate, especially when the local electorate demands more control over the local school and its programs. Often, state legislatures overreact to these pressures and mandate procedures that are sometimes detrimental to the students of the schools; however, many states now have the alternative available to enable a local school/district to embark on an SBM mode of operations. In some states, this involves the application for a waiver from state regulations concerning the operation of the local school/district, while, in other states, the process is mandated and each school/district must develop a plan for SBM to be implemented.

There are several important tasks for the state department of education to undertake if SBM is to be implemented in the state. These include the following.

Strategic State Education Plans

In order to establish expectations for the education of its citizens, the state must develop a strategic plan, which specifies the expectations for the local schools/districts and the students. This is usually done through the legislature, which passes the laws governing education, and the state department of education, which promulgates the rules that establish the specific expectations for the schools of the state.

The state board of education, through its staff, usually translates the legislative program into a specific state strategic plan for education, which should set the parameters for the development of district and school plans to implement the state's goals and objectives. The state board, through its staff, delineates what is appropriate for the schools of the state to implement and achieve.

The strategic plan of the state must start with an adequate needs assessment or context analysis, which delineates the current status of education in the state and builds an understanding on the needs and priorities of the state when it comes to the education of its citizens. The state department of education has all of the data about the accomplishment of local districts and schools and can develop an appropriate needs assessment from that data. This needs assessment should accurately reflect the current status of education in that state and should also reflect the prioritization of resources with which to meet those needs. Data used to initiate a strategic plans development include performance on standardized tests by the students of the state, an analysis of the demographics of the state, a summary of the opportunities available to the students of the state, and a description of the general condition of the educational institutions of the state. These data are then compiled into a summary statement of how the system serves the citizens of the state and where the discrepancies that must be corrected exist.

The state strategic plan formulates the educational needs of the state in broad strokes and sets the parameters for local districts as they develop their plans to meet the state's expectations. The state has a real vested interest in the education of its citizens and, for that reason, will not allow the local schools carte blanche in their operation. However, under the SBM mode of organization, the state will permit the individual schools greater flexibility in the delivery of services and in the development of particular methodology and pedagogy to meet unique student needs and styles of learning.

Because education is such a continuous process and each level must build on the previous level, it is imperative that the total educational effort be considered as the strategic plan is developed. This means that the total educational plans, ranging from preschool through graduate education, must be coordinated and interrelated. In some states, the higher education system is separate from the K−12 system, but the strategic plan should provide for continuity between the two systems in order to devise a cogent plan to meet all of the educational objectives of the state. While higher education boards often look down their nose at the K−12 levels of education, they are so dependent on the K−12 system for their own survival that they must become partners in the development of the strategic plan.

The state strategic plan attempts to answer the what, why, where, and when questions, while the local plans define the how question. Usually, the state strategic plan begins with a statement of mission for the education of citizens of the state. The appropriate role for the education of citizens and how such education is to be transmitted is also important to the strategic plan. Defining the appropriate mechanism for the delivery of educational services and who shall be the designated providers of such services is included.

Allocation of State Funds

The funding of public education is the single most expensive program that the various states must find support for. As costs continue to rise and as the demands for improved education services accelerate, new and different ways to generate resources are being contemplated by the various states.

Many states have initiated a state income tax for this purpose, while others have raised the state's sales tax with a certain percentage of the sales tax earmarked for the support of the public schools. Still other states have initiated a state lottery with those proceeds designated for support of the public schools as well. However, even the total receipts from the state lottery will only support a small portion of the state's share of public education costs; so the lottery, while advertised as being a major factor in support of education, actually provides a minor amount of resources.

Typically, the state must decide the extent to which each of several competing agencies deserve substantial support. These decisions are made at the state legislative levels and generate extensive lobbying efforts on behalf of the various agencies. Included are the following major agencies: education, higher education, state parks, mental health, social services, prisons, highways, health, and state police.

State legislative bodies, typically, do not guarantee any agency a certain allotment and, generally, allocate resources according to the political support generated by the particular agency. Thus, when the funding of education was questioned in many states because of the property tax inadequacy and because of the inequities rising from the property tax-based method of school funding, many states moved from an extreme dependence on the property tax toward a more equitable form of generating resources for public education. This, of course, meant that the dollars utilized for the support of public education had to be generated from either the state income tax and/or the state sales tax. As federal and state courts increasingly mandated the equalization of public education support between property-rich and property-poor school districts, the local dependence upon the property tax has been minimized and even eliminated. The state has had to replace the property tax with other forms of funding.

In most states, education is the single most expensive program that is funded through state efforts. Social services, health services, and prisons are the next most costly programs. Many states have bonded for the purpose of expanding their prison systems and now face the need to open and operate these new prisons with a limited source of dollars. This complicates the process because each of these agencies competes with the education agency for the scarce dollars for operations. As a result of equity lawsuits, many states are forced into supporting the capital expenditures of school systems in the state, something they had not had to worry about before. This new expectation for state participation further complicates the competition among the aforementioned agencies for a slice of the same total budget. Thus, most states are frantically looking for ways to increase their tax revenue while, at the same time, keeping the existing tax load constant and level. This is a most difficult task and one that gives state legislatures and governors a great deal of trouble.

Most states allocate a certain dollar amount per student as support for local schools. Often, the students are rated according to the type of program they qualify for. Thus, certain special education programs qualify for a weighted allocation ranging from 1.0 for the normal student to as high as 7.0 for students needing residential treatment. Vocational programs, for example, are also weighted and funded accordingly. The local district receives the dollar amount for each student in attendance at the local school and must stand the test of annual review and audit of attendance. Some states fund according to number of "teacher units" the local district qualifies for, although this system is less prevalent than the individual student funding.

In most states, the primary burden for the support of education is shared by the state and local unit of governance. The main mechanism for raising revenue locally is the property tax, of which many states are approaching the upper limits. Generally, the local district is permitted to levy a property tax to supplement the state funding although this method of school funding is rapidly becoming obsolete because of the legal requirement to equalize the funds to every student in the state. Thus, while local property taxes are levied for the support of local educational systems, a portion of the local tax must be given to the state in order to equalize the resources for every student.

Most equalization plans require that the combination of state and local resources generated must be approximately the same for all districts in the state. There is provision for some small "enrichment" factor, but that is all that is permissible among the various districts. Of course, those who are from property-wealthy districts charge that this is discriminatory because it equalizes down to the state norm, while those who are from property-poor districts generally support the method of equalization.

Monitoring for Compliance with State Laws

One of the more important tasks taken on by the state department of education is the monitoring of all state and federal education laws and regulations. The state department of education has, as its primary function, the obligation to enforce and assist local school districts in their compliance roles. This means that the officials of the Department of Public Instruction (DPI) must interpret and translate all laws pertaining to the educational system into meaningful regulations for the school districts of the state to follow. This is not always an easy task because, many times, the state and federal laws are, at best, ambiguous and, at worse, indecipherable. The professional employees of the state department of education must have the capacity to make sense out of many borderline laws passed by state legislative bodies and, further, interpret those state board of education regulations and rules that are equally ambiguous and confusing.

The compliance function is one of the more important duties of the DPI and takes much of the energy and time of the state education employees. In addition to monitoring state laws and regulations, the DPI staff must also monitor local districts for compliance with federal laws and regulations. This includes all of the equal opportunity laws, as well as the various legal safeguards intended to protect students and parents. Federal laws are particularly focused on services to the disabled and to those who have special education needs by virtue of a handicapping condition. The federal laws protecting the handicapped were passed as a result of local jurisdictions ignoring the need for special services and are intended to equalize educational services for all students.

The state department staff assigned to the monitoring function is almost always the largest numerically in the DPI. Personnel included in the unit are specially trained in the monitoring function and understand the laws and regulations being monitored. The DPI staff has the power to take corrective action against those districts not in compliance with the laws. This action can vary from citations to more stringent actions like state takeover of a local district not in compliance with state edicts. At the same time, they are trained to assist the local district in the interpretation of particular regulations and law so that the local unit understands the reasons for noncompliance.

State laws governing class size, courses offered, periods taught, length of school day, allocation of resources, discipline of students, extracurricular activities provided students, building capacity and condition, support activities provided, and many other state regulations and laws are monitored by the DPI staff. Federal laws concerning equal opportunity, affirmative action, equal employment opportunity, special education services, and other federal laws are also monitored by the DPI.

Because of this monitoring function, the DPI often gets the reputation of being overly bureaucratic in nature. While this is true by the nature of the organization, the members of the DPI staff are often very helpful in assisting the local staff in interpreting the many rules and laws governing education in the state.

With the introduction of the SBM concept in most states, the DPI staff has had to learn new behaviors and skills in order to assist those districts embracing the SBM concept. They, the staff, have had to become familiar with the SBM concept and develop a tolerance for those districts who choose to gain a waiver from the multitude of state laws and regulations and embark on a SBM course. This means that the DPI staff must acknowledge the right of the local unit to develop plans for implementation of SBM and must assist the local unit in getting the necessary waivers to permit the SBM process to work.

State Accreditation

In many states, the state department of education also performs the accreditation function for the schools/districts of the state. While many states utilize the services of the various regional accrediting agencies, i.e., the North Central Association of Schools and Colleges, the Southern Association of Schools and Colleges, etc., many states were allocated this function by their state legislatures as a result of 1980s reform acts. This was done specifically because the legislative bodies were reacting to public pressure for improvement in the education systems of the various states.

While the regional accrediting agencies will assist a local school in developing the accreditation process, the operating word is self-study, with assistance from the regional agency. In other words, the staff of the school collects the data deemed important to the accreditation process and submits it to the accrediting agency. After the data are compiled, the regional agency appoints a team of peers to visit the school to see if the submitted materials accurately reflect what is happening at the school. This results in the accreditation of the school or a series of recommendations intended to bring the school into compliance with the accreditation process.

States entered into the accreditation business at the request of the various state legislative bodies who, as the amount of state resources going into education accelerated dramatically, began to demand improvements in the education provided the students of the state. In order to monitor and affect the quality of the educational programs offered in the schools, several states initiated accreditation efforts conducted by state DPI personnel. The accreditation process then moved from the traditional accreditation concept of evaluation of school inputs to a more outcomes-oriented accreditation effort where what students learned became more important than how they learned it. Texas, one of the leaders in the state accreditation movement, reorganized the accreditation department in 1984 as a result of the Texas Education Reform legislation passed in that year. Other states approved state accreditation developments at about the same time, and all were concerned with the results of the state tests that all students were required to take.

This model of school and district accreditation requires that each district submit data to the state department of education on an annual basis. These data are the summary of local information required by the accreditation staff and permits a "desk" audit of each district in the state. After the desk audits are performed, about 20% of the school districts are visited each year for on-site accreditations. The 20% are selected in a variety of ways: either by a rotating schedule, by the results of the desk audit, or by the results of the state tests taken that year.

The DPI accreditation staff spends time in those districts selected for the accreditation visit and determines how well the district is complying with the state expectations and laws. Every school in the district is accorded a visit by the accreditation staff. Time is also allocated to listen to citizen comments about the local school district. After learning as much as possible about the local district, the DPI staff returns to its home base and develops a report that is sent to the local district after a few weeks.

Usually, several levels of accreditation ratings are possible, ranging from fully accredited, to accredited advised, to nonaccredited (correctable) and to nonaccredited (state take over). Each of the levels below fully accredited require some sort of remedial action on the part of the local district. These corrective measures can range from routine activities, such as keeping better records of the personnel files and assignments, to more dramatic actions, such as revamping the curriculum and reassigning staff to comply with state regulations, to requiring the board to submit itself to development of the appropriate ways to conduct school business.

The most severe penalty is the requirement that the local board submit itself to outside intervention and control by a monitor or master assigned by the state to govern the district. Such severe actions are taken only after much dialogue and discussion with those involved with the accreditation effort. If, in the judgment of the DPI, a district is cheating the students out of a fair and quality education, this severe action may be taken. Other cases where such severe actions are taken are cases where there is proof of illegal activity on the part of the staff and the local board, resulting in students being cheated out of an equitable education. Sometimes the board and the administration are at odds with one another, and the DPI is forced to recommend that a monitor be assigned so that the district can function. The hoped for result is, of course, to be fully accredited so the local district can proceed for another five years without fear of losing its status.

The ideal accreditation process results from the state setting measurable objectives in every area to be evaluated, while the DPI staff is able to gather the data on-site so the local district can be assured of fairness and equity in the accreditation process. This means that the state must have provisions for a data bank (management information system) that gathers objective data from each school in the state and provides these data in certain forms for the DPI staff to utilize in making accreditation decisions. These data, combined with the results of site visits, lead to a final evaluation of the school/district for accreditation purposes.

In many states where the state performs the accreditation task, the involvement of peer educators is also required. In Texas, for example, a "Texas School Improvement" initiative was initiated to train school district staff in the accreditation process so that they could supplement the DPI staff in performing school site visits for accreditation purposes. This effort also provided the opportunity for staff development in the various educational areas being probed by the accreditation process; thus, a marked improvement in the quality of education provided to the students of the educators involved in the "Texas School Improvement" initiative was realized.

The state accreditation process is a most important function for the DPI in those states that have a state accreditation program. Many states, Texas for one, have adopted the effective schools correlates and definitions as the focal point for the state accreditation process. For those districts wanting to move toward an SBM type of operation, the first step is to get state approval for such a reorganization by getting the state DPI to approve a waiver of all state regulations that might be too restrictive. Once this is done, the local district must develop its strategic plan so that the state goals and objectives are reflected in the local plan. Then, each of the sites in the district must develop their plans that reflect the district's strategic plan and the manner in which the site is going to implement achieving the objectives itemized in the site plan.

When the district is to be accredited, the accreditation team must consider the various school plans and evaluate according to those specific objectives itemized in the various plans so that the sites are evaluated against each of their individual plans, rather than the total district plan. While this somewhat complicates the accreditation process, it does make it germane to each school and accomplishes the task of accreditation in a fair and complete manner.

Other State Department Tasks Related to SBM

There are, of course many other tasks and duties performed by the DPI that impact those districts involved with the SBM approach to organization. Among them are the following.

Staff Development

The DPI usually has a unit devoted to providing staff development for the schools of the local districts. These staff development efforts encompass many needed activities, none of which is more important than those aimed at enabling the local staff to understand and appreciate the SBM type of organization. In those states where SBM has been mandated by state law, the topic for such staff development is prescribed by the laws that created the move to SBM; the DPI staff has quickly embraced the topic and developed appropriate training programs. Topics usually addressed in such staff development efforts include participatory governance and what it involves, how to gain consensus in decision making, the role of the various participants in the governance of education, strategic planning and how it is accomplished, cooperative efforts in education and how they are attempted, managing learning systems, setting the evaluation process, and other topics related to successful SBM implementation.

Curriculum and Instruction Division

Most state departments of education have many curriculum and instruction specialists on staff. These specialists perform the tasks associated with the introduction and development of curriculum that is required in that particular state. These are the experts in the particular field of study who provide their expertise to the schools of the state.

These personnel offer their expertise through seminars and staff development sessions for the schools. They travel the state and advise and consult with the districts and individual schools. These personnel provide the local schools with the assistance needed to implement an SBM program by assisting in developing the particular subject as a part of the SBM effort. Because the move to SBM requires a change in the way curriculum is transmitted to students, the specialists at the DPI develop the accommodation of their particular specialty in a manner consistent with the demands of SBM. Thus, they provide an important adjunct to the entire process of change from a traditional organization to an SBM-oriented organization.

Legal Staff

This division also assists the DPI in making the necessary adjustments in order to accommodate the move to SBM. Such matters as legal interpretations of state laws and the best approach to gaining waivers from existing state rules and laws are handled by the legal department. State tenure laws and contract disputes are also regulated by the legal division. Since the move toward SBM ultimately involves the changing of staffing patterns and some dispute with either tenure laws and/or contracts with individual employees will arise, so the legal branch of the DPI is always on call to intervene in these disputes. There are many, many areas in which local districts get themselves involved with the legal system, and the legal services division has more than enough to do. In some state departments, they also act as ombudsmen for the citizens of the state and investigate complaints levied against local schools and districts. The legal staff must review the local plans for SBM to assure that state laws and regulations are not circumvented in the process.

Finance Staff

Every state department has a financial staff to accommodate the transmittal of resources to the local districts and to track the use of state money. The finance department tracks the dispersal of state funds to see that it is consistent with state law. Local districts qualify for state funds according to the state laws governing the distribution of state funds.

As the state moves to accommodate the SBM pattern, some changes in how the state monies are divided could be in order. Because the state ultimately has the responsibility for educating all children, the DPI financial staff has the responsibility to track how the expenditures are allocated at the district level. The financial department, therefore, performs an annual examination of the systems books to see that all funds are dispersed properly and that there are no glaring deficiencies in the bookkeeping procedures of the local district. State financial forms are developed by the financial staff of the DPI, and every district is expected to follow the state form for tracking expenditures and income. The state financial manual is one of the more important tracking devices for the development of information for state legislative bodies.

Planning and Evaluation Division

The planning/evaluation function is crucial to the success of the educational system, and the DPI is the logical agency to provide the needed assistance in this function to all of the districts in the state. Planning and evaluation assistance is available from the planning/evaluation division of the DPI. This division develops the state's strategic plan and performs the evaluation function on a variety of state and local initiatives at the direction of the state board and/or legislature. They also provide the staff development component needed to make the local district viable in terms of planning and evaluation.

With the advent of SBM, most districts need assistance in developing local initiative for a move into SBM. The state staff can be immensely valuable in assisting the local district to develop its capacity to plan and to evaluate.

Evaluation tasks ranging from the analysis of state tests to an evaluation of the state's performance on nationally normed tests are common to the DPI division of evaluation. Recent evaluation tasks include the development of instruments with which to evaluate personnel and the evaluation of schools/districts as part of the accreditation process. Typically, the state department agrees on a standard evaluation design and then transmits this design to all districts in the state so that all are assessed on a similar instrument and design.

The state's strategic plan must be developed with the local needs and prerogatives in mind. From the state plan are derived the various local plans, which also must lead to the development of school plans that are the driving force behind the educational effort embodied under the SBM organizational pattern. It is, therefore, imperative for the state to have a well-defined system of providing planning assistance to the local districts, as well as a common evaluation design for use throughout the state.

Questions Often Asked about the DPI Role in Implementing an SBM Effort

Q-1: Our state does not mandate SBM. Before attempting such a move, should the local district inform the DPI of its intentions?

A-1: The local district should not only inform, but also develop a preliminary plan for submittal to the DPI. This preliminary plan should enumerate the possible conflicts between state laws/regulations and SBM and ask for waivers from those laws/regulations.

Q-2: Our state's financial reporting document has no provision for "carryover" funds on an item by item basis. How are we to provide these services to schools if there are no provisions for doing so in the state manual?

A-2: Provide for this transaction locally and notify the state of what you are doing. The success of the SBM program is often dependent on keeping faith with the school personnel by providing for the capacity to carry over funds to meet long range obligations and plans.

Q-3: The bureaucrats of the state department of education, or DPI, are often unwilling to permit deviation from the rules as promulgated by the DPI. How can we develop an SBM approach to school organization if we are held to stringent rules and regulations by the staff of the DPI?

A-3: Most states provide for waivers from state rules and regulations upon submittal of a plan for action that enumerates the laws and rules that must by waived. Develop such a plan and submit it to the DPI.

Q-4: Our state mandates the move toward SBM by every district in the state. In developing our SBM plan, we do not choose to go the route that the DPI mandates for every district but, rather, want to develop the program according to our defined needs and at our own pace by providing for all of the stakeholders a participatory role in the process. Can we develop SBM in such a manner, and how do we get the state's concurrence with this plan?

A-4: Develop your plan according to your own timetable and needs making sure that you include the rationale for the plan as presented and specifying the student gains projected from your plan. Submit the plan to the state and ask for their concurrence in its implementation.

Q-5: Our state guarantees a total reimbursement of $4,500 per student in average daily attendance. Our plan calls for money following student but does not follow state guidelines in pupil/teacher ratio or specific expenditures that are common throughout the state. Can we deviate from the state model in those expenditures?

A-5: Yes, provided that the expenditure pattern was explicated in the plan you submitted to the DPI originally. If, as the year moves along, you find that certain expenditure patterns are better changed to some new pattern, you should submit a changed plan of expenditure so you are protected from unforeseen emergencies.

Q-6: Our plan for SBM involves the reallocation of the instructional minutes of the day according to the needs of the students in each school as defined by the results of the state testing program. Will we be allowed to deviate from the state mandated instructional time allocations?

A-6: If your plan calls for a deviation from the state-mandated requirement and you have developed a rationale and a strategic plan for implementation that suggests the deviation from the state mandate, the state will permit it if the plan is submitted to the state with a request for a waiver from the state mandate.

CENTRAL OFFICE – SUPERINTENDENT AND SUPPORT STAFF

As a district moves toward the implementation of an SBM organizational pattern, the personnel at the central office must be the primary players in the move because they have the greatest investment in the process. A move toward SBM means that the role of the personnel at the central office must change dramatically from a directing role to a facilitating and supporting role. This is not an easy transition and requires significant mental and philosophical changes on the part of those employed at the central staff level.

Typically, those personnel located at the central office have worked long and hard to get to the position they now hold. They feel that they have earned the right to direct the various programs and will fight to retain that right. Additionally, they are often the products of the system and have touched all of the bases as they made their way to the central office position they now hold. They are protective of the status they have achieved and resentful of those who would take the status away from them. Besides, they are the stars of the system, and they know what is best for the students of the system. All of this participatory nonsense is just another way of diverting attention from the contribution that they (central staff) can and will make. The foregoing is an example of the typical central staff opinion about the severe changes that SBM implies. These are presented to show the degree of difficulty in making the transition from the traditional mode of operations. Those who want the rearranged form of organization will realize that, without the central staff to push a plan to fruition, the plan has little chance for success because the central staff knows how to make things run and how to get things moving.

Yet, under the SBM type of organization, the central staff is expected to adopt a changed pattern of behavior and to assume the support role that is often strange and awkward to the personnel of the central staff. The rationale is really quite simple and straightforward: those who are located where the students are, at the school level, know best about what is good for those students, because they have the best feel for what the students can and will learn and about how to deliver the programs to their students. All other personnel are support personnel and must behave as support personnel.

The major question of what is an effective support program and what the role is for those in support services must be addressed. While each system must delineate the particular role and define the support services function, several general statements are in order here. First, the members of the central staff who are called on to perform these support activities must learn to interpret school requests and pleas for assistance. This is best done by going to the school and getting to know the staff and students. Once the school staff knows and learns to respect the central staff member, they become less threatening to the school staff. This leads to a feeling that the central staff member is a support source for the school and also leads to requests for increased services and assistance. Second, the central staff member must learn the techniques involved with educational planning in order to be of assistance to the school staff in their planning effort. The central staff as planners is, perhaps, the most important role shift. Third, the central staff member must learn the evaluation role and how to implement the evaluation model chosen by the district. As the chief evaluator for the school, the central staff liaison person must perform the major evaluation thrust while still serving as the advocate for the school, interpreting their wishes and concerns to the central office of the district. Finally, the central staff person, acting as liaison to the school, must know where to find and generate staff development resources for the school with which they are aligned. This is very important because, through the staff development process, programs that lead to student growth are created and implemented.

Once the central staff are assigned their direct school liaison responsibilities, the process of making the relationship a lasting one begins. There are several specific obligations that the central staff liaison person assists the local school in developing. These include the following.

Assist in the Development of the District's Strategic Plan

As the district enters the SBM mode of operations, the central staff must shift from a directing mode to a planning/evaluation mode. This means that the superintendent must assist the members of the central staff as they learn this new changed role for them. They are now being asked to develop long-range plans for the district to follow as it enters the new age of educational decision making, where decisions are allocated to those closest to the students, i.e., those at the school level.

While the central staff members are known to be specialists in the particular subject matter field they head, the new demands are for them to be generalists and planners/evaluators able to assist all school-based personnel. As a district studies the changes needed to assist in the transformation from a traditional district to one that implements the SBM model of decision-making, the need for the total central staff of the district to become support staff becomes crucial to the success of the SBM model. One of the best and easiest ways for this to happen is through the participation of all central staff in the development of the strategic plan for the district.

The development of the central staff as planners and evaluators is one of the primary tasks in the move toward SBM organizational patterns. This is not an easy task but, rather, takes place over many months and years. As was mentioned earlier, the central staff has much to say about the direction the district will take during the preplanning process, and they must be involved in the development of the strategic plan for the district. It is this plan that will set the parameters for the development of the SBM mode of operations for the district. The superintendent must, with the rest of the central staff, become convinced that the move to SBM will resolve the learning deficiencies currently found in the district. The central staff's belief in the need for such a move will result in the development of a viable plan for implementation.

The strategic plan for the district must start with, and build from, the state's goals and objectives for the educational system. This means that the local strategic plan must recognize the main goals set for education at the state level and, in addition, develop local priorities and objectives for the schools in the district. These locally developed goals become the parameters for the schools as they plan for the direct education of the students in their care. These goals are not negotiable and must be part of the school plan for implementation. What are negotiable are the time needed and the methods and pedagogy to be used in achieving the goals/objectives. These methods depend on many variables, such as current achievement levels at the school, student needs priorities identified at the school, staff strengths and weaknesses, resources (financial and otherwise) available to the schools, and assistance expected from the community.

The district strategic plan must be a basic plan that describes the priority goals and the reasons therefor. It also describes the organizational pattern of the district and the responsibility of the schools in the development of their school improvement plans. The district strategic plan also describes the financial potential for the district and the other resources available to the schools as they strive to meet district goals. Additionally, the strategic plan describes the evaluation system to be used in determining the success and/or failure of the schools to meet their goals. It also describes the achievement minimums acceptable to the district. The plan is a written document that defines the elements of what the district is working toward over the next five years, with checkpoints for each of the years. The success of the district strategic plan is dependent upon the quality of the school plans developed around it and the quality of the evaluations conducted by the central staff of the district.

From the district strategic plan must come an annual work plan that specifies the particular activities of the district for the year. This work plan reviewed and updated each year is based on the strategic plan and becomes the basis for the development of each school improvement plan for the year. The work plan sets the parameters for the school plans and permits each school to set its own school plan within those limits.

Assisting the School in Developing Its Improvement Plan

Because the central staff liaison person has had the experience of assisting in the development of the district's strategic plan and understands the strategic plan, assisting the school staff in developing the plan is one of the more important obligations the central staff liaison must meet. This is why the central staff must become familiar with and well-versed in the planning process and must provide this expertise to the school.

The acceptance of the SBM model places most principals immediately on the defensive, because they have not been trained in the particulars of planning/evaluation/decision making that this model requires. In addition, the requirement for participatory decisions adds another new element to the process. Thus, the school principal must depend on the central staff liaison person for assistance and guidance in the process.

As the central staff considers the techniques they must learn, the strategic planning skills must take a high priority. They (central staff and superintendent) must learn the elements of a good strategic plan and must become familiar with the terms utilized in strategic planning and priority setting. The superintendent must lead in the setting of new and changed expectations for the performance of the personnel at the central staff level by becoming the leader in the development of the district strategic plan.

The setting of the vision and the expectations for the district are the sole purview of the chief executive officer of the district. He/she, in concert with the board of education, establishes what they want the district to be over a five- to ten-year period and set the expectations for each of the sites in the system. The central staff then participates in the establishment of the district strategic plan and then interprets the plan to the various schools so that their plans are compatible with and build on the district plan.

Once the district strategic plan is in place, the expectations for student achievement are established for each of the schools in the system. It is at this time that the central staff liaison to the school must become involved as the primary assistant (consultant) in the school planning process. The capacity of the central staff liaison person to interpret the district strategic plan to the school staff and community will determine the acceptance of the plan during the negotiations process utilized to finalize the plans. It is, therefore, extremely important for the central staff liaison to become well-versed in the planning process and to take an important role in the school planning activity. This is best done through establishing the central staff person's credibility and knowledge about the planning process and through establishing a relationship of trust with the school staff and community.

The superintendent, as the chief executive officer of the school system, must lead by example, as well as by interpreting the board's policies. The superintendent establishes the visions of what the district could be and leads the district toward that vision by translating all efforts into elements of the strategic plan and into efforts at implementation of that plan. The superintendent sets the stage for the involvement of the staff and the community in the total educational effort of the district by including everyone in the process. He/she must lead by example and insure that there are community representatives involved in all facets of the school district's operation. He/she must also develop the methods of community and staff participation and assure that all members of the school system staff also learn these priorities. The superintendent sets the pace for the rest of the staff to follow in the implementation of SBM for the district.

As the central staff initiates its school liaison role, there are several important considerations to keep in mind. First, it is crucial that the central staff member act as a provider of information about the process of involvement, rather than as an arbiter of the process. Thus, the central staff member explains the meaning of the several types of involvement and assists the building staff and the principal in sorting out the types of involvement that are best at the particular school. The central staff liaison person must always keep in mind the district's definition of inclusion and remind the school staff of the policy statement permitting the involvement of staff and community. It is equally important for the liaison person to differentiate between involvement and participation so that the various players do not get confused by the various roles and responsibilities for the conduct of the educational program.

The central staff member must assist the local staff and community in the development of as many alternatives as possible for their consideration. This means that the liaison person must know the planning process and the implications for alternative responses to a particular need. The translation of student and community needs into deliverable programs of education is a most difficult process requiring the very best planning expertise and the establishment of definite priorities.

It is essential that the central staff liaison person be the advocate for the school they are representing. In the performance of this advocate role, the central staff liaison must fully understand the school plan and what it is intended to accomplish for the students. In addition, the advocacy role requires that the person acting as advocate be knowledgeable about conditions at the school and in the community so that the advocate can interpret the realities to be found at the particular school.

As the primary support person, the central staff liaison person must know the nuances found at the school and be able to have dialogue with personnel and community members in order to draw out the best possible plan for the school. This must begin with a context analysis or needs assessment to determine what the highest priority educational needs are at that particular site. The context analysis, therefore, determines those items that must be included in the plan of action for the school.

Once the plan is completed and the final plan is negotiated with the central office and the board, the central staff liaison person assumes a new and slightly different role with the school. In this new role, they are the direct evaluators of program efforts on that site and also serve as evaluators of personnel at the school, in addition to the customary role as provider of support activities and staff development activities.

The liaison person must be careful to perform the evaluation role as it is intended, which is to assist the school to improve its performance and programs. A good evaluation design will encourage local staffs to improve programs provided the students by pinpointing the areas and specific programs that need improvement. The adoption of an evaluation design such as the CIPP (Context, Input, Process, Product) model will assist the staff in performing the evaluation function because the CIPP model is predicated on the need for accurate data and information as a prelude to decision making. It is only through such data and information that adequate decisions can be made as to the direction and scope of the instructional program for the school. Evaluation is intended to improve, not to prove, so that those involved with the evaluation function must make sure that all of the staff and students contributing to the evaluations are aware of this function of the evaluation design.

As data become available and as the planning process becomes more a part of the functioning of the school, the staff liaison person can proceed with his/her staff development role more fully as an adjunct to the planning/evaluation function. As an integral part of the planning role, the definition of those things needing development are gleaned, and, therefore, the staff development function is a natural outgrowth of the planning effort.

It is hoped that, after a few cycles, the planning role will become institutionalized and the staff liaison person will merely be a monitor in the development of future school improvement plans.

Monitoring Function—To Guarantee the School Will Address Priority Issues

SBM must be developed as a trusting relationship between the central office and the schools in order for it to work. The superintendent realizes that he/she cannot develop appropriate programs in isolation from the users of these programs and is, therefore, willing for the consumers to participate in the development of program efforts to meet the needs of the students at the school level. However, since the superintendent is held accountable for the success/failure of the school system as a whole, he/she must be assured that each school focuses on the high priority needs of the district. This is accomplished through consistent program development throughout the system. The central staff liaison person must also assume the monitoring function to oversee the activities and actions of the school relative to the district strategic plan. This includes monitoring the district work plans as they are written and implemented annually.

It is important that no school be left to drift under the SBM organization by being allowed to develop their own style and priorities without direction from the board and central staff. This is why the development of a strategic plan as a precondition to the move toward SBM is strongly recommended. This, along with the annual work plans, will establish parameters for each school to follow and will set the process in motion for the development of school focus on methods and pedagogy as they focus on student program needs. It is important for every school to realize that the district goals are an important baseline for every school and that the primary objective is to develop delivery programs that will reinforce the goals adopted for the entire district.

School personnel are pressured by their communities to deviate from the district plan, according to the proclivities of the community. The school must state loudly and clearly that the district plan is the parameter within which the school operates and that all efforts are to reinforce the district strategic plan. While the central staff liaison person assists the school in developing the school plan, they are, at the same time, monitoring the school activities to ascertain that the school focus is on the appropriate objectives and does not deviate from the district plan. If the school starts to stray from the district plan, the central staff person must quickly call this to the attention of the principal and suggest ways to assist in bringing the school back on track. If the community does not wish to develop programs according to the priority needs as defined by the district, the staff liaison person has the responsibility for assuring the community that they are off base in their focus and must return to the objectives as defined under the strategic plan of the district.

It is important that school personnel understand they do have the responsibility for the delivery of appropriate programs to students and that the monitor is there to assure that the priority items are tended to and appropriate programs developed for delivery to the students. The central staff liaison person, as the central staff member most familiar with the operations of the school, can be of great assistance to the school staff as they develop appropriate programs for delivery to the students.

Monitoring does not mean approving every transaction that is culminated at the school. It also does not mean that the monitor must approve every activity conducted at the school before the fact. It does mean that the monitor must gather the data necessary for the central officials to understand the activities being conducted at the school level and the rationale for these activities.

The central staff liaison to the school must assure that the right priorities are being stressed at the school level and that the district's objectives are being treated through the development of appropriate programs for delivery to the students. This places much confidence in the monitoring capacity of the individuals entrusted with the liaison function. They must be of the highest integrity and very capable educators for the function to be performed in a manner appropriate to the situation. The local staff must have faith in the person while the central office (superintendent) must have complete confidence and trust in the person as well. They are the keys to the flexibility inherent in the SBM type of operation.

The depth and quality of the monitoring depends on the capacity of the liaison person to become known and accepted by the staff of the school as an advocate for the school. Often, this will permit the central staff person access to data that would ordinarily be restricted to school staff. Having complete data available to the central staff liaison person will make advocacy a more attractive duty.

The best plan for monitoring a school is to give its personnel complete authority to suggest the types and kind of monitoring they will feel comfortable with, by providing them with a list of the things that are important to the monitoring function and then allowing them to suggest ways of getting the necessary information without threatening the process. For example, one of the main items involved with the monitoring function is how the students are achieving the criterion-referenced objectives in each class. Rather than insisting on reviewing every test and doing an item analysis on the tests, the monitor can ask for a summary of the materials and allow the local staff to assemble the materials as they review their results. This process will further assist in the local staff's acceptance of the central staff liaison person.

Staff Development—Assistance to the School in Staff Development

Among the more important duties of the central staff liaison person is the assistance they provide the school in the staff development area. Starting with the planning process and proceeding through the evaluation process, the central staff liaison person becomes as familiar with the school staff development needs as anyone in the district. In his/her role as support personnel and the main provider of staff development efforts to the school, the central liaison person has the opportunity to significantly affect the quality of education being provided the students at that site.

Rather than being the primary person for staff development at the school, the central staff liaison person is the gatherer of staff development resources to meet the needs of the local school. The staff, with the assistance of the central staff liaison person, identifies what the particular needs are at the school and the central staff liaison person gathers the resources from throughout the district to meet those needs. The central staff person knows who the experts in a particular area are and where they are located. Because the central staff personnel are comprised mainly of specialists in subject matter fields, it is likely that the person required to fill a particular staff development need is an employee of the district and can be brought in through a simple phone call to clear a date.

Some staff development efforts are best accomplished through the engagement of other schools for purposes of providing staff development sessions. Because the central staff liaison person has access to the resources of the entire district, such sessions can be readily arranged. Many school districts have a barter system where such staff development sessions are charged to the credit of the school providing the service and then they have access to the same number of hours from the district to fill one of their own needs. In this way, the talents of the entire system can be utilized for the good of the students anywhere in the system.

There are, of course, some topics the central staff liaison person can best perform for the school, particularly if the need is in the area of the central staff person's expertise. In these instances, the central staff person schedules the topic for a convenient staff development session for the school. It is also possible that the school staff has the expertise on staff to meet a particular need, and the only thing needed is to schedule the activity for the benefit of the total staff. Many times, individual staff development sessions are the best way to provide a particular individual with the opportunity to learn a new technique. In these cases, the provision of a substitute for the person giving the development must be provided. Again, the central staff liaison person can coordinate these activities as a service to the school.

Are there any examples of what could happen if the district does not do a good job of planning for the development of an SBM approach to governance? Yes, in one district known to the author, the decision was made to decentralize to the school level because of state requirements; however, the process was not preceded by the development of a strategic plan for the district, nor were any guidelines developed to provide parameters for the schools. Now in its third year, SBM has become a fiasco in this district because the schools are each going in their own direction, with absolutely no restrictions or guidelines to enable them to focus on common objectives. The central staff was not requested to serve as liaison staff with the schools, but were left to their own devices as to what their function would be. This resulted in a continuation of the status quo as far as the multitude of curriculum personnel were concerned, with little attention paid to what the staff development needs of the various schools were.

In this district, one of the larger districts in the country, only $.502 of every dollar finds its way to the direct support of the schools, while some $.498 goes to support the infrastructure with no visible results from the expenditure. The citizens of this school system are beginning to ask what the payoff is for the students from this very high expenditure for the central administration and bureaucracy. Incidentally, the $.502 spent at the school level includes all of the personnel (teachers, custodians, administrators, bus services, maintenance services, etc.) and support accorded to the school level.

When the district made the decision to decentralize, they did not consider the support needs of the various schools and the changed organizational needs of the district that come from a move toward SBM. As previously discussed, this invariably results in a changed responsibility pattern for the members of the central staff and a reallocation of those resources to the building level. In every district that has successfully accommodated the move to SBM, the net result has been a reallocation of personnel from the central level to the building level and a net reduction of staff at the central level. In this particular system, the net result has been to increase the central staff by eight persons in order to accommodate the decentralization effort.

Not only are the schools losing the expertise of the central staff members as they discover their staff development needs, but the central staff is also embittered because they feel that their expertise is not recognized by the system. This results in the waste of very valuable assets to the students of the district and is an enormous waste of resources to the taxpayers of the city. One of the major shortcomings in this city, which has over 100 schools, is that each school has now developed a strategic plan, and none of the plans have much in common with the other plans. Students who transfer from one school to another are left in no man's land when it comes to similarity of programs between buildings. Transition difficulties between elementary and middle school levels and between middle school and high school levels are also exacerbated by this strange set of circumstances.

Why did this happen and who is at fault? Many are responsible for the fiasco: the acting superintendent who was trying to appease the board of education and the members of the various staff unions; the board, which had always been a highly political and vocal board, with their roots in the various buildings throughout the district and a tendency to micromanage every decision; the school staffs, who wanted to avoid accountability responsibility; the various communities, who wanted control of their local schools; and the central staff, who were threatened by the state-mandated move to SBM and were protecting their jobs. All must share the blame for what has happened to the district as a result of this situation. Careful planning, evaluation, and decision making must be the watchwords for the district wanting to move to a SBM organizational pattern.

Evaluation of All School and District Personnel and Programs

Another of the important tasks for the central office personnel is the task of evaluating all programs that are a part of the district's offerings, as well as the evaluation of all personnel in the district. Indeed, the rationale for recommending that the district adopt a common evaluation model (see Chapter 4 of this handbook) is so that the central support staff can be introduced to the model as one that will be used in the evaluation of all programs and in the evaluation of personnel across the district. This gives the district's personnel a common base from which to be evaluated and judged.

It is important for the personnel of the district to recognize and accept the notion that evaluation is "to improve and not to prove." All personnel must stand the test of evaluation, as must all programs and efforts implemented by the various schools in the district. In the development of the school plan, the expectations for every program effort are itemized. The standards for the evaluation of all programs conducted in the district are the expectations for each program, developed at each site for the particular program and then judged. These expectations become the standard for evaluating the program at the end of a cycle. The evaluation leads to a shift in program emphasis if it is called for. The evaluations are mostly formative and lead to adjustments during the course of a cycle in order to make the program more effective.

Data are being developed at the National Center for Educational Evaluation located at Western Michigan University to incorporate the total evaluation process within a common model. This project should make the process much more amenable to the evaluation needs of every school and district. The Center, funded through a federal grant from the U.S. Office of Education, has studied and researched the current evaluation efforts in both program and personnel evaluation and has concluded that a common model can and should be developed for use in the field.

The author, working with Dr. Daniel Stufflebeam, the Center Director, and others, is currently involved in the development of a common model.

One of the primary tasks of any school district is the evaluation of programs and personnel in such a way as to make the process fair and cause improvement in the way programs are delivered to students. Personnel evaluation efforts currently being utilized are not always consistent and fair to the person being evaluated. Often, the evaluation process is developed for ease of operation and implementation and is developed around a particular bias, rather than involving the person being evaluated as one component of the instrument's development.

Ideally, each staff member develops objectives around his/her assignment, and, after concurrence with the supervisor, consensus is reached on the appropriateness of the objectives. Then, the subordinate is evaluated against the objectives developed by him/her around the particular job. Many districts involve several strands in the personnel evaluation process. These usually include at least five layers: self-evaluation, peer evaluation, subordinate evaluation, super-ordinate evaluation, and client evaluation. This provides a well-balanced evaluation effort that is fair, yet comprehensive. The instrumentation for these evaluation efforts is usually developed with the particular district's needs in mind.

The central staff person's role in personnel evaluation is to make sure that the instrument follows the dictates of the process and that the process is conducted fairly. Further, the central staff person may serve as the "other" outside evaluator if needed.

In the evaluation of programs and ongoing efforts mounted by the district, the central staff member serves as the main conduit of data needed for the evaluation process. While this sounds as though it is a tremendous task, the earlier planning process has served to establish the main objectives and expectations of the particular programs, and the evaluation process is merely a means to see that what was promised is actually delivered to the students. The best evaluation is always the evaluation that takes place when the person delivering the service or program compares what the student got against what the program promised.

As the system moves toward greater and greater accountability, the role of central office personnel becomes much clearer. The personnel at the central office are charged with the evaluation tasks for all evaluation efforts (program as well as personnel) being conducted by the system.

Questions Often Asked about the Role of the Central Office Staff in the Move to an SBM Type of Organization

Q-1: The central office person charged with being our liaison person always says that a suggestion is not possible and should be changed. Can we at the building level appeal that decision?

A-1: By all means. The central office person acting as your liaison does not have the capacity to make unilateral decisions concerning your school. He/she should be available for consultation and advice but should not be a naysayer to any ideas that crop up from the staff and community. Most districts have an appeal process to allow staff at the school to develop ideas against which the liaison person may be biased.

Q-2: As a superintendent, I am nervous about turning the decisions affecting students over to the various sites and staffs. How can I be assured that they will operate in the best interests of the students and not become self-serving?

A-2: If you have your district's strategic plan in place and if you have a developed evaluation design also in place, the task becomes much easier. The local schools are required to develop school plans that are compatible with the district plan, and then the agreements for implementation are negotiated with your office. You have the responsibility for evaluating the progress being made at each site on the agreed-to implementation plan for that school. If progress is not what you and the board expected and if there are no mitigating circumstances that preclude the school's making progress toward its goals and objectives, the task is really quite clear for you: you must make the necessary decisions to permit that school to show the kind of student growth that you and the board expect.

Q-3: The building staff have decided that they want and need a person trained in the development of cooperative teaching for their school. Through the elimination of two teaching assistants and the consolidation of several line items in the budget, they can see where they can find the funds to support a half-time professional for this duty. Is this type of barter permissible?

A-3: Of course, this is what SBM is all about. The local staff can adjust their budget and allocated resources to meet their prioritized needs.

Q-4: When we developed our school plan, we felt that the most important need for our students was a complete and rigorous approach to the teaching of reading. Therefore, we decided to allocate an extra period every other day to the teaching of reading. In our negotiations sessions with the central office, we were chastised for not including sufficient time for the teaching of science in our planning and were told to modify our plan to include the teaching of science in the time allocations. Can the folks at the central office do that?

A-4: Yes, they can. They are charged with seeing that every subject in the curriculum is given attention, and you must have slighted the teaching of science. If you can support a shortened time allocation for science because the achievement level of the students in your school in science is so high that this is appropriate, make the argument; however, if the science achievement of the students in your school is not appreciably higher than the district average, I'd suggest finding another way to allocate increased time to the teaching of reading.

Q-5: Our school has decided to accept a higher student/teacher ratio in order to generate sufficient resources to add a curriculum planning/instructional specialist to the staff. Is this move appropriate and can it be done?

A-5: Yes, on both counts. The school advisory committee has the obligation to see if the school can meet the highest priority needs by changing the traditional method of allocating resources and by permitting the staff and community to decide what is of utmost importance to the school. If the staff has decided that an important priority for the school is the addition of an instructional specialist to assist in the educational planning effort, they can, through efficient consolidation, generate the needed resource for the position.

Q-6: Is it appropriate to use the substitute teacher allocation to provide substitutes for a grade level so that they may have a day to develop instructional strategies?

A-6: Yes, it is. The best use of a particular budget item is when it is used to provide the students with an improved program of education. If the particular grade level staff want to have an extra day for planning a major change in the delivery system of the school, it is appropriate to use the substitute teacher budget allocation to permit this kind of activity. Care must be taken to maintain an adequate level of substitute teacher resources to provide for emergencies, but the distribution of those resources equally throughout the school is a fair use of the resource.

Q-7: Our principal is a wonderful woman, but she does not believe in staff and community participation in school affairs. She is threatened by such participation and refuses to open the system to staff and community involvement. Our district just mandated a move to SBM and has directed that the staff and community participate in certain decisions. Our principal has said that she will never relinquish control of the school and has ignored the directive to open the process. What should we do?

A-7: Organize a staff committee to explore the SBM process. Request a meeting with the central office liaison person for the school, share your frustration with that person, and solicit his/her advice on the topic. Support that person as he/she meets with the principal to initiate the mandated move toward SBM. Remain calm in the face of trauma on the part of the principal and show her that the staff wants only to become partners in the educational process.

Q-8: Our whole-language reading program has been poorly evaluated by the liaison person. We, as principal and staff, feel that a single year is not enough time to show growth trends for the program and are comfortable that, in another year, those trends will show positive and real progress for the program. Should we submit a minority report on the evaluation of the reading program?

A-8: By all means. If the staff has reason to feel that the whole-language approach to reading will ultimately produce the desired results, a request for an extension of one year in the summative evaluation is in order. However, if data show that the school is not making progress after a two- or three-year period, the staff must come to grips with that data and be willing to make changes in the delivery system.

Q-9: Our central office has been given two years to learn new and different techniques for the implementation of the SBM type of organization. If we do not learn these techniques, the threat is that we will be sent back to the classroom as teachers. Can they do this to us?

A-9: They can and will if they are serious about the move to SBM. This type of school organization does not require the number and type of central office personnel that the old traditional organization did. Therefore, if the central staff do not wish to learn such support activities and skills as planning and evaluation, their usefulness to the system is limited, and they become a luxury the district can no longer afford. Change is difficult but necessary if the United States school systems are to remain effective.

SCHOOL PRINCIPALS

The school principal is the key element in the move from a traditional system of organization to a Site-Based Management organizational scheme. Principals and superintendents are the two main school system positions that are considered generalist in nature. This means that the principal must have a broad general knowledge about the entire process and organization of the educational system in order to be successful, which is similar to the requirements of the superintendency. As a generalist, the principal has a vital role to play in the evolution of the school as the provider of instruction to the students enrolled at the site. He/she is also responsible for the allocation and monitoring of the resources available to the school.

In the traditional system, the principal was expected to implement district policies and procedures relating to the delivery of educational services. Any exception to the mandated practices were not condoned without first getting permission for the change before the fact. Under the SBM organization, the school is expected to generate new and different methods for delivering the educational services to the students. The principal, as the educational leader, must take the responsibility for directing the planning needed to make the school staff responsive to the needs of the students in their charge. Thus, the role of the principal is a changing and more demanding role than it ever was.

From Manager to Leader

The principal under the SBM type of organization must become a leader of the personnel and parents of the school for which he/she is responsible. Under the traditional organization, the principal was basically the manager of the school. As such, he/she made sure that the directives and processes ordered by the central office were implemented. Additionally, the principal organized the school in accordance with the wishes of the superintendent and the central office and managed the delivery system so that all of the main delivery objectives, as set forth by the central office, were carried out. The principal, if he/she was a risk taker, did some things that were best left untold to those in authority and, in fact, bordered on making some decisions that were for the benefit of students, but against district policy and procedure. In these cases, district personnel usually looked the other way if the principal was one of the "better" principals in the district.

As the move toward SBM becomes more entrenched and spreads to many districts across the country, the role of the principal becomes more defined as "leader" than as manager. The principal must acknowledge his/her role as the leader of the school or "learning community" housed at that particular site. As the leader of the learning community, the principal must utilize the strengths of the total staff and community to develop the best possible program of education for the students of that site. To do this requires a variety of strengths that are not commonly associated with the principalship. The principal should possess such characteristics as providing the vision for what the school could and should be, the ability to involve staff and community in decisions about the school and the programs offered the students, a commitment to risk taking for the benefit of the students, a willingness to permit the staff to plan and implement appropriate programs for the students at that site, the capacity to evaluate programs and staff so that the formative evaluations lead to better programs and methods for that school, the ability to generate resources from the immediate community and the broader business and commercial community, and the vigor and energy to accomplish the strategic goals and objectives of the district as translated to the needs of that particular site.

This is a far cry from the traditional role of the school principal and requires far more capacity, originality, flexibility, and strength than ever before. The school principal must come to grips with what he/she knows the school can become and show the staff and community the road to this vision. At the same time, he/she must involve all of the staff and community in the necessary planning required for success in reaching this vision.

Among the new and different skills the principal must exhibit are those enabling skills that are required to develop a consensus model for the school. This means that the principal must know how to work with a diverse clientele and staff so that they arrive at consensus on what, where, why, how, and when new adaptations and programs are to be introduced and implemented. Along with the previously required skills of managing an operation the size of the school, the principal must develop those skills that are required for the school and community personnel to become partners in the educational delivery system at the school. He/she must do all of this while never compromising the original mission of the school and district.

The task of being the educational leader of the school is one that calls for the best in the area of personal skills and requires the highest order of human and academic skills. It is not easy to lead a group of professional educators and the surrounding community into a serious examination of the existing conditions of the educational program being provided the students and to plan changes in the program to make it much more appropriate to the students located at that school. Such leadership requires strengths and firmness of purpose that few humans are capable of.

The planning function is the most important task area that the principal must learn and become proficient in. The generation and use of appropriate data on which to base decisions will greatly enhance the success chances of the principal. The recognition of what the needs are as described by the data and how they can be addressed becomes one of the more important skills that the principal must learn. While all of the traditional skills of managing the school remain, the new and equally important skills of planning, evaluating, and decision making become paramount for success. All this must be done while developing the staff and community to be partners in the process.

As the leader of a learning community, the principal must admit and accept that no one person has the total answer to persistent and demanding problems facing the school as it tries to serve the student's educational needs. It is only through close personal involvement of all who make up the learning community – the staff, the students, the parents, and the community at large – that the best possible programs can be developed to serve the students. The principal, through the use of consensus-building skills, assists the planning process in evolving into a decision-making process for that building.

The goal of the educational program will always be to minimize the differential between groups in attaining the educational objectives deemed important by virtue of the board's goals and objectives. Data are gathered, provided to the community and staff in a variety of forms, and disaggregated so that the planners can see in context how the various groups will greatly assist the planning process. The principal must recognize the differences between the groups in attendance at the school and make use of the data to emphasize the importance of equalizing the learning opportunities for every student at the school. Teachers must quickly recognize their role in the provision of equal educational opportunity to all students. Through the leadership of the principal, these nuances become highlighted for the staff and community and become important objectives for the school.

The principal must know how the staff operates when it comes to developing and delivering a program to the students. His/her main purpose is to allow the staff to have maximum flexibility in developing and implementing programs, while still keeping the objectives of the school as the guiding principle for such development.

Strategic Plan for the School

The development of the campus improvement plan is the first step in the move from a traditional approach to the SBM approach to school operation. In the traditional approach, the campus improvement plan was handed down from the central staff and made the focal point of all activities of the school. Under the SBM concept, the principal, staff, and community have the responsibility of developing the campus improvement plan using all available data derived from a variety of sources.

The first place to look when developing a school strategic plan is the district's strategic plan. Much of the data used to develop the district plan is applicable to the school as well and should be considered by the principal in the development of the school plan. Moving from the more general to the more specific is a part of the evolution from the district's strategic plan to the school plan. Certainly, the district goals are to remain a significant part of every school plan in the district. Since these are a part of the district's policies, they must become the highlights of the school plans as well. The school, however, has the responsibility of developing the specific operational plans with which to meet the objectives of the district strategic plan and annual work plans.

When developing a school plan, the logical place to start is with an examination of all of the pertinent data concerning the particular school.

This includes test scores and similar test data from the archives, records of achievement at the particular school, data concerning the students and their families, racial data, socioeconomic status data, descriptive data about the school and community, data concerning the school staff, fiscal data about the school, and all other data about the school and community and how they operate.

Next, the inputs or resources provided the school must be identified and listed. This includes budgetary allocations, as well as human resources and volunteer assistance available to the school. There are many resources that are accessible to most schools that are never identified as an input, because the school does not recognize their availability. Human resources are often overlooked because they are not specifically identified as inputs to a school. These human resources include staff, volunteer personnel from any source, donations and/or grants available, federal and/or state grants bestowed as a result of a winning proposal from the staff, adopt-a-school partnerships that generate resources for the school, and other such efforts to develop inputs for the school. Once these resources are identified, the principal and staff know what the limitations are as far as budget is concerned and, therefore, what they must do to supplement the available resources in order to make the school function for the benefit of the students.

The context analysis and the results of a survey of the inputs help define the strategies to be utilized by the staff and community in providing the best possible program for the students of the school. The best possible program of education must be devised within the budget parameters and delivered to the students at the school. Instructional strategies must be learned and implemented that will make the students of the school successful in attaining the educational goals and objectives as defined by the board in the district's strategic plan.

The principal must take the leadership responsibility for the development of the school plan and must provide the opportunity for all staff and community to participate to the extent they feel they can. At the very least, acceptance of the school plan by all stakeholders is required, while, at the maximum, direct participation would be appropriate. The involvement process is always difficult and should be approached with caution. People must learn how to become participants in a planning process and are, usually, required to grow into full participation status. That is why it is important that the district strategic plan be the model for the school plan because it sets the parameters.

The context analysis is, perhaps, the most important information-gathering phase for the school to initiate. Through the context evaluation, the school principal and staff learn what the most important and highest priority needs are at that particular site and can, thus, assign a higher classification to those emerging needs. After all, it is not as important to reteach those things that students already know, while it becomes crucial to teach those elements where the student body is not at the desired level of knowledge.

Developing the context analysis of the school is most important because the staff and community must understand what the highest priority needs of the student population are in order to develop responses to those high-priority needs. Reaching consensus on the priorities to be assigned also permits the staff to focus on these, while not wasting time and energy in meeting needs that are already met through the routine processes at the school. Complete understanding of the priorities at the school will also encourage the serious examination of budget allocations to determine where resources are needed to address the highest priority needs. It might be that certain programs may be found to be superfluous, and those resources may be reallocated to the high-priority needs. At any rate, this process is recommended as important to the involvement process at the school.

The strategic plan for the school must consider not only the context analysis, but it must be cognizant of every variable to be found at the particular school. By that we mean that, as the planner considers the priorities of the school in terms of meeting those goals/objectives as identified as important in the district's strategic and work plans, the focus shifts to the practicality of meeting the goals at the school level and to what resources are needed to predict success in the endeavor.

Collaborative Planning Process

The development of a strategic or improvement plan for the school demands a collaborative planning process involving the principal, staff, parents, community, and students of the school. Students, particularly those at the middle and/or high school levels, can easily verify the needs assessment and the priorities assigned to the needs at the school. Students, more than anyone else, know what the quality of their education is and how it can be better and more focused. They also have ideas about how to transmit good education to all of the students and about peer influence and cooperation in the instructional process.

In order for the school plan to be accepted and utilized by the entire community, it must reflect the involvement of the entire community in its development. While it is virtually impossible to actively involve every member of the school community, it is possible and recommended that a representative sample of each component of the staff, students, parents, and community be appointed as the planning committee, with the charge of developing a plan to be presented to the entire population of the school community at a designated time. Of necessity, this committee will be kept small enough to accomplish the task, because sheer numbers often make real progress impossible; however, these committee members must represent their constituency and reflect what the desires of their particular group are.

Involvement of the various stakeholder groups in the planning process often negates possible problems, because the various groups are represented in the original development and are familiar with both the process and the particulars of the plan. Consensus is possible when people of good faith meet together to solve particular problems. The principal has the responsibility to make the planning process work for the benefit of the school's students. He/she must understand the planning process and utilize good involvement procedures while drawing the best from the various elements of his/her community and staff.

Individual Educational Plan for All Students

Under the emerging technological developments now being made available to most schools and districts, combined with the organizational patterns suggested by an SBM type of organization, it is quickly becoming possible for the local school to develop a system of individual educational plans (IEPs) for each student enrolled at the school. The development of an IEP for each student is an appropriate goal for every school.

The technology is already available for such development, and, through the use of computers and software already developed, such individualized planning is possible for use at the school level. This will permit the utilization of much more data about each student and leads to the development of focused educational plans developed to meet the highest priority needs of that particular student.

The monitoring process is readily available through the use of technology, and all data pertinent to the particular student is examined and interpreted for the classroom teacher. The development of such individual student data bases will promote the use of different techniques for every student and force teachers to become aware of the differing learning styles of the various students in the class. It also will encourage the use of peer teaching arrangements, as well as individualized learning environments created on the basis of the demands of the student's particular learning style.

The use and development of IEPs will force the movement of the teacher from the current dispenser of factual information to that of manager of learning systems, responding to unique learning needs of the various students in the class. The teacher cannot be held responsible for all of the factual information that is now available to every student but can become the manager of the learning system that conveys that information to the student through the use of emerging technology and various information systems now available to the students and the schools.

The principal, as the leader of the learning community, must become aware of the emerging technologies available to the school and must transmit this knowledge to the staff and community. He/she must assist the staff and community in developing the appropriate appreciation and familiarity with what technology can do for the students of the school. As students become computer-literate at an earlier and earlier age, the need for staff and community to become equally computer-literate becomes very important. The principal can be of tremendous assistance in this process by making the technology available to the parents and by making sure that they understand the application of the technology to the school program.

Diverse Curriculum

The site must identify and develop the curriculum needed to permit every student to learn and to meet educational objectives as defined by the strategic and work plans of the district. This means that the school staff, with the assistance of their liaison person from the central staff and other specialists on the learning process, will develop the appropriate curriculum for the students at the site. Most often, this involves the development of different methodology and pedagogy for the individualization of instruction so that the IEP needs of each student can be programmed.

Techniques for integration of curriculum and for integration of multi-aged students based on their readiness must be developed at the site. The site staff, led by the principal, must identify the particular student needs on a curriculum by curriculum basis and develop the integrated responses to meet the students' learning needs. This involves the deep understanding of how programs are developed and applied to meet the diverse needs of individual students. The merging of the total curriculum of the school into a united program of instruction geared to meeting the unique needs of a diverse student body is a particular strength needed by most school staffs. The staff must be provided with training necessary for such development. Few, if any, districts have these particular strengths in their own central offices and must seek assistance in developing these unique attributes.

The principal must coordinate these efforts and be the person responsible for the lasting impact of such staff development on the total program of the school. Grouping similar curricula is an initial step in the direction of curriculum integration. Most schools start with the grouping of science and mathematics, English and social studies, art and music, and other similar groupings. The development of coordinated learning units reflecting these groupings requires staff with diverse backgrounds in learning theory and in understanding individual learning needs.

Evaluation Based on Student Outcomes

One of the major responsibilities of the school principal is the development of an evaluation system that is based on student outcomes, rather than the traditional input evaluation where the school is evaluated on the inputs made at the school level, and outcomes are then assumed.

As part of the school plan development, the school must learn to express plans in terms of what students will learn, subject by subject, so that evaluation will focus on what the school is going to teach. Such precise language is to be expected if the staff is going to assume responsibility for the learning rates of the students in their care. Teachers must take responsibility for student learning and must be led by the principal into the development of action plans addressing the priorities as established in the campus improvement plan.

The careful alignment of the curriculum with the learning objectives of the school will lead to an item analysis of the materials tested to determine how well the school's curriculum is aligned with the instructional program. An adjustment of the program may be made to guarantee its appropriateness to the curriculum. Many schools find that, through curriculum alignment, they are able to encourage great gains in test scores and other measures; thus, the school becomes an active participant in the development of appropriate curriculum. The principal is the staff member responsible for the development of this tool for improvement. He/she, through the involvement of the staff and community, generates the needed assistance for the development of a plan for curriculum alignment of the instructional program.

Needs Assessment for Staff Development

The principal should gather the staff development needs of the staff and community and use them to formulate a staff development/community development plan for the school. The principal should always remember that the staff members are at various stages in their understanding of the SBM process and their own roles in that process. After all, they are expected to learn new behaviors for which none of them have been prepared. There are few, if any, role models for the staff (and principal) to observe.

The wise principal requests that the staff itemize and express their own needs as far as development is concerned. No expressed need is too small for a response, and every attempt to meet that need should be attempted. In some cases, the needs expressed by the staff can be gathered into a common need, and a particular program can be mounted to meet those specific needs. When those needs are expressed by a majority of the staff, the wise principal attempts to provide staff development in that particular area of concern.

Staff development needs should be addressed in the context of a comprehensive plan for staff development, so that the scarce resources can be utilized in the most efficient manner. It is sometimes helpful for two or more schools to formulate development plans in cooperation with one another, so that the most common of the development needs can be met cooperatively. Typically, the needs related to the development of campus improvement plans and the development of an evaluation effort are best met through a common staff development effort. However, those development needs that are unique to the school, such as the particular data generated at that school and what it means to the plans for student growth, must be met in a manner that is unique to that particular staff.

Because of such unique and differing needs in the area of staff development, it is suggested that the staff development budget be partially decentralized to enable local schools to have some seed money for providing staff development efforts locally.

Questions Often Asked about the Role of the Principal in the Move toward an SBM System

Q-1: As a principal, I have a difficult time accepting the visionary role and am hesitant to express the dream I have for the school where I am principal. Is there assistance that I can get to assist me in the development of the vision for the school?

A-1: Yes, any number of publications are available for your use. Among your staff there should be several members who are quite visionary about what the school should and could be. Tap their vision and build a vision of the school that comes from the best thinking of the total staff and community. If you are able at this time to express the vision of the school as you would like, get the leadership team to collaborate in its development.

Q-2: I am good at the detail that must be accomplished at the school level but find that I am somewhat limited in providing the leadership to the staff. I prefer to have the staff develop the major plans and objectives for the school. Is this appropriate?

A-2: Yes, it is. Many principals have the same difficulty as you but are unwilling to have the staff take the leadership in the development of the school plans. By all means, have the staff develop the plans in concert with the community. Your role will be in the implementation and support of the plan as it is conceived.

Q-3: We are a strong union staff. Our principal and the leadership team have decided to exchange two teaching staff members for several aids and a curriculum specialist. This is in violation of the union contract. Should we support or reject the staffing pattern?

A-3: If you are convinced that the contract provides the best possible educational opportunity for students, by all means oppose the suggested staffing pattern; however, if the proposed staffing pattern is best for the students of the school, the thing to do is to support it. Remember that the school is there to serve the students, and the leadership committee has recommended what they feel is best for the students.

Q-4: Our principal is a strong person who wishes to make every decision concerning the school. As a member of the leadership team, I feel that our good ideas are not listened to, especially when they are different from the ideas of the principal. How can we get the principal's attention?

A-4: Convey to the principal that the leadership team wishes to contribute to the planning effort and to the decision-making process as it affects the school. If the principal persists in making every decision without any consultation with the leadership team, appeal those decisions that are most controversial to the wishes of the leadership team and demand a participatory role in the future. This should resolve the problem.

Q-5: The leadership team is composed of union members who defer to the union leadership on every decision. As principal, I want to make the leadership team responsive to the needs of children and not to the demands of the union. How can I exert leadership so that the decisions forthcoming will be in the best interest of students, instead of what is best for the union?

A-5: Among the steps to be taken are (1) expand the leadership team to include non-union members so that the balance of power is changed to members who want what is best for children, (2) provide a challenge to the current members of the leadership team by explaining the role of the team and its accountability for student success, and (3) develop a data base about the school and its students that will refute the feelings of the union group and make them pay attention to the reality of what is happening at the school.

Q-6: The staff of the school does not understand the strategic planning process and does not wish to assume stronger responsibility for planning activities. As principal, how can I get the staff to participate more fully in the development of the strategic plan for the school?

A-6: By requesting staff development activities for the staff that focus on the planning process and its importance to the development of an active plan for the school based on a thorough context analysis, and by getting the leadership team to work on the development of a plan for the school and sharing it with the total staff for their approval.

Q-7: Our teachers are used to a traditional mode of operation and wish to remain individual "cottage industries" in their self-contained classrooms. How can I, as principal, get extended staff participation?

A-7: By providing the staff development activity needed to get them out of the traditional mode of operations. Most teachers are comfortable with the status quo and do not wish to change. Through careful discussion and examination of the data (context analysis) about the building and through the introduction of ideas regarding the opportunities accruing as a result of the SBM organizational process, the staff of the building will get the idea that you are wishing them to participate in the decisions affecting the students of the school. A slow, careful weaning is indicated in order to change the culture of the school.

Q-8: Our staff is resisting the move to an IEP for every student. How can I, as principal, get the message across that this is the wave of the future and we must all get on board?

A-8: Again, through staff development sessions utilizing the technology that makes an IEP for each student possible. When teachers learn how much better they can serve the students through the IEP and related data, they will get on board and implement the process.

Q-9: We are having trouble integrating the curriculum at our school. The teachers still want to isolate each subject and develop teaching units based on individual subjects and do not wish to integrate the subject matter as a way of presenting a problem-solving solution.

A-9: Once again, the best approach is to present a staff development program that shows how a group of teachers did solve the same problem by arriving at an integrated solution to the merging of several individual subjects into a whole range of problem-solving activities. Imitation is the best form of flattery, and the teachers at your school will quickly develop an appreciation for the merged curriculum.

TEACHERS

Teachers at the school are the most important actors in the SBM process. They can subvert the process by not participating in the various committees that are so essential to the success of SBM. Remember that the SBM process demands the most from the teaching staff of the building. They are asked to change the culture of the school by changing long-established behaviors that are imbued in most teachers from the day they entered the classroom.

Teaching has always been a cottage industry because what the teacher does when he/she closes the classroom door is sacred to the teacher. Teachers have been accustomed to making every decision about the learning process, about what is best for the students in their charge, about how much emphasis to place on the various subjects, about how much time to devote to particular activities, and so forth. Now, they are being asked to focus on outcomes rather than inputs, to be held accountable for student learning, to individualize the instructional program, to adopt cooperative learning and teaching techniques, and to permit the student and parents a role in deciding what is important to the student.

This new role for the teacher is without precedent in the field of education. Not only must the teacher change his/her behaviors, they must do so without the benefit of a carefully planned behavior modification program. Few, if any, universities have embraced the emerging role for the teacher, and fewer still are prepared to create models for the changed behaviors expected of teachers under the SBM mode of operation. While it is unfair to expect teachers to learn the new mode of operation without the benefit of assistance from the institution of higher education that produced them originally, the reality is that teachers must develop for themselves a new culture for the school. The principal and various support staff are there to assist in every way possible, but the bulk of the work is the teacher's. Teacher participation is often an "add-on" to the normal work day and takes its toll on the teacher wishing to be a participant in the SBM process. Fortunately, once plowed, the ground becomes easier to work, so the recycling process is not as time-consuming as the original participation effort. There are a number of areas where teacher behavior must change under this type of organizational structure. They include the following.

From Provider of Facts to Manager of Learning Systems

Even without the generous use of the exploding technology now being made available to the teacher, good educational planning suggests the development of an IEP for every student, in order to best serve that student. This, coupled with the move toward outcomes-based instruction, are among the biggest changes imagined for the classroom teacher.

Employing the technology permits the teacher to become a manager of learning systems with the system selected for each child dependent upon his/her learning style. It no longer is necessary for each student to accommodate the teacher's teaching style, but, rather, the teacher now must recognize the learner's style and accommodate it. The work of outstanding educators like the Dunns and others make the recognition of learning styles easier and available to all educators in the country.

The day when a teacher could assimilate all of the factual knowledge about a subject and develop lesson plans around that knowledge is long gone. Knowledge and facts are exploding with the quantity of new knowledge doubling every five years so that it is humanly impossible to keep up. The technology is already available for tracking the knowledge explosion, and, once harnessed, it is available for all to partake of. The computer with CD ROM disks is a primary source of factual information, and interactive television makes it possible for students far removed from the source of a presentation to communicate with the instructor on a very intimate level. Fiber optics wiring is now being accomplished in a variety of ways and in most educational systems. The promise that cable operators will make fiber optics available to the schools adds another dimension to the technological capacity of the school.

All of these developments portend change and dramatic shifts in posture for all educators, especially teachers. Rigid union attitudes will have to change to accommodate the emerging technological age. As with all organizations, education must embrace the opportunity for improvement promised by the technology and must learn to use it to full advantage. Teachers must become computer-literate and use the technology to improve what happens to and for students. In those districts where a commitment has been made to embrace technology, dramatic and unforeseen changes are occurring. For one thing, the students are becoming so literate about the emerging technology that they are pushing the staff toward learning more and more about the technology or they will become obsolete. This is frightening to some staff members, but they quickly adjust to the reality of the times and embrace the new "tools" of education.

The Teacher as Diagnostician

With the emerging need to develop IEPs for each student, the teacher becomes a diagnostician and user of the available tools to diagnose and prescribe corrective action to the student. This is a takeoff on the physician model and extends the notion of the teacher as a professional educator who knows how to use the resources available to him/her for addressing the needs of each student on an individual basis.

Perhaps the most important change for the teacher to contemplate is the transformation from a person who lectures to a class, to becoming a person who diagnoses the instructional needs of each student and then sets out to provide the activities that meet these needs. While a certain amount of lecturing will still be necessary in all schools, the need for the lecture method as the sole mode of delivering educational services is gone and deservedly so. We have learned that there are several other more effective means to transmit learning to the student. Probably the best way to induce student learning is to develop an understanding of the particular student's learning style and then make the appropriate presentation based on it.

Because of emerging technology, the teacher has most of the needed tools and data available to him/her. Minute data about each student are available and can be utilized for diagnostic purposes. Knowledge about the things that could hinder learning and the rate of learning are easily accessible to the teacher about every student. The use of this data to develop appropriate delivery systems is one of the major charges to the classroom teacher.

The teacher as diagnostician is a relatively new concept and promises to have a lasting impact on how teachers are viewed. Accceptance and use of diagnostic techniques to gather, sort, and interpret student data to arrive at appropriate programs for students is an important use of the diagnostic capacity. Applying the medical model to education is an important first step in the professionalization of the teaching profession. The use of diagnostic techniques as the basis for the development of IEPs for every student gives credence to the claim that teachers are professionals in every sense of the word.

Cooperative Learning Leader

A rapidly emerging technique for assisting the student to become a self-directed learner is the cooperative learning approach to teaching/learning across the curriculum. In this approach, the teacher leads the students as they cooperatively dissect and examine a topic and sort out the essential elements that they must master. Cooperative learning provides more exposure and greater retention than does the traditional lecture/response method. In the cooperative learning approach, the student is directly involved with the planning and implementation of the lesson and is a direct participant in the teaching/learning process. Students develop a greater sense of urgency and pride in the topics to be learned because they are an integral part of the teaching/learning process.

The classroom teacher provides the appropriate climate for the involvement of the students in their own programs of education by guiding them into a careful examination of their learning needs and styles. From this "context analysis," the students can assist in the determination of the priorities involved in a particular assignment and arrange the subject matter in such a way as to be most responsive to student needs. Usually, students will also demand more from themselves than the teacher normally does and extend themselves into a higher order of thinking skills than is normally the case when the lesson is solely teacher-directed.

Cooperative learning offers the opportunity to select topics for focus that will permit the integration of several curriculum areas into a single examination of a topic. Over time, this permits a natural integration of the curriculum into the resolving of a topic that is germane to the students' learning needs. The teacher must learn techniques that encourage student involvement, which is a different technique than the traditional lecture approach. This approach requires greater tolerance for ambiguity on the part of the teacher because the students are not attuned to this type of classroom operation. They, the students, must be given greater leeway in expectations until they become used to such free-wheeling operations.

The Teacher as Planner and Visionary

As a primary participant in the development of the school approach to mitigating the students' learning difficulties and to developing educational programs that meet the primary needs of the students, the teacher must learn to see himself/herself as a planner and visionary. The capacity to dream and to visualize what the program could do for each child at the school is the first step in developing programs with the individual student needs in mind.

Teachers must learn planning techniques in order to be successful at harnessing the potential of each student. Because each student is different from each other student, the teacher as planner assumes a far more important role than ever before. As a full partner in the development of appropriate educational programs to serve the students, the teacher must learn to utilize the planning techniques that make for a far more efficient use of scarce resources. The setting of educational priorities and the establishment of a chronological order for meeting those needs is also important to the planning process. The teacher is crucial to the development of a strategic plan and a working plan for the school. These plans become the basis upon which the school and staff are evaluated for the subsequent year.

Because the teachers are the persons who know the students best, they must come forward and act as student advocates in the planning process. As student advocate, the teacher must defend the student's capacity to learn, identify his/her learning style, and reflect on appropriate programs to meet that particular student's academic needs. The teacher must use the analysis of each student's context to determine the best approach for solving the student's learning difficulties. This involves knowledge about the student, the family, the environment around the family, and the economic realities impacting the student's life.

The teacher, as planner/visionary, can adjust programs to meet the realities of the student's environment known only to him/her. Many variables impact the student, and the teacher, because of his/her intimacy with the student, knows about these variables and can protect the student when the time for protection is at hand.

The Teacher as Evaluator

The teacher as evaluator performs the customary student evaluations as before but now must, in addition, assist in the evaluations of the ongoing programs of the school in order to develop improvements in the school's delivery efforts. The involvement of the classroom teacher in evaluating the effectiveness of school programs is an important step in the SBM process, for it is because of such evaluations that the needed improvements are made to the school delivery process, to make it more acceptable and useful to the students at the campus.

The teacher is the best person to utilize data developed through the evaluation process and match that data with the appropriate delivery system so that maximum effectiveness is realized in all programs. Given the knowledge about the student that the classroom teacher possesses, the use of that knowledge to improve delivery systems so that they are more effective in their service to the students is essential.

As the prime user of evaluation data, the teacher must become a prime participant in the development of evaluation designs for the school. These designs are intended to provide critical analysis of the programs being implemented at the particular school and to assist the staff in developing a recyclable program that more effectively meets the needs of the students.

The teacher as evaluator must utilize student outcomes as the prime source of data for the evaluation effort. Outcomes, rather than inputs, should provide the essential data upon which to base the evaluation of a particular program. For far too long, we have utilized inputs as measures of progress. Inputs measure what the organization invests in a particular program but not how effective the program is. Essentially, outcomes tell the user how effective the program is and what must be done to make it even more effective.

In addition to being the prime evaluator of student performance and a participant in the evaluations of the programs offered at the school, the teacher plays an important role in acting as a self-evaluator in judging his/her own performance, as well as acting as a peer evaluator in assisting in judging of the performance of colleagues. Another segment of the evaluator role is teacher participation in the evaluation of the principal and superintendent. In this dimension, the teacher acts as a subordinate evaluator and provides valuable information for the formative evaluation of these personnel.

The Teacher and Staff Development

As the school unit moves into the SBM concept, the teacher must also assume some responsibility for the total staff development program located at the school. The teacher, in cooperation with the rest of the staff, can quickly determine the staff development needs of the local staff. If these needs are not met centrally, the teacher must work to get the necessary resources to meet them locally. The teacher must be a participant in the development of the school plan for staff development in order to make it as meaningful as possible.

Among the topics that are appropriate for teacher staff development are the following:

(1) Classroom use of technology
(2) Integrating instruction in all curriculum areas

- *(3)* Developing cooperative relationships among staff
- *(4)* Planning/visioning techniques
- *(5)* Gathering and sorting data about students
- *(6)* Evaluation and what it means to the classroom teacher
- *(7)* The development of cooperative learning methods
- *(8)* Consensus building and how it is done
- *(9)* Personal health and staff wellness
- *(10)* Developing the IEP

The Teacher as a Member of the Site-Based Leadership Team (SBLT)

Perhaps the greatest change for the classroom teacher under the SBM type of organization is the need to become a participating member of the decision-making process. This is accomplished through a member of ways, the first of which is as a member of the site-based leadership team, which participates in the decision-making process at the school. Not all teachers desire to participate in every decision made at the school, but for those who do, the opportunity for participation is there.

Historically, teachers have traded the opportunity for greater participation for absolute, de facto power of decision making in the classroom. Since this mode of classroom operation is going to be gone with the need for cooperative planning and teaching under a changed management system, the classroom teacher must consider new opportunities for participation in the decision-making process. SBLTs, consisting of teachers, support staff, parents, principals, and students, where appropriate, provide the necessary balance for needed decisions concerning student program improvement. A well-balanced leadership team represents all stakeholders in the educational process and considers all viewpoints before making a decision that impacts the students of the school. While the principal is the chair of the team, he/she should strive for consensus and equity in all decisions. The leadership team has as its prime responsibility the support of decisions that meet the test of equity and fairness to all, especially to the students.

Teachers, because of their close relationship to the students in their class, should be able to contribute an introspective view on the decisions being contemplated by the leadership team. Such introspection is important to the quality of the decisions and should focus the attention of the team on the welfare of the students. The planning/evaluation/decision-making function performed by the leadership team is crucial to the success of the school in meeting its educational goals and objectives. Participating and understanding the planning process and what it means to the school are prerequisites for a successful experience as a member of the leadership team.

Most teachers have real insights into the planning process because of the experience gained in developing student lesson plans over the years. They bring to the planning process a certain reality and "real world" orientation that gives credibility to the entire exercise. In addition, they are committed to implementation if they are involved in the original planning. Teachers are most capable of exercising leadership to their peers and to the community. They have, by virtue of their classroom experience, a wealth of understanding and knowledge about the student and what he/she needs. That, plus a firm desire to serve the students of the school, makes the classroom teacher a natural participant in the site-based leadership team.

Questions Often Asked about the Role of the Teacher in the SBM Type of Organization

Q-1: As a teacher, I do not have time to participate in all of the "busy work" presented to the leadership team by my principal. How can I get the team to focus on real matters when the principal always brings trivia to the table?

A-1: Don't fall into the trap he/she is setting for you. Refuse to take all of your time on trivia; rather, bring up items of importance to the school and suggest that an agenda be developed with input from all members of the leadership team. The principal will soon get the message that the team is there to assist in real decisions and not as fun and games.

Q-2: All of my education and preparation for becoming a teacher has served me to be able to lecture and drill my students on factual information. Now the demand is for teachers to work cooperatively and enable the students to master data and use the data to develop higher order thinking skills. How can I learn the emerging teaching techniques and styles?

A-2: By participating in the staff development offerings provided through the district and by initiating a school staff development process, whereby you and your colleagues can study and develop a teaching/learning style that meets the needs of your students.

Q-3: I read about the need for an IEP for every student and am sympathetic to that need; however, I have been teaching for ten years and have yet to be taught the techniques for performing an IEP. How and where do I learn about the IEP?

A-3: Participate along with the special education teachers in a real IEP development and ask questions about what you are seeing. Special education teachers have, for a long time, actively produced IEPs for every one of their students. It is time we all learn from the special education teachers the techniques and methods of producing the IEP for every student in our charge.

Q-4: I've always been comfortable with the fact that, once I closed my classroom door, I was in complete charge. Now I'm being forced to open the door to a variety of techniques and any number of cooperative ventures. How do I cope with this new demand?

A-4: Start with a serious examination of the results of your labors to see if there is room for improvement. If your students are performing as well as you think they should and your principal and peers agree with you on the assessment, they will probably not bother you as you continue to act as a "cottage industry." If however, you feel that there is something you can provide your students, initiate a cooperative venture with one or two colleagues and share your efforts toward providing an exemplary program for the students under your charge. As you become comfortable with opening the classroom to others, there are absolutely no limits on what can happen to and for your students.

Q-5: Our principal wants all of the teachers on the staff to make themselves available for the monthly leadership team evening meetings. He suggests that our presence will convey to the parents that we are truly interested in what is happening at the school. Our union contract specifies that we must attend only three evening meetings a year and should be paid for any other meetings required of us. The principal says that, if we choose not to attend the monthly meeting, we shall have to abide by the decisions made at the monthly meeting and follow those decisions in our daily activities. Can he do that?

A-5: Yes, he can. If your principal permits you to be absent according to the union contract and you choose to miss the monthly meeting, you forfeit the right of participation in those decisions made during the meeting. Parents have a right to attend some meetings that are planned around their schedule. Since most parents are working parents, some accommodation must be made of their schedule, and that means some meetings will be in the evening hours. SBM means the involvement of all who are stakeholders in the school, and that includes parents, as well as teachers.

Q-6: Our building is at loggerheads with the teacher's union over the flexibility permitted under the SBM type of organization. We, the staff of the school, wish to staff the building according to our needs and not according to the union contract. The union says that we cannot do this but must conform to the language in the contract. We say that we must do this or risk not adequately serving our students. The district says it will fund, according to the average teachers' salary, those positions we qualify for, according to our enrollment and that we can staff according to our improvement plan for the school. Can we ignore the union's insistence on staffing according to the contract?

A-6: If, after repeated requests from the union for a variance from the contract, the union still does not see fit to grant you permission for the variance, you must ultimately use your own judgment and do what is best for the children of the school. The district can make the claim that they funded according to a staff/pupil ratio as agreed to under the contract and that they approve of your schools' decision to staff according to your perceived needs. This is a common union grievance and one that must be faced by the teaching staff of each school in the district. Do student needs or union contracts determine the staffing pattern of a school?

Q-7: We have a group representing the religious right fighting and gaining control of the Site-Based Leadership Team at our building. They have done so because not many of the parents will give of the time necessary to participate in the SBM process while the religious right wants to gain control of the school and its activities. How can we, as staff, strike a balance between the religious right and the normal parent group who, typically, are most supportive of the school?

A-7: Recruit parents to the team by expressing the concerns that you feel. Parents do want the best for their children and often are deluded into thinking that certain parents represent them in their thinking but find that they are not representative at all. Open meetings and exploration of all of the issues often places extremists in an uncomfortable position. The truth never hurts, and, by telling the truth about representation, you can permit the parents of the school to defend their turf. Open, honest discussion never hurt any school, and this is an important option that you must explore.

Q-8: At our school, we have a site-based leadership team, a planning committee, an evaluation committee, a parental involvement committee, a student development committee, a facility committee, a budget committee, and a program committee. With only twenty-two teachers on staff and so many committees that require staff participation, we are stretched almost to a breaking point. How can we, without hurting our principal, suggest that there are far too many committees and that the leadership team should make most of the decisions now being allocated to the various groups?

A-8: You can suggest to the principal that, while all of you are desirous of participating in the affairs of the school, you do have other responsibilities at the school such as teaching and working with students. While you appreciate the opportunity to have such extended participation, you trust the members of the leadership team to make the decisions and express your thanks to the principal for taking the opportunity of involving all of the staff. The wise principal soon gets the message and makes adjustments.

Q-9: The members of the leadership team are at a stalemate over what to do about student truancy. The teacher members want to hold the parents responsible, while the parent members want to hold the staff responsible because of the inappropriateness of the programs to student interest. How can we resolve this issue?

A-9: By visiting several schools where they have resolved this issue through close cooperation between the parents and the school teaching staff. There is some validity for each of the groups' postures on this major issue. Programs should capture the interest of the students to be most effective, while parents should encourage their sons and daughters to attend school regularly. Visiting effective schools would give each group support and ideas with which to determine the answer to the problem.

Q-10: Our district has made a commitment to embracing emerging technology as a tool for improving the educational delivery system. The teaching staff is quite frightened by this approach and wants to have some time to think through the implications of becoming a high technology school system. How can we, as teachers, influence the district's decisions concerning technology?

A-10: Technology often threatens teacher morale. It is something new and different and is making inroads into the status quo. You all must face reality and agree that technology is already here, and your best approach is to embrace this as an appropriate development. Ask that the staff be provided with staff development programs in technology and that individual schools be provided the capacity to participate in developing the use for the technology to be provided at the school level.

Q-11: Our teachers are split between those who embrace the SBM concept and those who do not want to participate in anything but, rather, wish for things to remain as they were. How can we get the faculty to coalesce around the SBM concept?

A-11: Through constant dialogue and exploration of what is best for the students of the school. Assure the doubters that they will not be expected to change all of their behaviors at once but that they will have time to grow into a new culture. Things are different, and everyone must recognize that. Teachers now have the opportunity to participate in the decisions that affect them. This is a major step in the right direction, and they should support it.

PARENTS AND COMMUNITY

Other important and often overlooked elements in the SBM process are the parents and community of the school. Besides being important stakeholders in the educational process, they have entrusted their most valued family members to the school for purposes of assisting in their education and the "rite of passage" into adulthood. The school is an important adjunct to the neighborhood and must always interact with the community to establish expectations and delivery systems for providing the educational product to the students.

Parents are an important source of added human resources for the school to call on. Many parents have special skills that add immeasurably to the pool of resources available to the community. The school, in its wisdom, must find a way to tap these human resources to the benefit of the students of the school. Other community members also are able and willing to contribute time, effort, and sometimes dollars for the benefit of the students at the school.

The school should make a systematic study of the context of the neighborhood in order to develop an appreciation for the talents and resources available to assist in the delivery of educational services to the students. The identification and development of such a rich resource is often the difference between success and failure in the educational delivery process. Most community members, if approached in the right way, will be eager to support the educational effort of the school either by direct involvement or by supporting the effort in a variety of ways.

There are some specific ways that the parents and community can and should be involved with the school under the SBM type of organization. These include the following.

Involvement in Planning

As members of the site-based leadership team, the parents have full participatory rights and obligations. The leadership team assists in the development of the school strategic and work plans and sets the priorities for the school during the academic year.

They help develop the context analysis and assist in the identification and development of a data base upon which most decisions are based. They, more than any other group of stakeholders, can provide the explanation for the variances and differences found in the context analysis of the school as compared to other schools. They know best the needs of their children and the community since they are part of the community and know it well. Through examination of the community and school context, they can assist the staff in developing the kinds of program thrusts that are appropriate for the students of the local school.

Often, community members have special skills that enhance the planning effort and provide extra resources for use by the school. These special skills may take the form of specific talents and/or knowledge that will make a program extra special at the school. Perhaps, a parent's occupation lends itself to supporting the curriculum of the school. Other talents such as photography, writing, or the arts also provide opportunity for the school's students to benefit. Often, the act of volunteering provides the school staff with relief from routine, ordinary tasks and allows teachers to focus on the more creative aspects of delivering education to the benefit of the children.

The context analysis or needs assessment is best done through a cooperative process involving all stakeholders of a school community, because each has something to offer and a point of view that is unique. Typically, the SBLT, which has representatives from every group, develops the context analysis for presentation to the total school stakeholder group. As the leadership team learns to prioritize the needs of the school, the allocation of resources can proceed with minimum dialogue and argument. The data developed during the context phase of the planning process will largely determine the item by item resource allocations for the school.

Establishing the priority concerns for the school are perhaps the most important efforts of the SBLT because the priorities should drive the allocation of resources and programs. This is sometimes called "input analysis" or "input evaluation," which means the way in which resources, human as well as dollars, are allocated. Certainly, if the resources are not allocated according to agreed-upon priorities, the whole question of the validity of the planning process comes into question.

The process analysis is mainly a professional issue where the professional staff makes determination of the appropriate programs to meet the priority needs of the students at the school. This involves the choice of appropriate programs, the best methods for delivery of these programs, the choice of the pedagogy to be used in the delivery of programs, and other strictly professional matters and concerns. However, the parents and community can and should participate in the evaluation of these efforts to ascertain whether or not the methods and pedagogy appropriately deliver the programs to the students.

A more important role for parents and community is their participation in the establishment of product expectations for the school. The board of education establishes the district-wide expectations, and the SBLT establishes the school product expectations, which are in concert with the district norms. The leadership team usually sets the time frame for expectations to be met and the design for evaluating the efforts of the school.

School-Site Councils

School-site councils, often called site-based management or site-based leadership teams, are important vehicles for the parents and community to use as they become involved with the school. It is the legitimization of a process of community involvement that permits the voice of the community to be heard as the leadership teams accomplish the planning, evaluation, and decisions needed to make the school a viable part of the community.

The site councils perform many valuable duties and have a real impact in the operation of the local school. Membership on the site council or SBLT is through a selection process determined by the school's principal, staff, and parent groups. Usually, there are up to seven members of the SBLT, with the principal as the chairperson of the team. The remaining six members of the team are usually selected from the staff of the school (3) and the community (3), providing equal weight for both staff and community. In many middle schools and high schools, the number of members of the leadership team is increased to ten or eleven, giving students a voice in the deliberations as well. A total membership of eleven is not too much to enable dialogue and consensus to be arrived at about the various issues.

A seven- to eleven-member leadership team permits all of the members to participate, without allowing any one of them to become domineering and have undue influence over the decisions made. The leadership team usually meets weekly or whenever there is business to take care of. Meetings are more frequent during the budget season and when the plans are being crafted for presentation to the central board. During the school year, leadership team meetings are whenever the principal and/or members of the team call them.

The duties of the SBLT are varied and multiple. They largely depend on how much autonomy the principal is willing to share, what the district guidelines are for community participation, how the staff of the campus feels about such participation, and how comfortable the community is about the school. In many states, the limits for community participation are spelled out in the state code, which specifies the actual responsibilities the community may be allocated. In other states, the community may participate as much as the district permits and as far as the elected board of education is willing to share their power.

Participation on the school council is not a frivolous activity but a most important commitment on the part of the community and parents. The opportunity to share in the planning and evaluation of the school's programs is an indication of the worth of the SBLTs and the esteem under which they are held. It is certainly much more meaningful than participation in the local PTA being used to raise dollars for whatever the school needs and cannot afford. While the PTA is an important and well utilized support mechanism for the school, parent and community participation in the SBLT is much more than being a part of the school PTA. Membership on the leadership team means sharing in the planning/evaluation/decision-making responsibility for the school.

Staff Evaluation Responsibilities

The community is expected to share in the evaluation of staff at the school through participation on the site-based leadership team. As customers of the school and as consumers of the educational programs offered by the school, parents and community members have a vital role to play in the evaluation of both programs and staff of the school. As stakeholders in the school community, parents do have an important opinion about the quality of the staff and the propriety of the programs offered at the school. They can become one strand in the evaluation of the staff, by participating in the examination of the effectiveness of the staff as it affects the students at the school.

Emerging evaluation designs encourage the widest stakeholder participation in the evaluation of professional educators. Research by the Evaluation Center located at Western Michigan University on the development of evaluation models with which to evaluate professional education personnel reveals that the accomplishment of a fair and equitable evaluation that meet the widely circulated Joint Committee on Standards for Educational Evaluation criteria is possible through the involvement of all stakeholders in the education community. The Joint Committee Standards, totaling twenty-one are grouped under the following major categories: propriety, utility, feasibility, and accuracy. These standards must be met for the evaluation design to be judged acceptable and usable.

The research staff at the Evaluation Center studied all available staff evaluation models currently in use across the United States and then developed a hybrid model that meets the criteria and involves the various stakeholder groups as participants. During the 1994–95 academic year, the Evaluation Center will incorporate a comprehensive model for educational evaluation that will permit the use of a single model for the evaluation of both personnel and programs. This design will become most important to the members of the SBLT as they devise evaluation designs for use under an SBM system.

Questions Frequently Asked by Parents and Community about the SBM System of Operations

Q-1: As a parent, I am really interested in the educational program offered by the local school. However, when I inquire about program specifics, I am usually referred to the central office and made to feel inadequately prepared to deal with such delicate matters. How can I become involved with the planning of appropriate programs at my daughter's school?

A-1: By insisting on your right to know and understand what is being provided your daughter at the school and by becoming a part of the site-based leadership team and/or the community organization that names the community representatives to the committee. As a parent, you do have a right to participate in those decisions affecting your children, and you can choose to exercise those rights through participation in the school leadership team or its sponsoring organization.

Q-2: The parents and community who are the patrons of our neighborhood school are quite satisfied with the programs and curriculum at the school. They are very complacent about participating in the activities at the school and feel that the programs implemented at the school are the purview of the professional staff, and their role is to support the staff in whatever decisions they make. Is there a better way of supporting the offerings of the school and of providing a sure means that the program will remain flexible enough to change if such change is needed to serve all of the students at the school?

A-2: Yes, there is. By becoming more involved in the affairs at the school, parents and community can exercise their right to participation at the site level. Under the SBM organizational pattern, the local board of education sets the parameters for parent/community participation, and, through the establishment of site-based leadership teams, the local school encourages the involvement of parents and community on all phases of the instructional program.

Q-3: My husband and I are desiring a more participatory role in the education of our children. Our school board recently adopted a policy that encourages each building to develop an SBM type of organization and to involve parents in the decisions made at the school. The board also adopted a decision matrix, which specifies which decisions are to be made at the school and which are to be made centrally. How can my husband and I assure ourselves that we are heard when we express our feelings about certain programs and staff members who have such power over our children?

A-3: Inquire about the opportunity for parental volunteering at the school. As you become more familiar with the operations of the school and learn what the faculty and principal feel is important for the children, you can submit a plan for your activities as a volunteer. You can also begin to get involved in the various school committees, leading to participation in the SBLT, which is about the most involved that a parent can be. Involvement at whatever level is best for the individual parent should be the objective of the school and parents.

Q-4: Our principal is a fine person and a good educator, but he does not wish to involve the parents in any meaningful way. He prefers to have the staff of the school take full responsibility for all programs and expects the parents to support whatever the staff proposes. How can we, as parents, become more fully involved?

A-4: By showing the principal and staff that you, too, have ideas to contribute to the planning process and that you wish to make this contribution. Impress upon the staff of the school that you are the real owners of the system and that they work for you. Give them full responsibility for the professional development for which they are trained and hired, but impress upon them that you are fully capable of participation in the planning and evaluation of those professionally developed programs.

Q-5: A certain group of parents at the school are the most demanding of the parents at the school. They preempt all efforts at involvement by taking over a meeting and demanding services for their own children whom they consider to be gifted and a cut above the other students at the school. Rather than sharing and cooperating for the betterment of every student, they make demands that take most of the resources of the school and force the school to provide programs for few students. How can we get ourselves heard and become a part of the allocation process?

A-5: By becoming as vocal and demanding as the other parent group. If your school has moved toward an SBM organization, become a part of the school-site committee process and express your feelings. Always demand equity and fairness in all appropriation discussions. Provide rationale for whatever you recommend and make sure that equity always prevails.

Q-6: Our SBLT has made the development of higher order thinking skills the top priority for our school, in spite of the fact that over 50% of the children are not reading at grade level. We wish to change the priority system to refocus priority on the academic needs of the students, one of the biggest of which is the improvement of reading to guarantee that every child will read at grade level before leaving the elementary school. How do we go about that?

A-6: By expressing the data and factual information at the meeting where priorities are approved. Armed with accurate data that tells of the reading achievement levels of the students, recommending that the top priority should be the reading improvement of the students, rather than the development of higher order thinking skills should suffice. If not, bring the recommendation to a vote, and, if you have support, the reading skills improvement will prevail.

VIGNETTE #1

Effect on Participants of SBM

One district in Texas, which utilized the author's assistance in the development of an SBM approach, is a district of approximately 18,000 students located along the Rio Grande River on the border with Mexico. This district is almost entirely Hispanic in its student composition, and over 75% of the students are from lower socioeconomic levels. Indeed, approximately 75% of the students participate in the free and reduced fee lunch program.

The parents from this district are mostly migrant workers who are residents of the notorious *colonalias* that dot the Rio Grande Valley. These settlements, or *barrios,* are best known for their lack of sewage, running water, and other amenities that are expected and common across the United States. When implementing the SBM legislation, the staff of this district decided to explore the flexibility and participatory provisions of the law and made the effort to involve the parents of the community in their planning and also in the implementation of their design for improving education in the school district. In order to provide maximum participation, the staff of one elementary school decided to open the doors of the school to the extended community and to provide food service and support services to the entire community in exchange for parental involvement in the education of the students. Over the past three years, this also provided an excellent means for adult education and literacy training of the parents, who felt the need to partake of the adult education opportunities in order to be of assistance to their children. Because many of the parents are unemployed after the migrant season ends, they are readily available for program assistance and involvement at the school for most of the school year.

Through the completion of a work plan constructed after the district developed a strategic plan and specifying specific objectives for the site, the following objectives were adopted for the school:

(1) Every child shall approach the appropriate grade level in the basic core subjects.
(2) Attendance shall be over 96% in average daily attendance for the year.
(3) Each teacher shall visit every home of every child in her/his room annually.
(4) Parents shall be comfortable at the school and shall participate in the adult literacy classes offered at the school.
(5) Every lunch room, custodial, and teacher aide position shall be filled by a parent at the school.
(6) Monthly meetings of the site-based management committee shall take place during the evening hours to enable parents to attend and participate.

(7) All soft money (grants, special projects, contributions, etc.) would be allocated to the various priorities developed by the SBM committee.

In the first year under the new administrative arrangement (SBM), the faculty had several disagreements with the principal and the community. Great care was extended in explaining the needs of the students and the role of the staff in meeting those needs. Those staff members who felt they could not devote the necessary time and commitment to the primary objectives were encouraged to transfer, with no hard feelings or repercussions. Of the total teaching staff of twenty-five, four were transferred to other assignments, and the community and faculty participated in the selection of their replacements.

When, before the second year began, the staff developed the objectives listed above, the staff was together in their belief that the children of the school could learn and could become model students and learners. They set out to prove that, even in schools where the expectations were not always the highest, students had the capacity to become good learners and achievers.

Today, five years later, this school is one of the highest achieving elementary schools in the state of Texas, and the staff and student body have one of the lowest turnover rates in the state. This, when once the turnover rate of students was in excess of 100% annually. A visit to the school reveals the consistently high morale of the staff and students. The parents are always welcome at the school, and they take the opportunity to avail themselves of adult literacy programs offered at the school.

This case study is indicative of the influence that a dedicated teaching staff, a highly committed principal, and a receptive community can have on the learning rate of students. There is none of the graffiti and other earmarks often found in less than effective institutions to be found here. Indeed, when such graffiti are found at the site, someone from the community quickly covers the defacement, often without saying anything about it. It is easily seen how proud of the school everyone connected with it is and how they all want to preserve and protect the institution for the sake of the students. Talking with the staff of the school reveals the struggle that took place to establish the relationships that are so important to success and the way that everything fell into place once these relationships were established. The fact that the staff and the principal did not place themselves on a pedestal and were available to students and parents did much to assure the success of the school. The staff is confident that the pattern now accepted as the norm for the school will provide the energy for continued success.

One of the important features about the staff and principal of the school was the fact that virtually all of the staff were bilingual and could communicate with the parents in their native tongue. This enabled the parents to feel comfortable with the school's staff and broke the ice as far as common expectations were concerned. The staff and community are comfortable with their respective roles and work well together in developing programs that improve the learning of the students.

VIGNETTE #2

Effects on Participants

A district in the state of Washington adopted, in 1991–92, the SBM mode of operation. At the same time, the district made a commitment to become the top district in the country in the adoption and use of technology for instructional purposes. The district passed a $45 million elementary building program, which provided for several new elementary and middle schools (3), as well as the initiation of a planned expansion of the technology to every other school for classroom use. It was decided that, while the three buildings were under construction, staff development in the use and application of technology was to be the primary focus for the district and that the definition of SBM was going to be developed as well. The provision of the staff development effort was enhanced by the provision of a $500 per teacher allocation from the state of Washington for that purpose. This allocation enabled the provision of technology instruction across the board for the teaching staff of the district.

While this was proceeding, the superintendent and his staff, along with representatives of the administrative and teaching staff, were attempting to define what the parameters of the SBM effort would be. It was decided that the first step in the development of SBM would be the development of a district strategic plan that would provide the parameters for the schools to adhere to. In the spring of 1992, the board of education adopted the strategic plan for the district, and schools were instructed to develop school improvement plans that were in concert with the district's strategic plan.

While the schools were developing their improvement plans for submittal, the superintendent and his staff were restructuring the support staff of the district. They decided for and the board approved a major change of duties for many of the staff and the retirement and/or reassignment of many other central staff members. Those remaining central staff became planners/evaluators and had to learn new techniques and skills. At the same time, the district adopted the CIPP model for evaluation, and the central staff had to learn the application of the CIPP model.

During the 1992–93 academic year, each of the schools presented their work plans or improvement plans and negotiated with the central staff the expectations for the school. It was decided that the primary emphasis would be on the elementary sector because they were the recipients of the new buildings and the bulk of the technology resources and that the secondary would become the target after a secondary bond issue was passed.

The use of computers and technology became the focal point of every development in the district during the year. As a new elementary came on line, the facility became the focus of the use of technology, and its staff was provided the opportunity for extended learning in the application of technology. A lesson quickly learned was that there had to be some consistency in the application of technology; therefore, the district adopted a standard for each piece of equipment and for every computer purchased for use in the schools. This enabled the training of maintenance personnel so the repair and maintenance of all technology could be accomplished with little fanfare and disruption to the students. Also a teacher's committee was established to develop, purchase, and adopt software suited to the needs of the district. This, too, assisted in keeping the technology in its proper place and perspective.

Evaluation at the end of the 1992–93 academic year indicated a positive trend in student growth and that the use of technology was proceeding very well. It also indicated that the SBM concept was being embraced by the staff and community and that they were anxious to extend the concept. This external evaluation was also a first among the districts of the country and attempted to measure the accomplishments of the district in relation to the board-adopted strategic plan and objectives.

During the 1993–94 academic year, the district was able to pass a $120,000,000 bond issue for new and rehabilitated secondary schools and for completion of the technology effort across the system. This issue passed with a 72% plurality, a significant success among the districts of the state. The external evaluation for the 1993–94 academic year shows that the success rate is continuing and expanding with virtually every elementary and middle school showing improved learning rates and with the high schools also giving promise of meeting and exceeding expectations.

After observing the elementary and middle schools get active and energized by the technology project, the high schools became active in the SBM effort by becoming involved in the necessary planning activity and reorganization needed to accommodate the expansion of learning activities necessary to keep students involved and in school. Each of the three high schools (plus the alternative high school) developed their own approach to serving all students. Because the district adjusts the school budget according to the active enrollment every six weeks, it quickly became important for buildings to keep their students and prevent dropouts because they would lose staff and dollars whenever a student drops out of the school. Thus, a series of efforts to develop alternative programs were started at every school, and the resulting reduction of dropouts was evident in the external evaluation done during the summer of 1994.

A fourth high school is being planned, and a new alternative high school building is also contemplated. These two facilities, as well as a rehabilitation of existing facilities and the expansion of technology, is now being implemented. The school system has proven that an urban center of approximately 20,000 students can adjust its academic programs and develop initiatives suited to urban communities such that the clientele will make significant progress in gaining educational parity with its suburban neighbors.

VIGNETTE #3

Effects of Participation in SBM

One of the most dramatic and rewarding experiences springing from the movement into SBM was the experience the author had in one of the larger urban districts of Texas. The district had undergone several years of transition from a traditional organizational pattern to an SBM approach. One of the first things established was the fact that all student data would be disaggregated into the major student groups, i.e., ethnically, racially, socioeconomically, and by sex, to make sure that the system was serving all groups equally and that all groups were making progress toward the major objectives established by the board in the strategic plan and the subsequent work plans that followed.

In an effort to reward those who made the best progress toward becoming exemplary schools, the board established a category called "outstanding school" and had plaques made up to portray such achievement. Those schools who thought they deserved such status could proclaim their right to the status of "Outstanding School," and the district would examine the data, and, if the school warranted such acclaim, it was given with attendant fanfare and public recognition.

One school, because of its high average score on the ITBS and because of the feeling that it was one of the best schools in the district, laid claim to the "Outstanding School" status and asked for the award. Upon examination of the achievement data, it was found that, while the average score on the ITBS was very high (over 90%) the disaggregated data told a much different story. Two years prior to the date of the application of the school for the "Outstanding School" status, the district had undergone a mandated desegregation program in which students from other sections of the city were transferred in to the school to meet certain desegregation standards. The students transferred to this school were inhabitants of a public housing development in another part of the city and were mostly African-American, with a few Hispanic students as well. Examination of the achievement records showed that, while the indigenous Caucasian students did, in fact, achieve at a rate well above the 90th percentile, the minority students were at the 30th to 35th percentile. Additionally, these students missed more days of school and were cited repeatedly for disciplinary infractions. The disaggregated data were provided the school staff and the community advisement committee, and they were told that they did not qualify because they were not serving the entire student population.

To the everlasting credit of the school and its community, they accepted the findings and reworked the school improvement plan to incorporate the needs of the total student body and began to make an effort at involving the total group in the process. The effort was tedious and slower than the staff expected, but they persisted. Slowly, the parents from the minority community became convinced that the school was really committed to serving their students and began to participate on the various community involvement committees at the school. The attendance rate of the minority students increased dramatically until they approximated the attendance rates of the majority students.

The staff developed several approaches to meeting the needs of the minority students, including peer tutoring, computer-based instruction, individual IEPs for every student, and an effort to initiate cooperative learning efforts at the school. After three years had gone by, the school again applied for "Outstanding School" status, and this time the results were very positive. Average achievement rates were much higher than the last time the school applied, largely because of the dramatic increase of the achievement scores of the minority students. While not yet as high as the Anglo achievement rates, the trend line was well established, and the gap was markedly narrowed with no loss in achievement for majority students. Other marks of quality included the participation rates of minority and majority students being almost identical, while attendance rates of all students were at a very high level (over 97%).

This is, perhaps, the best example of a staff and community accepting their responsibility for the complete education of the students assigned to the school and working together to develop appropriate programs to serve the students at the site. The school continues to make progress and is acknowledged as the best school in the district. There is pride and respect for diversity present at the school that has much to say about how the SBM process can and should work. Professional educators can develop responses to differing conditions once they make up their minds that it is in the best interest of all involved.

Chapter 3

PITFALLS, HURDLES, AND OPPORTUNITIES UNDER SITE-BASED MANAGEMENT

As with any system of organization, Site-Based Management (SBM) poses a variety of opportunities, hurdles, and pitfalls to those who avail themselves of the organizational structure. Foremost are the new requirements for professional behavior and for changing the work environment of educators. For those who are committed to the traditional mode of operation and for whom change is difficult, SBM poses a real threat. Because the concept is predicated on the notion that those who are in close contact with students on a daily basis best know what the student needs and is capable of performing, this mode of operation is vastly different from the traditional mode. Those professional educators embracing SBM must have a working knowledge about the student, and this, along with their understanding of how learning takes place, enables them to provide the educational programs that are student-based.

There are, of course, a number of challenges, opportunities, and adjustments to be considered as one travels the road to cooperative decision making and to the organizational pattern that SBM envisions. First, the false assumption that SBM will make the task of educating students easier and less demanding is simply not true. The premise that SBM will solve all of the problems of public education is as wrong as assuming that SBM can solve all of the problems of society. What SBM can assist in doing is in providing the opportunity for local schools to work at solving their problems without having to pay blind obedience to a central office that tends to impose solutions on schools whether or not they have the problem. SBM is a mechanism for local schools to involve their communities and staffs in developing mutual solutions to existing problems by, first, identifying the problem and, second, involving all of the stakeholders in the development of a solution that encompasses the best thoughts that they have as a collective group. Such close collaboration provides a real advantage in problem solving and should be the primary goal of all SBM ventures. In the final analysis, SBM is another tool available for educators to use as they strive to develop the best possible program for the students in their charge. While not the ultimate tool, it is an approach to collaborative decision making that permits all stakeholders a role in the process.

There are a number of issues that impinge on the successful implementation of an SBM approach to school governance. Among them are legal issues, union/contract issues, and governance issues. While the impediments to successful implementation of SBM are many and varied, there exists, under an SBM arrangement, a window of opportunity for professional educators to participate in the decisions concerning their future that has not been available heretofore. Examination of broad areas by presenting obstacles and opportunities will permit the initiation of a plan for surmounting these pitfalls and broaden the benefits for students at the school level. In each of these broad categories, there exists a number of opportunities that should be exploited in order for SBM to exist and survive. This chapter will explore the various issues and suggest a number of alternatives for consideration.

LEGAL ISSUES

Because the state is the legitimate governing body for education, it must be involved in the formulation of a state policy enabling the SBM organizational structure to operate. The state, by virtue of the federal Constitution not mentioning education at all, has the power to set and govern public education and to set the laws impacting public education. Most states, Hawaii being the exception, provide for a state department of education, or Department of Public Instruction (DPI), to act as the enforcer of state laws concerning education and as the state agency having direct influence over the public schools of the state. Usually, DPI has, as its chief executive officer, a state superintendent of education. The titles of the state's chief executive education officer vary from state superintendent to state commissioner to state director of education.

These positions are either appointed or elected with the majority being appointed.

The state superintendent reports to a state board of education, which is also elected or appointed with the majority of states having elected membership to that office. The state board sets the educational policy for the state and, with the state superintendent, monitors the school districts of the state. State boards establish textbook purchasing procedures (some states buy all textbooks for the schools of the state, while others provide revenue for assisting local districts in purchasing the locally adopted textbooks), provide for state adoption of textbooks, set curriculum for the state's public schools, establish certification standards for professional educators, set minimum requirements for student achievement across the state, establish the minimum calendar for the schools of the state, provide for the distribution of state funds to the school districts of the state, establish accreditation standards for the school districts of the state, provide certification services for the professional educators in the state, provide for cooperative purchasing of certain big ticket items like buses and major pieces of equipment, monitor the expenditures of the school districts of the state, act as the staff development agency for the state's school districts, interpret the state education laws into rules and regulations for local districts to follow, establish modes for evaluating student performance, and set the general expectations for the districts of the state.

The state legislature is also a major participant in the establishment of the state educational policies and laws. Legislators, who must respond to their electorate, often propose educational legislation that beg the issue of whether it is well conceived and appropriate to a particular situation. Sometimes, this bit of legislation passes the legislative body and becomes state law with some dramatic consequences for the member public school districts of the state. For example, most of the reform legislation of the 1980s was inspired, by either the governors and/or the legislative bodies of the state, because of a rising concern for the achievement rates of students and because of the feeling among many constituents that the education system needed reform. Such major reform events as the Texas reform of 1984, the Kentucky reform of 1990, and other state reform efforts have served to place educators on notice that the public is desirous of improved education for their children. The nation's governors, being political experts and noticing that the bulk of their states' resources were going to public education, were the driving force behind much of the reform efforts of the 1980s and 1990s. Moderate voices were not heard during the time of the greatest upheaval—voices like those of Gerald Bracey, who has researched the so-called decline of the SAT scores and found them to be a myth because, if there was any decline, it was largely due to the expanded numbers of students taking the test and not to a fall in actual scores. Indeed, Bracey found that the real scores for the same population on the SAT were increasing, rather than declining.

Even such outstanding research organizations as the Sandia National Laboratories, who, in their 1991 unpublished report, "Perspectives on Education in America" stated that the general condition of American education was healthy and strong, could not stem the tide of damaging public documents that tell of major shortcomings in the American school systems. Incidentally, the Sandia report has never seen the light of day, perhaps because it rebuts the claims of severe shortcomings in the American school system. Starting with the *Nation at Risk* report, in which the public schools of the country were declared to be at risk, and continuing through the Bush administration, most of the reports and declarations about public education were that the schools of the country were failing the students. President Reagan used these reports very effectively to make the claim that the public schools of the nation were using money frivolously and were not giving the public quality education for its tax dollars. School bashing seems to be a political art form and is always a sure vote getter in the political arena. Such entrepreneurs as former education secretary William Bennett and undersecretary Chester Finn, reinforced by former assistant secretary Diane Ravich, have set a pattern of doom and gloom about the state of American education. Part of this is due to their political leanings, which range from the right to the far right, and part is due to their lack of success in becoming the seers of the educational establishment, precisely because of these political leanings.

In this atmosphere of gloomy predictions for public education, the SBM type of operation was born. The predictions that all public schools were failing the students gave emphasis to the need for a major restructuring of the nation's school districts, particularly the major, large urban centers that, because of the age and era of specialization and uneven growth, had become huge bureaucracies that were completely out of touch with their constituencies and had become bloated and ineffective as school organizations. The need for a decision-making process that was located closer to the student became very apparent to most observers of the education scene. Also, a closely related need to divert more of the tax dollar to the direct service of the student made the SBM approach to the delivery of services an appropriate approach for exploration. As the concept developed, equity issues began to crop up in those districts that embraced the concept.

When considering legal issues in education, the question of equity is never far from the concern at hand. Equity issues have dominated the field of education from the beginning of American education. The issue of education for all Americans started when the first public educational ventures were initiated in the common schools of the original colonies and have never been far from the surface in the years since then.

Our forefathers felt that the provision of a common elementary education was sufficient for the day and did not provide for high school public education, reasoning that the provision of the high school and college years of education was the prerogative of the family and should not be the responsibility of the state. The famous Kalamazoo case of 1837 decided the issue of public support for public high schools, and, since then, there has been no question about the right of all Americans to partake of public education through the completion of high school. Some states have made a concerted effort to provide community college education to all citizens, and others have made a full four years' college experience quite moderate in cost to its citizens. At any rate, the principal of free public education is well established in the United States. A growing minority has long lobbied for comparable support for private and/or parochial schools with, so far, little success. Those who want support for nonpublic schools argue that they alleviate the public schools from dangers of overcrowding and provide a valuable service to those communities in which they are located. They argue that the patrons of the private and parochial schools are being taxed twice for the support of education and that this is an unfair burden on them. So far, the courts have held that, while it is the right of every parent to send his/her children to nonpublic schools, they must pay for the costs incurred as a result of that decision.

Equity Issues

Among the major equity issues being faced by the educational system are those issues predicated on racial and sexual equity. While racial equity issues have been in the courts for almost five decades, starting with *Brown v. Topeka I* and continuing to this day, the sexual issues are of a more recent origin. The *Brown v. Topeka I* was a repudiation of the *Plessy v. Fergasson* case, which decreed that equal but separate was appropriate and desirable in the United States. This case, decided in the 1890s, set the federal and state policy concerning school desegregation for over half a century until the 1954 Brown case was heard before the Supreme Court.

Brown I led to Brown II, and a staggering number of similar cases were heard before the federal courts over the next forty years. These cases were more important for what they tried to do than for what they actually accomplished. They did set the stage for a national policy of equity in educational programs for all children, regardless of race, creed, and/or national origin.

The ebb and flow of opinions by the various courts have prevented a national policy from being set and followed because, just when a case establishes a national trend, a new and different case undermines that policy, and it becomes a new ballgame again. For example, the use of transportation systems to address corrective measures, once the best tool for true desegregation in the schools, became questionable when those who had the most to gain or lose by transporting their children began to question why their children were always the ones to be loaded on a bus and transported to another school. Thus, began a "cross busing" approach to school desegregation, which was not appreciated by everyone. The minority families then began to question why they were required to sit next to a white person to achieve equal education. Why couldn't their schools provide the same education as the schools in the white section of town? This led to a series of cases where the plaintiffs requested that the courts assure that their schools were of the same quality as all of the schools in the city and also requested a return to the neighborhood school concept. The net result is that the country, as a whole, is not much more desegregated today than it was before the first Brown case in 1954, although predominately minority schools are not as deficient as they were then. Then, too, housing patterns are not too terribly different from the 1950s, so that there is much to be done in that arena before neighborhood school desegregation can be achieved. However, the early desegregation cases led to the development of a series of "magnet" schools across the country. These magnet schools provided one of a kind programs that were made available to students of every race that wanted the particular magnet program for themselves. This provided a measure of desegregation, particularly when the magnet program was located in a minority school and was the only such program in the school district. If Caucasian students wished to avail themselves of the program, they had to attend the minority school, leading to some measure of desegregation in that school district.

The issue of sexual equity is more difficult to examine and, while seemingly more straightforward, is no easier to rectify than are the racial equity issues. Sexual equity requires a new definition of the inequities that exist in today's schools. While it is easy to count the number of minorities involved in providing school experiences and strive to equate these experiences for students of all races, sexual issues are not that easy to define and take much reflection and thought. There are two types of discrimination involved with both racial and sexual inequities. The first, and easier to rectify, is the numerical balance that should be the norm in all organizations, particularly school systems. The second is the equalization of program opportunities and the corrections necessary to make all curricula reflective of the equity needs. This balance is much more difficult to achieve and takes several turns and starts in order to comply. School systems have devoted much time and energy to the resolution of these equity issues with varying results. There is a growing feeling that the issue of curriculum balance and equity will be a long-range process and be dependent on the ability of the local districts to make curriculum decisions based on racial and sexual neutrality. This involves the submersion of long-held biases and feelings and the true testing of reality in all curriculum offered in the public schools. It also involves the change of attitudes of educators and communities, as well.

There is a mounting body of evidence that indicates that serious discrimination has been perpetrated against women in the hard sciences and mathematics because of the traditional view that girls are not suited to the study of the sciences and mathematics. This has been confirmed by analysis of test data for the past decades. It is also reinforced by the hard data about employment in those fields demanding knowledge about science and mathematics like the various engineering fields, research science activities, Ph.D. enrollments in the sciences and mathematics, and other indicators of the availability of the area to women. This is being addressed through a concerted effort to make the study of the sciences and mathematics sexually neutral and through efforts at providing extra counseling for girls concerning those fields. This, of course, will take at least a decade to rectify, and the results will not be known for a length of time.

At the same time, equity in curriculum and instruction for all races is proceeding. A number of task forces, state departments of education, and school systems are addressing the need for equity in the school curriculum as it applies to equity between the races. Minority schools are being assisted in the development of programs aimed at providing the necessary background for minority students to compete in advanced academic work. Many colleges and universities are seriously recruiting minority students with scholarships and assistance to enroll in those fields previously denied minorities. Most urban districts and many state institutions of higher education have an active recruitment policy concerning minority faculty, with preference given to those minority candidates who meet employment requirements. The number of minority students enrolling in many of our state universities continues to grow although they are not yet enrolled in the numbers their population distribution would indicate as parity.

We have seen the demographic reality of the United States become stratified, with most big cities becoming majority minority, while most of the suburbs remain majority Caucasian. This has happened in the decades since World War II and has been assisted by the minority movement from the rural South to the northern cities. This movement was precipitated by the job opportunities developing as a result of the era of mass production demanded by the war effort of the 1940s and continuing through the 1950s and 1960s, with the high consumer demand requiring continued production of goods and services.

Indeed, many of the large cities of the country are almost totally minority and ringed by almost totally Caucasian suburbs. True, there are some suburbs that are starting to become multiracial because of the various open housing laws passed during the 1960s and 1970s, but these are relatively minor adjustments in demography and are more related to economics than anything else.

An interesting phenomena is now starting to appear, and that is the recycling of cities from the inside out so that there appears to be a movement back to the center city as it is being revitalized and rebuilt to accommodate families. This phenomenon is best exemplified by what is happening in Chicago, Washington, and Boston where entire blocks of the city are being gentrified and rehabilitated to house young families of every race and culture. Here, too, the public schools will play a major role in the process because these families demand good public education, or they will defect to the private schools of the area. Again, equity in education becomes an important consideration for the homeowner.

Because education has always been a field of endeavor that has attracted a majority of women to it, the numbers reflect the preponderance of women. However, when administrative ranks are folded into the picture, the data reflects that most of the high-level administrators are male, with over 90% of school superintendents being of the male gender. While women have made some inroads in this arena in the past few years, the disparity is much too great to permit it to continue. Actually, the domination of women in the teaching field is more a function of the restrictive nature of other fields to women than to the natural affinity of women to education. For decades, the only fields open to women were nursing and teaching, and the numbers reflect that reality. It has only been in the recent past that other fields have been opened to minorities and women, and their growing numbers in those fields are now showing that fact.

There exists, under the SBM form of school organization, a real chance that the equity issues will be neglected because of the homogenized quality of neighborhoods that comprise the school neighborhood. In some instances known to the author, community groups act to favor their particular interests, against the best interests of a minority group and/or women. Care must be exercised by those in the planning/evaluation/decision-making capacity that the rights of everyone are protected and that no damage is done to any group in the greater community. An example of that kind of activity can be found in the "book burning" and sorting activities promulgated by some of the more extreme Christian Right groups now coming to the fore in the public schools of the country. By denying the placement of certain books in the school library and demanding the removal of other books from the shelves, these extremists try to influence the entire school to accept their point of view concerning public education. Protection against such extremism and unilateral action is needed. The central board, when adopting a policy permitting the initiation of an SBM form of organization, must stipulate that any activity and/or action of the site council must be in conformity with the laws of the state and the policies of the board of education. In this way, such extremism is negated, and the local schools are available for everyone to use as they deem important. One of the main reasons for the adoption of a district strategic plan is to set the parameters for local school SBM to operate.

Legal issues usually revolve around three basic groups of stakeholders: students, staff, and community. These three areas must always be a prime concern for the board and for the site-based management team. Careful planning and evaluation will prevent becoming ensnared in any of the three areas.

Student Legal Issues

Legal issues involving students include such legal concerns as the placement of students in the appropriate grade; recognizing religious beliefs of students and adjusting accordingly; impinging on the student's right to acquire an education by restrictive actions; denying the student access to the education provided other students; acting in a discriminating manner toward the student; abusing the student either physically or emotionally; denying the student access to equal treatment accorded every citizen under the bill of rights; denying the student benefits of education because of race, creed, or national origin; denying the student access to programs because of sexual orientation; and other such individual protections that may be implied by the federal and state constitution.

In addition, there are the various equity issues that guarantee the individual student his/her equity under the laws of the state and nation. Among the more important state and federal laws are those guaranteeing the student equal access to programs needed for admission into one of the professional fields. Such courses are sometimes denied those of minority extraction, and sometimes the only recourse is through the court system. In these cases, the local school system is called upon to justify why the particular courses are not offered at every school. With the advent of computers and the capacity of most school districts to provide interactive television contact, this element of discrimination is being eliminated because every school can now have access to one-of-a-kind programs that were once so expensive and hard to mount. Indeed, the so-called distance learning techniques are increasingly being utilized to circumvent this issue of individual student equity.

Under SBM, every school must be aware of the legal entrapments likely to hit them when they plan the programs to be provided the students at their site. That is why strict attention to the district strategic plan is necessary. Adherence to the district strategic plan will provide the local school guidance as to how much leeway they have in developing approaches to programming for the students at that particular school. As can be seen, the district strategic plan sets the parameters for the school plans and establishes the limits for the school.

Staff Legal Issues

Legal issues concerning staff also cover a multitude of topics and must be dealt with. First and foremost is the area of equal employment. This always rears its head, particularly under an SBM approach. It is in the decentralization of personnel decisions that the district can get into equal employment difficulty. Sometimes, when filling positions, the SBM personnel committee will let personal preferences dictate the selection process and not consider the equal employment needs of the school and district. If, for example, two candidates are equated equally in every area of evaluation and if the school has no minority staff, the minority candidate should be chosen, or the school is guilty of a violation of the equal employment practices. Community groups often pay little attention to such requirements unless they are called to the attention of the group before the selection process begins.

Again, the district personnel office can be of tremendous assistance to the local school by advising the local personnel selection committee as they start the screening process. Often, the district human resources staff provides the service of prescreening applicants to the top four or five candidates for the school committee to select from. In this way, such dangers as neglect of equal employment practices are mitigated.

Other staff legal concerns are of the treatment of the individual type where the principal and community sometimes equate SBM with totalitarianism and make demands of the staff that are absolutely extreme and unusual. In these cases, the individual staff member can get relief by threatening legal action under the fair employment standards as established by the state. Such concerns as the hours and length of the academic day, class assignments, numbers of students assigned to the individual teacher, curriculum areas assigned (whether they are in certified areas or not), and similar concerns are the subject of these matters. The showing of partiality to any group or individual is strictly forbidden and should not be tolerated at any school.

One of the possibly more prickly and serious staff equity issues could arise from the move toward cooperative learning/teaching. Under this arrangement, the school divides into several teacher/learner groups, and the professionals in each group are held responsible for the teaching of all of the subjects in the school curriculum to those students. This arrangement sometimes ignores certification areas of teachers and assigns teachers to teach areas where they are not certified. Those districts entering this type of grouping pattern should get a variance from the DPI before entering into this type of organizational pattern, to avoid such equity issues.

Community Legal Concerns

School communities can get embroiled in a variety of legal issues, most of which are really inconsequential to the problem at hand. Some communities become involved in the power game and feel that they, as a community, have the right to make every decision that arises at the local school, whether or not it is made in concert with existing state and federal laws. The mistaken assumption that, under an SBM approach to school organization, the community becomes the sole source of decisions and can do as it pleases is totally wrong and not to be tolerated.

In such cases, the central board must exercise its authority and retrieve control of the local school. One of the serious pitfalls of the Chicago plan for decentralization is the fact that many local councils feel they are totally autonomous from the central board and can make any decision they wish about their school. Events in Chicago are concluding that the parameters must be more exactly spelled out for the local councils and that, unless personal equity issues are carefully identified, this form of decentralization will not last or even approach a successful educational experience for the students.

The Chicago experience reveals the major pitfalls inherent in the SBM approach to school organization. It also suggests why the central board should establish a strategic plan for the whole district as a parameter for the local site councils as they operate. The Chicago plan was a result of strong community objections to the way things were going at their schools and a desire to participate in those decisions affecting their students. It was born of political expediency and was imposed on the entire system without any training for those persons who soon were to be elected to community school councils.

The resulting chaos was the separation of power from the central board, which still has the power of budget allocations and still maintains a strong presence in the local schools, to the local school council, which makes all of the personnel and program decisions at the local school. Rules governing these two entities were never spelled out, and they are now struggling to define their respective roles and duties. In the meantime, students are the pawn in this power struggle and are being sacrificed to appease the political goals of their parents. This is a classic case of a state legislative body, because of political agreements and deals, mandating certain operational procedures and imposing them on a single school system. The deal was made to prevent a teacher's strike in Chicago, and the Chicago Teacher's Union became a victim, as well as the thousands of students in the city who realized little, if any, improvement in the education accorded them. While gaining the monetary benefits they worked so hard to achieve, the teachers also placed themselves at risk because of the desires of the local community for control of their schools. This control is best illustrated by the power to hire and fire staff at the local school. Chicago is being watched, and many court cases will evolve from that situation.

Resource Allocation Issues

The move toward an SBM form of organization raises many concerns about the allocation of resources for a system utilized by the central district. The issue of equity in resource allocation is always an important one, and, under the SBM form of organization, this becomes an even more important issue for the school system. As with any new and different system of organization, the budget allocations under SBM are open to discussion and debate among the participants. In the traditional school system, budget allocations are usually made on a per student allocation system, with schools qualifying for certain basic per pupil allocations for school supplies and equipment. Teachers are furnished on a given pupil/teacher ratio prescribed either by the state (as in Texas for grades K−4) or by board policy. Variation from the prescribed pupil/teacher ratios are approved on a case by case basis for certain preset reasons and conditions. Some districts adopted a "money follows child" policy where special grants and granting conditions are allocated special funds with which to address the special condition that the particular child met. Such conditions as poverty, special bilingual language needs, and other specific student needs were addressed by these special grants and distributed to the local districts that qualified for these monies. Where the federal guidelines suggest that certain schools, as entities, qualified for these grants, some districts adopted a policy that said the grant money follows the individual child so that all children who qualified for a special grant would benefit from those funds.

As a local district prepares for the advent of SBM, there are certain allocation decisions that must be made initially for the process to have a chance of succeeding. The first of these decisions is how to charge the staff of the school to their local budget. Should the staff be charged on the basis of actual salary or should the average salary of each employee group be determined and that average salary charged to the budget of each school in the system? Most authors would argue that an average salary allocation is much more fair and realistic for purposes of devising creative staffing patterns. After all, the message is that creative personnel assignment procedures will provide the school with many alternatives for using the staff salary.

Thus, a school can qualify for the equivalent of twenty-four classroom teachers at an average salary of \$35,000 for a total of \$840,000 (24 × \$35,000) so that, if the school decides to forego three teachers for a different staffing pattern, they can realize \$105,000 (3 × \$35,000) to apply to the new staffing pattern. This gives every school in the system the same opportunity for exchanges and does not penalize any of the schools for having a staff that is more mature and higher on the salary schedule.

In addition to the normal budget allocations for staff salaries, supplies, equipment, travel, and conference expense, the school budget also reflects an allocation for substitute teachers and for damage caused by vandalism and other mischief during the academic year. These costs are usually prorated according to the average per pupil expenditure averaged over several years. The school is usually permitted to utilize these funds, if any remain after the academic year, for any purpose as deemed important by the school leadership team. Thus, each school can generate added funds if they can monitor their own use of sick leave and reduce the amount of vandalism at the school. Also, there is usually a grant-awarding procedure that permits each school to write a proposal for seed money for specific purposes that the staff of the school feels strongly about. These grants range in size from several hundred dollars to several thousand dollars and provide the startup costs for many projects intended for the improvement of conditions at the school.

Individual schools can, thus, generate some resources that are unique to that site and are provided for the betterment of programs at that school. Individual staff members can also apply for special individual and/or small group grants intended to spark the use of a particular innovation on the part of staff.

It is a reality that there are never enough resources to do the job in its entirety. However, through the careful allocation of funds in as fair a manner as possible, the school system using the SBM approach to organization can equalize the resource allocation process. The intent is to make available to the school as much of the education dollar as is possible, by minimizing the expenditures for the infrastructure of the school system. In this way, the students receive the maximum benefits from school budget expenditures.

State and Federal Mandate Issues

One of the major inhibitors to the move toward an SBM form of organization are the multitude of state and federal regulations and laws that, while their intent is to assure equity and fairness, function to inhibit local decisions. That is why most states have a system for granting local districts waivers from state and federal regulations that permit creative forms of responses to particular problems to be implemented.

Most states and local districts that have encouraged the SBM form of organization have, as a precautionary measure, proclaimed that all decisions made at the site will be in conformity with state and federal equity laws and will not be permitted if not in compliance with state and federal laws and regulations. In this way, the schools are notified that any rule or method implemented locally must be in strict conformance with all applicable laws and rules.

One of the reasons for the possibility of gaining a waiver from existing regulations is to explore the potential for creative staffing, which sometimes calls for a deviation from state mandates on pupil/teacher ratios. If, for example, the school decides to utilize a cooperative approach to educational delivery and if their plans call for the addition of a curriculum person in place of a regular classroom teacher, they can request a waiver from the state-mandated pupil/teacher ratio so the curriculum person can be added to the staff. In this manner, the local staff meets their responsibility to improve the delivery of educational services to the students under their charge and can do so within the restraints of the budget.

Another area where waivers may be utilized are those areas where the state mandates require certain time periods be allocated to the various subjects. Again, for the school that has gone to the problem-solving approach to instructional delivery, these mandates are not very conducive to the implementation of the problem-solving curriculum. Waivers from the state mandate are in order for this type of school.

It must be stated strongly that, when applying for a waiver, the local school must present the rationale for the waiver and the expected outcomes resulting from the granting of the waiver. Usually, the waivers are for a particular period of time, and a careful review is projected before the waiver can be extended.

The use of waivers are becoming an important adjunct to the SBM mode of operation. Local districts, too, make use of the waiver system to enable the school to depart from the board-mandated procedures and processes. Again, these waivers are followed by a period of evaluation before renewal of the waiver.

Questions Most Often Raised about Legal Issues under an SBM Type of Operation

Q-1: Our school's SBM leadership team has determined that a full-time curriculum specialist would be of great assistance to the classroom teachers and would assist in developing a problem-solving approach to the delivery of educational services. We have advertised and, upon interviewing the four candidates sent from the central office's department of human resources, have decided that none of the candidates meets our expectations. After we declined to employ any of the candidates sent for our consideration, the department of human resources opened the application process but informed us that we should consider minority candidates because the racial balance at our school was not in conformity with district guidelines and should be rectified. Can they do this, and how should we react?

A-1: They can and should. Every school in the district must participate in the equal employment process and should meet some self-imposed guidelines for affirmative action. Whenever a position opens for new employment, the department of human resources must inform the school of those employment needs that they can assist in meeting. Your selection for the position should reflect careful consideration of the equal employment needs of the system.

Q-2: After providing guarantees that all budget balances would be protected as carryover funds, the district business office took every one of the carryover fund balances and restored them to district fund balance for the coming school year. Can they do this?

A-2: Not after guaranteeing you the ability to maintain carryover balances as part of the budget balance for your school. Establish a meeting with the business office immediately and demand to know why the promise was not kept and why your (and others) budget balances were absorbed in the district's fund balance. Demand the restoration of those fund balances as they are a part of the ongoing effort to build toward a major expenditure for the school.

Q-3: Our school is being challenged by a group in the community for not placing enough emphasis on the basic skills. This is in spite of the remarkable growth in student achievement springing from the move into a cooperative learning environment resulting from our move into SBM. The group feels that, because we do not have regular periods devoted to the basic skills instruction, we are not focusing enough student attention on learning those skills. This developed after a careful review of what the test data show and after a review of how the teachers feel about how well students are learning. What should we do about this challenge before they proceed to the courts?

A-3: Plan and conduct several information sessions with the members of the group that are challenging the school. Gather and present the data that show the relative position of the school before and after the move to a cooperative learning type of instruction. Provide data to refute the claims that the school is not doing as well as they did before the change in instructional delivery. Advise the group of the opportunity to raise the issue with the central board before going to the courts. Try to gain the respect and confidence of the group by sharing all of the developmental work that went into the move before it happened.

Q-4: Our school has decided to attempt to group students heterogeneously rather than homogeneously. Immediately, a group of parents have threatened to take us to the central board because we are doing away with the gifted program. Our response is that the school leadership team decided to utilize the scarce resources available by using the gifted students to provide peer instruction to the rest of the students and that this in no way suggests the elimination of the gifted program. What can we do to further assuage their concerns?

A-4: Again, involve those parents so they may learn what the school staff and community decided through the site leadership team. Careful and repeated discussion of the issue and the requesting of input from those parents will go a long way toward resolving the issue. Permit the parents to participate in the decisions made by the leadership team and request their participation on the various committees at the school.

Q-5: The leadership team at our school has decided to extend the academic day by fifteen minutes every day so the staff can have a half day of staff development every three weeks. Can they do this and what about the needs of those parents who work and must have their students taken care of every day?

A-5: Yes, they can. The school, while functioning as a custodial institution, must have the flexibility to provide staff development so new educational delivery methods can be explored. You will have to make other plans for the custodial care of your children. I'd suggest you talk to the principal about the dilemma to see if there are other options worthy of consideration.

Q-6: Our school system has recently initiated a move toward an SBM form of organization in which the local schools are able to set some priorities and programs for themselves. How can I, as a parent, be assured that the local school will continue to perform as well as they always have?

A-6: By becoming involved with the site-based committees so you will know what is happening at the site. As the site considers the decisions to be made, you can have a participatory role in the process. Take advantage of the opportunity to become involved with your local school.

Q-7: Our school has decided to go to an ungraded organizational pattern. In addition, the leadership team has decided to develop a student portfolio evaluation design to replace report cards. I (and several other parents) oppose this and wish the school to continue the traditional report card system of student evaluation. Can the school adopt this procedure for student evaluation?

A-7: Yes, they can. If the board gives the local school the right, under the SBM type of organization, to establish their own grading patterns and methods, they can develop a system of grade reporting that is unique to them.

Q-8: As a minority parent, I wish for some additional role models for my children. Our school, under the SBM type of operation, has replaced several staff members but has not seen fit to employ any minorities in professional positions. I contend that they are not following equal employment practices because there are no minorities among the twenty-four professional staff members of the staff of the school. How long can they delay the employment of a minority?

A-8: Ask the question of the school board. The board has made a commitment to become an equal employment organization and must provide equal rights for employment for qualified minority candidates. A reminder to the board and the superintendent will provide the right emphasis for the employment of qualified minority candidates at your school.

Q-9: Can our school, if the leadership team chooses and with community concurrence, depart from the traditional courses of study and develop an entire project-based curriculum for educating our students?

A-9: Yes, you can, provided you do so in response to the priority objectives listed in the district's strategic plan. You will be held accountable for achievement under the emerging curriculum and must show acceptable gain scores in all disciplines (subjects) mentioned in the district's strategic plan.

UNION/CONTRACT ISSUES

The union movement came late to education, but it has arrived with a vengeance! Granted that the force for the development of a strong teachers' union was the arbitrary way in which teachers were treated by many boards and superintendents over the years, the organizing of teachers into formal unions was nonetheless slow in coming. This, coupled with the near starvation wages paid to teachers for most of the 20th century, made the profession ripe for a strong unification move. Both the American Federation of Teachers, an AFL/CIO affiliate quite powerful in the major urban centers, and the National Education Association, with the largest membership of the two main teacher groups, have become adept at representing their members' interests and are formidable foes across the bargaining table. The National Education Association, arguably the oldest teachers' group, was started as an association that focused primarily on educational processes and methods. It started as an all-encompassing organization open to everyone who was involved with the educational process. By the late 1950s, the National Education Association decided to become the sole representative of the teachers within their organization and separated those members who were administrators and/or supervisors. Thus, they joined the American Federation of Teachers as the two major national unions to which teachers can belong.

By the early 1960s, several states had passed legislation permitting the withholding of services (strike) when the negotiations process was not succeeding and at a stalemate. New York and Michigan were among the first to pass such legislation, and the first teacher's strike took place in Michigan in 1964. Since that time, the use of the strike has become a powerful weapon for the teachers in the bargaining process. In fact, the teachers' strike has come full cycle with Michigan, one of the first states to require teacher negotiations and condone strikes, passing legislation in 1994 that outlaws the use of a teachers' strike in collective bargaining. The Michigan statute mandates fines for the bargaining unit (union) in the amount of $5,000 per day if there is a work stoppage. This legislation shows the opinions of the public over the granting of negotiation rights and contract bargaining to teachers across the country. As teachers salaries have become competitive, public sentiment has shifted from feeling sorry for the teachers to a feeling of resentment toward a group who have made such gains over the previous thirty years.

Historically, because the majority of the teachers were women and because they were not given to complaining about working conditions and wages, the profession made little progress toward becoming competitive with other professions. It was after the teachers' unions became involved with the negotiations process that the teachers made major salary gains. These gains were precipitated by state legislation that was passed in many states permitting salary negotiations for the teaching profession. Indeed, some states are still prohibiting negotiations between boards of education and the teaching staff. In these states, what is called "meet and confer" takes place and leads to an agreement on matters such as salary and working conditions. These states do not permit work stoppages in education, and, thus, the teachers' unions are prohibited from using their major weapon in formal negotiations: the strike. Average teachers' salaries, in those states that are well organized, are most competitive with the salaries found in other professions. The disparity between those states and the states in which negotiations are not legal is substantial with average teachers' salaries considerably lower.

Of course, there are other matters of importance to be resolved during formal negotiations between teachers and the various boards. Among the more serious matters open for discussion are such things as hours, wages, and conditions of employment, which include most matters involved with the teaching/learning act. Lately, a growing demand for evaluation and accountability have made their way to the negotiations table as important topics for discussion. As the public stridently demands that all educators be held accountable for student progress, teachers' organizations are becoming increasingly reticent about permitting individual evaluations based on student growth to become part of the teacher evaluation process. They are more disposed to having the traditional "input" evaluations remain as the prime method for teacher evaluation. However, since outputs have become the norm for all evaluations, the teacher unions are having a difficult time justifying their position. Several national studies and research efforts, some funded through the U.S. Office of Education and all headed by outstanding evaluators, are now being conducted—all aimed at developing a model for teacher evaluation that considers how the students perform as part of the evaluation.

The National Center for Evaluation in Education is located at Western Michigan University. The Center is directed by Dr. Daniel Stufflebeam, best known as the person who headed the team that developed the Context, Input, Process, Product (CIPP) model for planning, evaluation, and decision making and who has been among the foremost evaluators in the country for the past thirty years, is currently developing a teacher evaluation model for use in several test sites. This model will include a variety of elements, including student outcomes as an integral part of the model. The Center is developing models for evaluating other educational professionals (administrators, supervisors, support personnel), which also will be tested in various districts across the country. This process will take several years and will lead to the endorsement of models for the optimum evaluation of all educational personnel.

There are at least four major contract issues that are constantly arising in teacher union bargaining sessions. We shall deal with the most important of these in the subsequent pages of this handbook.

Staffing Patterns

One of the signs of the strength of any labor organization is how successful it is in determining the number of employees an organization will have, as well as how they are to be paid for their labors. In education, the student/teacher ratio is a major measuring rod for determining the success (or failure) of the union to gain advantage for their membership. State legislation placing limits on student/teacher ratios are a favorite mechanism for assisting the union in their claim that they have succeeded in limiting the size of classes for their members. The lobbying effort causing these state limitations on class size is a favorite tool of the union because it sets the limits for the entire state and does not require a district by district negotiation over this particular issue. In many states, the lack of such legislation has caused a district by district effort, resulting in a variety of limits on class size that depend on the strength of the union in the particular district.

Site-Based Management is a real threat to the issue of class size and also to other staffing patterns that may crop up under an SBM approach. Teachers' unions take a very dim view toward having the capacity to set staffing patterns moved to the school level and will fight this with every bit of strength they have. They view such flexibility (with some validity) as a method to eliminate, or at least negate, unions from the educational equation. For example, if a campus decides to change from the union negotiated 22/1 student/teacher ratio and use those funds realized from adopting a changed ratio to provide for other professional services as called for in the school improvement plan, the union almost becomes extraneous to that effort and does little to further its claim as being the representative of the teaching staff of the district. This type of activity makes union heads very nervous and causes them to fight against most

SBM efforts. They know that, when a school by school proviso for setting staffing patterns becomes a reality, they will no longer be vital to the welfare of the teaching staff and, thus, the union becomes a much weaker force.

It cannot be denied that the union movement created vastly improved working conditions across the country and that, because of the formal negotiations process, teachers have arrived at a point where they can aspire to competitive salaries with other professions. However, the demand for improved outcomes and for holding teachers accountable for the results of classroom instruction have served to alert the unions that they could be easily ignored in the process of improving education for the students if they become too obstructive and protective. Thus, it is in the best interest of the union to become a participant in the evolving SBM process, rather than the opponent of such a restructuring effort. Unions are slowly coming to the realization that they are best served by coming into the planning process and protecting their members' interests as full participants, rather than as obstacles to such development.

The SBM movement is predicated on the close and continuing involvement of the school's professional staff in the decisions that are made at the school level and affecting the students. It is, in our minds, perhaps the last chance for teachers to gain professional status and take their rightful place in the hierarchy of occupations that are recognized as professional pursuits in our country. To do so requires that the teachers behave in a professional manner and make decisions that are aimed at improving the delivery system for the benefit of their students. This is not an easy task and deserves some careful consideration by the teacher. It also means that, in some cases, the teacher must participate in a decision that is contrary to what his/her union wishes and recommends. In those instances, the teacher behaves in a manner that provides the best for the students of the school without consideration of his/her personal preference.

While such different staffing patterns are not the usual arrangement, there still must be flexibility available to the school to permit a staffing pattern that responds to particular needs as they arise. The contractual arrangement between the district and the union should not preclude such flexibility. After all, the teachers at the site are part of the decision made to depart from the union-negotiated staffing patterns and move toward a new approach to serving students. The district must assure that the funding is based upon the normal staffing pattern that has been arrived at through the negotiations process and that the school will have those funds available to them as they strive to provide instructional experiences for the students. Thus, the union concern for equity is satisfied, and the school may use those resources according to their improvement plan.

The keys are the school strategic and improvement plans and the requirements they impose on the staffing arrangements for the school. As the site improvement leadership teams operate to develop the school plans and staffing patterns, they must have the flexibility to staff according to the emerging needs of the school and, more particularly, the learning needs of the students located at that site. To have the union contract determine the staffing pattern of the school is not an appropriate response to the student population. The assignment of staff and their function as part of the resources of the school are, perhaps, the most important decisions impacting the success and/or failure of a particular program.

As schools move toward the project type of program delivery and because there is less need for teachers certified in particular subjects and more need for teachers who are generalists, staffing patterns take on a different connotation. Particularly at the secondary level where, increasingly, groups of teachers are taking the responsibility for the entire curriculum for those students assigned them, is flexibility in staffing necessary. Waivers from state and district mandates are essential as schools and communities develop their most appropriate response to learning deficiencies and staff to mitigate these deficiencies. Given the rigid guidelines for the employment of teachers at the secondary levels, with strict requirements for certification in the various subjects, an "Essential School" could not be initiated without a waiver from state guidelines and without a commitment of the local staff to teach the students, regardless of the certification of the particular staff member. The curriculum of the "Essential School" is not as important as the grouping of students with staff who provide the total educational experience for the students. Research conducted by the Coalition of Essential Schools describes the success that this approach is having and the growth experienced by the students enrolled in such a program. The "Essential Schools" program is but one example of the flexibility needed by schools as they tailor their programs to the needs of their student bodies.

Emerging concepts such as project learning approaches, cooperative learning, and other modes of teaching the student according to his/her needs and learning style require different staffing patterns, and the capacity to deviate from the state and local mandate for staffing becomes even more important to the district embracing the SBM approach to organization.

Class Size

Closely related to the staffing pattern issue, but a more individual concern, is the class size issue. Teachers have, for years, given the impression that the larger the class, the harder it is to provide educational services on an individual basis. Research has shown that the class size must be reduced below fifteen for it to have an impact on student learning, but teachers have always felt that they can provide a better learning environment with a class size between twenty and twenty-five than they can with a class size that is twenty-eight to thirty and higher. While there is some credibility to the feeling that, with classes of more than thirty students, the individualization effort amounts to little or nothing, research does not accurately predict any significant student gains resulting from class sizes that range from twenty to twenty-five. True, if the teacher feels better about the numbers in the class, the possibility for improved student gains is greater than if the teacher feels the situation is impossible. There is emerging research that suggests that the frame of mind of the teacher affects student gains so it might be very important to arrive at a compatible class size figure.

Historically, in the old one-room school, the teacher taught all of the students who came to school and had the responsibility for multi-grade and multi-aged pupils. Under this arrangement, the concept of peer instruction first came of age with the older, more advanced students assisting the teaching of the younger students. Research supports the notion that, by teaching a particular topic, the peer instructor learns about the topic more than he/she would as a student sitting passively in the room.

As schools grew and as the era of specialization came upon us, the teachers began to specialize in the grade level that they fancied and, in fact, were certified according to the level that they chose to specialize in. Thus, we see that there are certifications for early childhood education, lower elementary education, higher elementary education, middle school education, and high school education in this age of specialization. Each certification requires certain age- and grade-level curricula that supposedly prepare the prospective teacher to better educate the student at the particular level.

Class size has become the rallying cry for teachers across the country as they strive to improve the working conditions for themselves. It is interesting to note that, in Europe and Japan, the average class size is much higher than it is in this country, and it is not an issue with the teachers in those systems. In the United States, this issue has become the most important issue in the collective bargaining process with many a strike revolving around resolving the class size demands.

At the elementary levels, the issue is straightforward and clear—so many students assigned to each teacher. However, at the secondary level with its higher degree of specialization and multi-grade assignments, the issue becomes one of the number of students assigned to each teacher during the school day. In most middle and high schools, where the teacher teaches either six of seven periods or five of six periods, the issue becomes the number of students seen during the day. This number is particularly important to those teachers teaching classes where there is a high number of written assignments and/or themes to grade. As a result, we see a number of teacher union contracts where English teachers are limited to a certain number of students during the day. If this number is exceeded, the school is to provide an aide to assist in the grading and reading of papers.

At a typical high school, certain classes have facility-imposed limits on class size, as well. For example, the chemistry laboratory has twenty-four work stations, so the class size limit is twenty-four, while the gymnasium holds upwards of 100 students comfortably, so the class size limit for physical education is 100. Other classes must be large for reasons of program, such as the high school band, which is often over 100 to 200 members, while the choir class also can accommodate a large number of students.

It is also interesting to note that, when elementary teachers are given the option of having a few more in their classes in exchange for adding a music, art, or physical education specialist to the staff, the teachers invariably choose to add more students to their class in order to provide the specialists to the school. This is because, with the advent of specialists in those fields, the classroom teacher can get a planning period while his/her class is in that particular subject for instruction. Typically, the physical education, music, and art teachers relieve the classroom teacher during their instructional period with the class.

Class size varies in accordance with the capacity of the district to generate tax revenue with which to support education in the district. In states where the greatest amount of equalization has occurred, class size has become a state issue, rather than a local issue because the dollars available for education are almost equal throughout the state. In many of those states, Texas for one, the state mandates a pupil/teacher ratio of 22/1 at the K−4 level. In Texas, if the ratio in grades K−4 exceeds the 22/1 ratio in more than one section of a K−4 enrollment in a particular school, the school must employ another teacher at that level. If there is only one section over the mandated level, the school may get by with adding a teacher aide for that particular section. Efforts to have the district-wide averages serve as the criterion have been to no avail because each school in the district must meet the mandated levels. As expected, this issue has generated much heat and discussion because it is an expensive mandate to meet since students, in some schools, are almost transient in their attendance. Incidentally, there has been no appreciable gain in student achievement in the ten years since this mandate was put in effect. Teachers, however, feel that their task is somewhat easier when the class size is fixed at a lower level.

School Day, Week, Year

The school calendar is also an issue with most union contract negotiations. Because most teachers take advanced graduate work and since they must enroll when the university offers the needed course work, the teachers are most dependent on the university schedule as they contemplate furthering their education. Typically, university schedules for summer courses provide such academic work on a late June to early August schedule; therefore, the academic year must conclude by early June for the teacher to take full advantage of the university schedule. However, many schools and districts have found that there is much less learning loss if the academic year is scheduled on a 45−15 schedule so that the students (and staff) are in attendance for forty-five days and receive a vacation for the next fifteen days, and the school year is a full year rather than a nine-month academic year. This, of course, does not meet with the full approval of the teachers since it precludes advanced graduate work during the summer.

With SBM, such decisions are usually made locally at the site where the parents and community combine to apply pressure for such academic years. In these cases, the teachers usually see the advantage of such a schedule and agree on its implementation. In one district known to the author, the district entered into an agreement with the local state university, whereby the university made certain classes available on the schedule of the teachers involved and permitted the teachers to take the needed courses at their convenience. This is an unusual move for a major state university and one that bears repeating all over the country.

In addition to the normal calendar issues, many schools have a donnybrook over the length of the school day. True, most states set the required number of hours in attendance for children during the day, but the district must set the exact times of attendance. If the district has a significant transportation system, the transportation system's requirements often set the school day because, typically, the transportation system must make two runs to transport all of the children to and from school. Therefore, if the secondary run is first, the elementary run must occur after the buses have had a chance to complete their secondary runs. Thus, the times of the school day are established by the transportation needs, rather than the desires of the school.

Increasingly, under the SBM mode of operation, the staff of a particular school, wishing to develop times for staff development, will bank ten to fifteen minutes daily to make up for the half day every two weeks that they wish to devote to staff development activities. By adding ten to fifteen minutes to the school day, a half day's staff development can be banked every two weeks, and the total minutes of instruction for the students is not compromised.

If the school, under the SBM decision-making capacity, decides to bank ten to fifteen minutes per day in order to have a half day staff development every two weeks, they should consider what the student's needs are as far as child care is concerned. In many instances, the school's volunteer parent group will provide for the child care during the half day so that the working parents are not required to provide child care during that period.

Teacher bargaining representatives (unions) feel they should bargain the hours of the school day and often will not accept the transportation needs of the district as an explanation for the specific hours required of the teachers. It is only after the transportation needs of the students are carefully explained to the bargaining unit that they will attempt to compromise this issue.

Many school districts also refuse to honor teacher personal leave or business days on the days immediately before and after a vacation period because they have found that these are the days that staff most abuse the leave policy. Therefore, the district will rarely accept a contract proposal that permits the use of personal business days on the day before or after a vacation period. Teachers would like to have these days available to them, but they understand the reality of student needs enough not to make a major issue of this.

Under the SBM type of organization, the local school has the right to determine many of these issues, with their own staff and their own community making the final decision. This gives the local school great flexibility but also great responsibility in this area. The district must insist that the local school meet all of the state requirements for school day, week, and year and will force the school to recognize the realities of the transportation system, but, other than that, the school can determine what the schedule of the school will be. This, of course, complicates the bargaining process because the bargaining unit (union) cannot anticipate the needs of all of the schools in a multi-building school district. The district, wishing to keep as flexible as possible, usually attempts to ignore this issue during bargaining, other than to stipulate the state requirements for attendance and time of school day and provide for each school to meet these requirements.

Another district concern must be the equity factor between the various schools. The district must enforce the need for the various schools to be somewhat together as far as time spent in school and on task are concerned. The time on task issue has not been a major sticking point so far, but common sense suggests that it is an important issue as far as student growth is concerned. Indeed, two decades ago, while the author was the superintendent of a major urban school system, the district undertook to make a "time and motion" study of the teaching staff and found that over 40% of the academic day was being wasted on such superfluous tasks as attendance, announcements, collecting lunch money, and other routine tasks. The district established a policy that no more than 15% of the day could be used in these pursuits, and student achievement accelerated remarkably. The time the student spends on the education learning tasks really does make a difference.

Resource Allocation

The issue of the allocation of scarce resources will always be with the school system. It is exacerbated when there is a formal collective bargaining procedure, because this area is one that defies reasonable solution. The district must always remember that the school budget must provide for the numerous support activities that make the operation of the district possible. Yet teacher bargaining units do not feel that they should take less for their needs to subsidize the various support activities.

Actually, because the school budget is so heavily weighted in the personnel area (roughly 86% of the budget goes for personnel salaries and fringe benefits), there are few discretionary dollars left in the budget after the salaries and fringe benefits are allocated. After salaries and fringe benefits are encumbered, there is approximately 14% of the budget left to pay for fixed costs (utilities, insurance, etc.), school operations (custodial services and maintenance services), supplies (student, as well as other), capital outlay, transportation, food services, and community services. As can be noted, there is little room for the discretionary use of any of the budget in this breakdown.

Because the union's major task is to get the most possible remuneration for the staff of the district, they are sometimes accused of taking everything and leaving nothing for the other major expenditure area of the school budget. Such charges, while sometimes true, do nothing to enhance the reputation of the teachers to other staff members of the district. With the advent of SBM, the cooperative feelings and respect of the various staff groups toward one another must rise above such petty differences and build the team concept. In districts where the teaching staff is viewed with some disfavor, this is a difficult objective.

Once the salary issues are resolved, there exist several other resource allocation issues that remain for resolution. These include the disparity between the elementary and secondary as far as student allocations for supplies and capital outlay are concerned. The harsh fact is that the secondary program receives much more on a per pupil allocation basis than does the elementary program. This is because of the many sophisticated and esoteric programs that are offered at the typical secondary school, as opposed to the offerings at the elementary level.

For example, the per pupil allocation for school supplies at the high school is often twice as much as the elementary school level, while the per pupil allocation of supply funds for the middle school is at least 60% higher than at the elementary level. The reason given for this is the higher costs for the supplies and equipment used in the instructional programs at the middle and high school levels as compared to the elementary level. This is true especially in those areas where consumable supplies in such subjects as chemistry, geography, industrial arts, and art are of such a sophisticated nature. Also, the music budget for a typical high school is tremendous when one considers the outlay for instruments and uniforms needed to place a school band in operation. Some states have established guidelines for supply and capital expenditures by size and grade levels served. While not absolute, these suggested allocations establish guidelines for school districts to use as they work on their budget allocations.

The bargaining unit is, thus, trapped in a no-win situation because, on the one hand, they wish to get as much of the school dollar as a salary commitment, while, on the other hand, they recognize that the teaching act requires substantial support activity in order to succeed. Thus, the bargaining unit is often in a dilemma as to where to draw the line on demands for teacher salaries and fringe benefits. It has been the experience of the author that union heads have a fine sense of the realities of school budgets and will make rational judgments when given the opportunity to do so.

A growing and important part of the teachers' salary and fringe benefit package is the insurance package. Health care is becoming the most costly and important part of any fringe package because of the rapidly increasing costs of health care. As these costs increase, the district must carefully track these expenditures for future negotiations and agreement opportunities. Many major urban districts are moving toward self-insurance in the area of health insurance. By taking catastrophic insurance to provide for extreme cases of high-risk claims, the district can save money by self-insuring for most coverage. In this way, the district can provide the staff with the best coverage within the means of the district. Smaller districts are forming insurance co-ops to generate the same coverage possibilities as the large districts have because of size.

Such major budget items must always be considered a responsibility of the central office and could be classified as a support activity since it has little to do with student learning yet had much to do with the wise use of resources.

Other union/contract issues include such items as released time for union representatives, released time for union leaders, union mailboxes at each school, teacher's union meetings on school time, teacher overtime pay for extra duties, stipends for particular job performance and assignments (coaching, directing plays, musicals, performances, etc.), planning periods (number and length), participation in school decisions, personal leave days, evaluations (number and type), classroom visits (observations) by principal, payroll deduction for union dues, teacher/parent conferences (number and type), required night activities (number), and other such activities. The resolution of these and similar issues is what makes the union a strong organization. Under SBM, the need for flexibility to resolve these issues at the school level with differentiation permitted by school makes this a bitter pill for the union. The capacity for each school to resolve many of these issues makes the union feel unwanted and irrelevant. If the staff wishes to depart from the negotiated agreement and resolve to operate in a different manner, they have that right under the SBM mode of operation. Such deviation from negotiated rights can be devastating to the union and makes the union seem frivolous. The emerging management/union contract negotiations model must evolve into a "win-win" model, with both parties gaining from an agreement, but the students gaining most of all. This new type of contract negotiations requires that both sides place the welfare of the student above the desires of the parties. It requires complete honesty and little gamesmanship. Some states are hastening the process by requiring a last best offer type of negotiations with a state monitor arbitrating the difference between the two sides. This places the heat on each side to extend their best offer and allows a professional arbitrator to decide who has the most compelling offer on the table.

Questions That Arise When Union Contract Issues Are Examined

Q-1: Our National Education Association bargaining unit gained a class size limit (22/1) for all elementary schools after years of hard bargaining and a bitter teachers' strike. Now with the SBM type of operation, several schools are moving toward increasing these class sizes in order to provide other support personnel and programs. Can they do this, and what do we, as an association, do about it?

A-1: If your district or state has a waiver process and the schools affected have applied for and received the appropriate waivers, there is little that you can do about it except to monitor and insist that the district provide the money freed up by the higher class size so that the school(s) are given the resources they made the sacrifice for. If the district or state has no waiver process, you can object that this is in violation of your duly negotiated contract and file a grievance about the contract violation. However, if the staff of these schools participated in the decisions to permit an increase of class size in exchange for other resources for the school, you might be in some difficulty with the prevailing attitude of the teachers in your district.

Q-2: Our teachers' contract with our district calls for the provision of physical education, music, and art teachers at the elementary schools of the district. Now, under the SBM operation, some of the schools are trading these positions for added classroom teachers so that they can reduce the class size below the 22/1 limit reached under the contract negotiations. Can they do this, and what can we do as a union?

A-2: If the district has accepted an SBM approach to operating the district and has spelled out the potential for making those decisions for the local schools, there is little you can do but file a grievance and hope that it will produce the result you desire. Most states and districts adopting the SBM approach have a system to allow individual schools to apply for waivers from contracted agreements as to class size, assignments, etc. If the schools have been approved under the waiver system, there is little you can do.

Q-3: I teach at a high school and am certified in mathematics and physics. Our school has recently entered into a program called Essential Schools, whereby four teachers take on the total responsibility for 100 students and teach them every subject in the curriculum and work with these 100 students until they graduate from high school. Since this program requires that I teach outside my areas of certification, we must apply for waivers from the state's certification requirements. I am torn between becoming part of the team and developing a program for the 100 students in our charge and remaining at the school as a mathematics/physics teacher. What can you advise?

A-3: This is the dilemma facing many high school subject matter specialists. On the one hand, they have studied long and hard to gain a certificate in one of the many subject matter disciplines and are rightly proud of gaining that certification. On the other hand, they recognize that many difficult changes and many new techniques and skills are going to prevail over the course of the next two or three decades. The introduction of technology alone will make many subject matter specialists obsolete because the potential for having master teachers provide courses in the advanced curriculum is expanding dramatically. As the teacher becomes more and more the manager of learning systems and less and less the provider of factual information, this problem will accelerate. You should accept the invitation to join the team and learn to become the manager of learning for those 100 students in your charge because this is the wave of the future in education.

Q-4: I am an elementary teacher, and I really love my class. I feel that I have been an effective elementary teacher and want to continue to be an effective teacher. To that end, I am pursuing a master's degree in elementary education at the local branch of the state university. Our school's leadership team recently announced that our school would enter into a year-round school program so that our students could have greater continuity and would not lose the learning gains made during the academic year. Since the university offers the courses I need for my master's only during the summer session and since I am very close to earning the degree, should I ask for a transfer and move to another school?

A-4: That is certainly an option for you; however, if this is a movement that is growing in your state and district, why not ask the university to structure a graduate program around your school's calendar? In this way, you might be able to have your cake and eat it as well. Universities are going to have to adjust in order to accommodate the needs of their students as well as the public school systems do. It will not do any harm to inquire about the potential for such accommodation from your university. Better still, request the district to inquire for you so they can bring the total impact of this decision to bear on the university.

Q-5: Our school's leadership team has recommended that we bank fifteen minutes per day to give us a half day's staff development time every two weeks. As the parent representative on the leadership team, I feel I must call attention to the fact that many parents work and cannot be home at an earlier time in order to accommodate the staff development program. In addition, to have a half day of staff development every two weeks will create an undue hardship on those working parents. What should I do?

A-5: Make your objections known to the leadership team. You do represent the parents of the school and know that there are some real difficult issues to the proposed program. Search for some compromise to the situation, such as encouraging the use of parent volunteers to conduct activities at the school to keep those children who cannot go home to be involved with a constructive activity. The awareness of some of the realities faced by some parents will make the school sensitive to the needs faced by certain students. This could be a major breakthrough in the development of the SBM leadership team for your school.

Q-6: Since we have entered into an SBM mode of operation, our high school principal has asked that all departmental budgets be gathered under the control of the leadership team at the school. He wants to involve all of the team members in the dividing of the budget and insists that we should give that prerogative to the team. I feel that my budget (music department) is mine alone and that I must have complete control of the budget in order to protect our gains made over many years. Besides, our booster club supplements our budget with donations of several thousand dollars every year, and I do not want to give that up. What should I do?

A-6: Because the funds provided by the district for your departmental budget are tax monies, you must follow the district guidelines for their monitoring. Your principal is within his rights to request that all of the departmental budgets be centralized at the school level to provide a better distribution of those funds to meet highest priority needs at the school. However, those booster club funds that are provided to the band are really "single-purpose" funds and are provided for specific expenditures for the school band. Those are your (the band's) funds and should remain with the band. Remember, however, that these funds must also stand the test of an outside audit annually.

Q-7: Our school wants to enter into a computer-assisted instruction program. The program promises to raise the reading and math skill levels of our students above the national norms over a five-year period. Our SBM leadership team has approved the exploration of this program, with the thought of recommending it to the total SBM community. The cost for the program will be $100/student, including the costs of the necessary computers. Our enrollment is approximately 500 students, so the cost is projected at $50,000 per year for a five-year period, after which the cost will be reduced to $30/student annually, or $15,000 per year. One of the options we could use to provide the needed resources is to trade in two certified teachers for $70,000. This would pay for the $50,000 in direct costs for the computers and the program and also provide $20,000 for the needed personnel to monitor the computer laboratory. To give up two classroom teachers would raise our average class size from twenty-two to twenty-four students per class. What should we do?

A-7: If you and your colleagues on the leadership team are convinced that this approach will provide the kinds of gains for students that you want, then go for it! One of the beauties of SBM is the flexibility to make such decisions for the school there at the school. If, after careful study and research, you decide that the computer-assisted instruction is the best approach that you can provide, you have the flexibility to adjust your staff to permit the accommodation of such a program.

Q-8: We have a school adopter who wishes to enter into an agreement with our school under which he will provide thirty computers for our use at the school, but he insists that we only use one make of computer, which is not the preferred make as expressed by our teachers. We already have twenty-five computers of another make, and he wants us to discard them when we accept his brand of computer. He will train us in the use of the selected computers and will provide software for each of the machines. Is this a good arrangement for us, and, if so, what should we do?

A-8: This is not a good deal for you, and I would reject it quickly. The adopter is asking you to give up twenty-five computers that your staff likes and can operate well, to accept another brand of computer that the staff does not like as well. Thus, for a net gain of five computers, you are placing yourselves at risk of having an arrangement that you will be very sorry for later. My advice is to reject the offer.

Q-9: Our district, under the provisions of SBM, has decentralized the budgets for substitute teachers and for vandalism-related (glass breakage, etc.) expenses. In our case, the substitute teachers budget will be $9,000.00, which will provide for approximately

180 days of substitute teacher time, and the vandalism budget is approximately $3,000 for the year. We can gain access to whatever is left of these funds provided there is a balance at the end of the year. We can use the balances to use in our staff development efforts or for any approved purpose at our school. Since our school had used an average of five days per teacher in the past years, is this a good approach for us and what does this say for our previous use of the sick leave?

A-9: It is a good deal for you. It recognizes the reality of sick leave use and makes it possible for the school to monitor their uses of sick leave and to gain dollars for their own use by minimizing the use of such leave. The use of sick leave and the abuse of school facilities are two of the more obvious areas for effecting a savings for the school district. It is a good plan to deal with these areas of abuse.

GOVERNANCE ISSUES

Under the SBM type of organization, there are quite a number of governance issues that arise. These issues range from state board/state legal requirements that impinge on the SBM mandate to central board/school issues that arise from day to day operations. Because the state has the legal mandate to provide for all decisions made on the development of educational services for its citizens and because the state's contribution to the payment for educational services is the largest and most rapidly growing part of the state budget, state legislatures and governors are most interested in the delivery of educational services to the citizens of the state. In addition, the members of the state board of education are also interested in what is happening locally with the delivery of educational services. These three entities, the governor, the state legislature, and the state board, provide the majority of state edicts under which local schools must operate. In some states, the state superintendent of public education has certain powers monitoring and enforcing the state laws and regulations, but the majority of the emerging edicts concerning education are the result of state legislative, state board, and governor mandates.

Once the laws are passed, the rules are promulgated and turned over to the chief executive of the state for enforcement. Usually, the state department of education develops the rules that govern the activities of the particular law to be met. This is when the state educational bureaucracy gets into the picture and provides enforcement, as well as explanatory interpretations, of the various laws and regulations. When there are no state laws or state rules on a specific activity, the local district has carte blanche to develop their own interpretation and resolution to a particular problem. In such instances, the state bureaucracy will stand by and observe how well the local option is working, and, if it is working, the state may adopt it as the solution to the problem and insist that all districts follow that particular solution.

Site-Based Management poses a variety of issues and problems for the state department of education, the state board of education, the state legislature, and the governor because it proposes that each school have the flexibility to set, within state guidelines and parameters, school-level objectives and processes. This is something that all bureaucrats are inherently against and will fight to the maximum because this mode of operation obviates the need for a large bureaucracy to interpret the state laws and promulgate enforcement.

The same is true, to a lesser extent, at the central office levels of most school districts. There, the central staff interprets and enforces the state rules and regulations to make sure the district's schools are in conformance with what the state requires. They also add their interpretation to those of the state department of education, and the local school is under the threat of severe restrictions if they choose to ignore those parameters. Of course, the best principals and the best teaching staffs soon learn to give lip service to the bureaucrats and then go their own way and really serve the students entrusted to them. After all, the state and central staff do not visit the school that often, and, when they announce that they are coming, the staff quickly develops the appropriate "show and tell" routine.

State/Central Board versus Site Council Issues

Perhaps the biggest and most disturbing issue that arises under the SBM mode of operations is the lack of flexibility under most state regulations and rules. Education policies and rules are developed from the perspective of having a common base from which to operate. Often, these rules are promulgated in order to make enforcement as easy as possible. Such a posture is not always in the best interest of students who.

come from varied and different backgrounds and bring with them to the school a vastly differing need for educational services.

As state laws are interpreted into the state rules and regulations for local district operation, the rule is applied indiscriminately to every district and school in the state. While such fairness in the application of a particular rule is fine and expected, the applicability of the rule to a situation is never questioned, and it should be because that is where the problem starts. Quite often, state legislatures pass a law to correct a particular situation and, in so doing, manufacture several other, more damaging situations. For example, in the Texas restructuring act passed in 1984, the legislature felt that they had to make attendance a prime issue and passed the law requiring every student to be in class, when permitted a maximum of ten absences per year, no matter what the circumstances. As one might expect, this soon led to a variety of extenuating circumstances and the development of a variety of reasons why certain students could not follow those rigid guidelines. Many school districts used this law to keep students from participating in many of the athletic events that dot the calendar of the typical school. It was noted that a maximum of ten absences for whatever reason was going to cramp the calendar of many schools. This law, while very appropriate and necessary, ran afoul of the athletic interests and other cocurricular activities and soon was eased, by permitting certain school functions to be considered as school attendance.

If, under SBM, the local school decides to invoke a rule determining attendance of students, can they be in direct opposition to existing state laws and rules? Certainly, they can because it is the domain of the school to decide what the students in attendance at the school should have as their guidelines for attendance. However, if the local school neglects to gain a waiver from the existing state rule governing attendance, the school is liable and vulnerable to citizen complaints about its policy and rule.

That is why, in those states having a strong commitment to SBM, the requirements for a defined state strategic plan, which sets parameters for the district's strategic plan, as well as the schools' strategic plans, are so important. Also, those states must have a well-defined and easily implemented waiver system, which permits local districts and schools to apply for a waiver to a particular rule that would impede SBM.

It is virtually impossible to implement an SBM type of operation if the state does not provide the options for local operation that are so important to implementation of the SBM principles. Because of the increasing demands for reform of the traditional system and organization of education, most states have taken steps to insure the flexibility needed to implement SBM practices. Indeed, some states have gone so far in mandating decentralization that the local schools are almost inoperable because of the new state laws concerning governance. When the intent of such legislation impedes the operation of a school, the law is obviously ill-conceived and ill-advised.

The state department of education, in its role as monitor and accreditation office for the schools in the state, must develop a system of accreditation that permits the local school/district the flexibility to function under the SBM mode. That is why, in those states who have a sophisticated SBM mandate, the state must first develop a state strategic plan for the districts to use as the parameter for the district strategic plan. From this, the school develops its strategic plan and the working plan for the immediate year.

The monitoring teams from the state department of education, or DPI, must utilize those school work plans to determine the propriety of the local effort and the impact of the local school on the learning rates of its students; therefore, each school should have a slightly different level of expectation that it is held accountable for.

Such flexibility is uncommon among state departments, but the fact that they must individualize their expectations to compensate for the differences in students found at the various schools is paramount. If such variance is not possible, the SBM initiative will be lost, and the state restructuring effort will be for naught.

Staff Selection/Employment Issues

Assuming the state impediments to SBM are resolved, what then become the major stumbling blocks to successful implementation of the SBM mode of operation? The remaining issues are largely central office versus school issues, the prime one being the staff selection/employment issue.

Typically, most districts have the central personnel office perform the major preselection tasks needed before employment. Traditionally, the personnel office, or human resources office, did all of the selection and placement of new personnel to the district. This permitted the office to closely monitor the staffing patterns of the various schools and to regulate their compliance to state and federal guidelines for equal employment practices. However, in the years leading up to the adoption of an SBM posture for school operations, the demand for local participation in the selection of staff for their building were heard and operationalized. Thus, we see that local school staff, principals, and community are participants in the selection of new staff for their school. The advent of SBM as a tool for the reform of education merely strengthened the need to decentralize the selection and employment process.

Typically, under the SBM mode, the human resources office provides the prescreening effort needed to generate the pool of candidates for a particular position. Then, the top candidates are invited to interview with the site personnel committee for the final screening. The site personnel committee then recommends their choice to the personnel office for submittal to the superintendent and the board for confirmation.

Because the local school has such power to determine the type of personnel and power over the final selection of who shall fill a particular position, the human resources office must exercise careful monitoring of the personnel function as it is performed at the school level to insure that district equal employment goals are met. Failure to do this will lead to a disruption of the personnel balance so vital to the success of any school system.

Local schools, while having the final say in who is employed and for what position, still must conform to the equal employment policies as set by the district and state. If equal employment is to establish a model for the country to follow, the local school must be the first link in the chain of responsible model establishment.

Budget Allocation Issues

The issue of budgets and budget allocations are never far from the top in any school system. It seems as though the allocation of scarce resources equitably and fairly is an ongoing issue in school districts. Under an SBM mode of operation, the issue becomes even more important because the local school must reallocate those dollars among the various divisions and departments of the school.

Typically, each site has a functioning budget committee. In some instances, the site leadership team assumes this responsibility because it is one of the more important duties at the school. The obligation of the finance or budget committee is to handle the final distribution of the funds that accrue for the site, in such a way as to insure fairness and equity. They, the finance committee, must answer the questions of fairness and equity, as well as insure that the long-range plans and work plans are attended to. It is sometimes necessary to provide extra incentives for a particular department during a current year, in exchange for a lesser allocation in future years. Such recommendations are the responsibility of the finance or budget committee and should be made with the strategic plan of the school firmly in mind. The principal plays a major role in the development of a budget for the school as he/she is the one who must implement the day to day operations of the school. Principals primarily must assure that the budget reflects the priorities of the school and provides fiscal support to those priorities.

The SBM finance committee also can assume other financially related duties. These might include such activities as monitoring the budget to make sure that monies are not expended other than for what they are intended and to enlist the assistance of the community in providing other resources to the school in the form of volunteer assistance or gifts and grants for specific purposes. The committee can develop a potential list of givers for particular programs and explore this list for volunteers to contribute to the expansion of the school's resources.

As mentioned earlier, the only real way to extend the school's resources is to modify the personnel allocations of the school to reflect the priority concerns of the school. By that, we mean that those personnel on board must be directed toward the prime needs of the students at the school. This means changing the primary assignments of the existing staff and/or adding staff trained to perform those duties deemed important to the school. Because approximately 86% of the school budget is allocated to salaries and fringe benefits, the amount of discretionary resource available to the school is very limited. Therefore, any large amount of dollars to be freed for other uses must come from the personnel allocation of the school. That is why the ability to exchange personnel at the average salary rate across the district is so important to the implementation of SBM.

Under SBM, the local schools should work to have as much of the budget decentralized as possible. This includes such items as supply budgets, capital outlay budgets, staff salaries, substitute budgets, vandalism budgets, utility budgets, and other direct costs charged to the school. Once these line items are decentralized, the local school can work on saving as much of that particular budget as possible, with the agreement that everything that is saved can be used for the program costs at the school. Potential savings from this approach are great, with every school using its own method for effecting this savings.

The schools should always work to increase the amount of the total budget allocated to the cost of operations at the school level and to diminish the amount of the allocation to the infrastructure of the district because these costs are not directly related to student growth and improvement of the instructional program. With the implementation of SBM, there should be a corresponding decrease in the need for the members of central office personnel because many of their former duties have been allocated to the school or deemed no longer necessary. Such decreases can enable a dramatic increase in the allocation for school- and student-related costs. In districts known to the author, this amount resulted in a staff increase in salaries of almost $5,000 per person. Districts have reported a decrease of central staff in the range of 50% with implementation of SBM.

Above all, it must be remembered that the SBM mode of operation is not an end in and of itself but a means to restructure the school system and move it towards a better program of instruction for the students of the district by giving the school the flexibility to implement programs developed locally with the students in mind.

Program/Curriculum Issues

As a district moves from a traditional organizational pattern to an SBM mode of operations, the flexibility provided by the SBM approach is in direct controversy to the traditional approach to program development. Traditionally, the central instructional/curriculum staff was responsible for introducing all innovations to the program, and, with this introduction, they usually permitted a few schools to implement the program for a test run. Local schools could innovate, but only after presenting their program to the instructional staff for approval. There was no formal approval process for locally developed programs, and local staffs were usually content to permit the central curriculum staff to do this development.

With state departments coming to the fore and determining the content of the public school curriculum under existing state law, the need for such large curriculum and instruction staff decreased. However, districts were reluctant to restructure their central office staffs because of the political fallout and because they did not yet grasp the significance of the state-driven curriculum. Thus, the huge bureaucracies that were developed as a result of the high degree of specialization of the school programs continued to grow. Because of the real need for understanding the many variables found in the demands for services, these staffs began to feed on themselves and continued to grow and flourish. When the SBM mode first began to develop, the realization that the day of the huge central instructional and curriculum staffs were numbered began to emerge. The central staff needed under the SBM mode was to be a totally different kind of staff than was there under the traditional mode of operation.

As the parameters of SBM are developed, it becomes apparent that the school has great flexibility in making program and curriculum decisions based on its school strategic plan and work plans prescribed for the students. As the concern for developing IEPs for every student becomes paramount for the school, the demand for increased flexibility in programming and in methodology continues to mount. Such flexibility demands that local staff develop the expertise to become curriculum experts and knowledgeable about change techniques and learning styles of students.

The concept of cooperative learning and teaching forces a change in the way curriculum is conceived and developed. Local school staff must participate in this development in order to have the knowledge to implement the program. As project learning becomes a fact of life in the schools and as such program realities are shown to provide a greater opportunity for student growth and engagement, the local staff must become knowledgeable about these innovative methods of student learning.

Related to program and curriculum issues is the staff selection and employment issue because the school must have the professional staff recognized as important to the implementation of particular programs. This can mean that certain staff must have particular and unique skills in order for the school to be able to implement a particular program. As these skills become identified, the school staff should be matched with the needed skills, and, if there is a discrepancy in skills needed and skills available, either the program must be changed or person(s) having these skills must be employed. Often, a mixture of the two approaches is required to make a program work at optimum levels.

Then, too, the community is always involved with emerging program issues because, if the community has not been involved in the development phase, their understanding of the new approach is so limited that they will be quite doubtful about the approach, particularly if it is a departure from the tried and true.

That is why it is so important to keep the community involved at every step, by including them in all of the working committees of the school and by reporting progress often and repeatedly to the broader community. In this way, the school provides the community with information about what is going on at the school and with a participatory role in the developments.

Governance of program and curriculum issues are resolved at the board level because of state laws establishing the role of the board of education. However, with the introduction of SBM as a method of operations, the central board shares certain powers with the community involvement committee and provides them the opportunity to function as a governing body over certain prerogatives, including program and curriculum development.

Equity Issues

It is a central responsibility for a board to provide governance workshops for the community involvement committees as they begin to function at the school level. These seminars should cover the multitude of laws and regulations that set the parameters for local district operation. Included in these laws and regulations are the state and federal laws governing equity for students, staff, parents, and community.

Equity requirements have become a major part of the law, and every state must take responsibility for enforcing these equity measures. The federal government has developed these laws because of the way that local governments treated its citizens over the years. Starting with the laws enacted to protect former slaves and other members of minority groups and continuing to more recent laws enacted to protect members of the female gender, these laws reflect the unfair treatment of these groups over the years. Many times, this treatment is not even recognized by the perpetrator of the treatment. This means that, in addition to stopping the activity that causes the treatment to be unfair, the school district must also educate the persons involved as to what constitutes the unfair treatment.

For example, the treatment of girls as far as achievement in mathematics and science is concerned had been proven to be a bias of the system against girls. Most educators do not recognize this as unfair treatment and continue to do as they always did. However, equity requires that each school system examine their practices in these curricular areas and make adjustments to reflect equal treatment of the sexes. Initial efforts are already showing dramatic gains for girls in these curricular areas. The most effective manner of dealing with this inequity is to prove that girls have as much talent in these areas of endeavor as boys and to provide encouragement and counseling to the girls at the appropriate time in their school career.

Equity also means the fair treatment of the various religious groups found in the school/community. While the first amendment prohibits the teaching of religion in the public schools, it does not permit the unfair treatment of any religious group that might think differently about who and what their God means to them. Often, the schools inadvertently discriminate against Hebrew children or Muslim children by the conduct of everyday activities. That is why the celebration of such religious holidays as Christmas are concerns for the public schools. It must be remembered that, while the practice of religion is prohibited, the study of religion is not. It is appropriate for the public schools to have a program of study of the various religions found in the typical American community. Indeed, our experience is that there are many community members who will volunteer to share their religious beliefs with the students at the local school.

Equity issues are of several general categories. These include personal equity (job or personal rights), group equity (racial, ethnic, or gender), and religious equity. Each of these has much case law to interpret the particular inequity committed, but the final analysis is the fair application of the laws and the fair treatment of every individual regardless of the group they come from and regardless of the religion they practice. School systems and schools must always consider the impact of unfair treatment of students, staff, and community on the program of education provided their children.

Questions That Arise about Governance When Considering the Impact of the SBM Mode of Operations

Q-1: Our site-based leadership team has presented an instructional plan to the total school community, which calls for a waiver application to permit the increase of the average class size from 22/1 to 26/1 and to add two specialists in exchange for the added class size. This will permit the school to move toward individual assessment and IEPs for every student, as well as provide for cooperative learning arrangements and for project learning and multi-aged grouping throughout the school. The state requires a waiver for schools to depart from the 22/1 class size ratio and also insists on the school submitting a plan that will specify how the student learning rate will increase with the new plan for instruction. While we can, we think, improve the current levels of student learning, we do not know how much the improvement will be. How should we develop the plan for submission to the state, and how can we project student learning gains without having any experience with these new procedures?

A-1: Provide as much information as possible and project, with caution, the proposed student gains under the new delivery system. You must have some idea of what the new system will do for the students' achievement at the school and what will accrue for the students at the school level. State the expected outcomes and request a three- to five-year continuance to establish the new programs before a summative evaluation is made. This will provide a sufficient length of time to determine the value of the approach you propose.

Q-2: Approximately 250 of the 800 students at our school qualify for state bilingual funds, and approximately 200 of these also qualify for federal Chapter I funds. Because our school does not have a high enough proportion of its students qualifying for either of these programs to be on the list of schools who qualify, we do not receive any bilingual or Chapter I funds. Since this means $25,000 ($100 × 250) in bilingual funds and $14,000 ($70 × 200) in Chapter I funds, for a total of $39,000, we contend that we should be the recipients of these funds under the theory that money follows the student wherever the student is located. What can we do to qualify for these funds and for the district to allocate these funds to our school to use in the provision of instructional services for the students who qualify for the program?

A-2: Arrange a meeting with the district person(s) in charge of the bilingual and Chapter I programs and submit your rationale for receiving the funds. If you get no satisfaction from these people, submit your request to the superintendent and board, taking care to emphasize that the qualifying students from your school have not received any services for the programs that provide the special resources to the district and that you feel that you should receive a proportionate share of those funds. If this fails, submit your request to the state, indicating a lack of response from the district and a desire to improve the program for those qualifying students.

Q-3: We have requested a curriculum specialist at our school to assist in the transformation from a traditional delivery system to a cooperative delivery system. While the central office (human resources office) has approved the request, they have insisted that we hire a minority for this position because we have no minority professionals at our school and the district is committed to approaching the district-wide minority count of 45% of the students. Can they do this and why?

A-3: Yes, they can. Every district in every state is committed to becoming an equal employment district or agency. The task of the human resources department in most districts is to monitor and assist local schools in meeting the equal employment guidelines. The human resources department is held accountable for the schools in the district meeting these guidelines and must prevail in cases like this. They will insist on having your school participate in meeting affirmative action policies as adopted by the board.

Q-4: Our school has, as part of the school improvement plan, a restructuring of the school staff, with a reduction of three classroom teachers in exchange for the addition of three professionals we feel we need to assist us as we embark into a technologically driven curriculum. These professionals will prepare the staff for the use and application of the latest technology as a crucial component of our instructional delivery system. Because we have three openings at the professional staff level, we are searching for three persons who have certain technological skills as part of their training. The human resources department is assisting us in the search and advises us that they will have five candidates for us to interview by next week. Because we are a majority Hispanic school, we would like to have the candidates capable of speaking

Spanish, as well as able to perform the technological tasks that are part of the job specification. The human resources staff informs us that only one of the candidates has the bilingual capacity. What should we do?

A-4: Interview the candidates and, if the Spanish-speaking person meets your expectations, hire that person and have the two remaining positions readvertised, with capability in Spanish added to the job description. It was a mistake to develop the job description without having the requirement for capability in speaking Spanish a part of the job expectations. Apologize to the other candidates and to the human resources department.

Q-5: Our district has embarked on an effort to start an SBM mode of operation for all of the schools in the district. We have been chosen to participate as a model school to initiate the process during the next academic year. Because this is so new to the district, there are no guidelines for determining which decisions are to be made at the site and which are to be made centrally. We want to initiate a creative staffing pattern but do not know how to prepare the plan required for district waivers. How do we do such a thing?

A-5: By developing your school improvement plan so that the plan reflects the emerging staffing pattern you wish to implement. When you negotiate the instructional improvement plan with the central office, make sure the waivers are discussed at the time the new staffing patterns are discussed. As part of the school improvement plan, develop a waiver request for submittal.

Q-6: Under the SBM concept, our school has decided to develop a phonics approach to the teaching of reading. The central office personnel in charge of reading do not believe in the phonics approach and have refused to approve our request to implement the phonics approach. Out staff believes in the phonics approach and wants to proceed with this approach. What can we do to assist the staff in implementation of the phonics approach to the teaching of reading?

A-6: Appeal the decision and support the request with the best rationale you can engender. If the staff at the school has the knowledge and expertise to implement a phonics approach to the teaching of reading and do not know or like the district's decision on the delivery of reading instruction, it seems that, under the SBM mode of operation, the school should have the right to decide and to implement.

Q-7: Our school has made the decision to focus on the teaching of the basic skills for the coming academic year. The district has chosen to emphasize creative thinking and problem-solving skills because they feel we have done as well as we can in the basic skills areas. Since we are not yet at the 50th percentile in the basic skills areas, we feel that our students will profit more from an emphasis on basic skills, rather than problem solving. Under the SBM mode of operation, can we prioritize the basic skills rather than follow the district's lead into the problem-solving, creative thinking priority?

A-7: If the district has determined that the priority instructional effort shall be creative thinking and problem solving and has made that the top priority in their strategic plan, there is little you can do to change that. However, you can propose your priorities with the submittal of your school improvement plan and negotiate priorities with the central staff. If your argument is persuasive enough, they might permit you to follow those priorities you have developed but do not count on it. Have a plan prepared that meets the district's priorities as well.

Q-8: By extending the school day and banking fifteen minutes per day, our school can provide for a half day's staff development every two weeks. Then, students will not be turned out to go home because we have a plan to provide for their participation in a school activity during that time and have arranged to have volunteer parents provide special "field trip" experiences during the days we have the staff development. The district has raised the problem of liability for the parents, while the students are on the field trips accompanied by parents, rather than certified teachers. What should we do?

A-8: Check with the insurance carrier to see what must be done to enable the field trips to continue. Perhaps a rider to the policy will suffice. In some instances, the carrier will write a policy for just the particular days that are involved and at a minimum cost to the school. If all else fails, be prepared to have some of the teaching staff accompany the students and parents on the field trip. Find out the minimum of professional staff that must be there to have the policy cover the staff.

VIGNETTE #1

Pitfalls and Opportunities

In the Oklahoma district mentioned earlier, the superintendent and board were most concerned about the way decisions would be made and at what level under the SBM mode of organization. As consultant to the district, the author felt that, until this issue was dissected and analyzed, the district would not arrive at an appropriate SBM concept. Therefore, the board and superintendent were encouraged to appoint a representative committee to develop a "decision matrix" for the district to use as it moved forward under the SBM arrangement. Serving on the committee were central staff, building principals, teachers, support staff, and parents. It was their responsibility to recommend to the superintendent and board the appropriate level and location for as many decisions as they could identify.

This committee worked for two years on the development of such a matrix, and, after extended discussion and study, they made tentative recommendations to the superintendent and board. In the meantime, the district had gone far beyond the committee in its expertise in dealing with the issue, so the matrix was really an "after the fact" *fait accompli*. However, from its inception, the decision matrix committee served a very valuable purpose and was proof of the seriousness with which the district considered SBM.

The committee started with a request to the various departments of the administrative structure of the district and solicited from them a list of decisions they felt were their province to make. From this data, there were six major decision-making areas that evolved. These were:

(1) Goal setting included the district mission statement and strategic plan, district goals and objectives, school mission statement and strategic plans, school goals and objectives, and school improvement plans, which included the setting of priorities and strategies for implementation, establishing time lines, and evaluation of projects.

(2) Budgeting included the district budget, the school allocation

process, capital outlay projects, school budget monitoring, and school budget amendments.

(3) The third area was the staffing and staff selection area, including recruitment, selection/placement, teacher job description/responsibility, evaluation/contract, school staffing, school planning for staffing under the equivalent allocation system, noncertified staffing, equity considerations, and new teacher induction.

(4) The fourth major area was the school organization, including the makeup of the leadership team, procedures of operation of the team, assignments of staff to particular duties, safety issues, staff development, calendar of events, student grouping, classroom locations, state-approved course offerings, department chair selection, coaching assignments, textbook selection, implementation of required district plans, implementation of state-required plans, record keeping, school discipline, parent/community involvement, and use of buildings.

(5) The fifth area of concern was the curriculum content area. This included federal/state requirements, core curriculum, enrichment, supplementary, textbook usage, resources/materials, new courses, new programs, staff development, instructional strategies, curriculum innovations, and assessment/evaluation.

(6) A final area of concern was the governance area, with particular concern expressed for the role of the site-based leadership teams and their role in the process.

As the committee met and developed their methodology and understanding, they arrived at a system of classifying the decisions and their appropriate location through utilizing the three major locations for the decision:

(1) The campus
(2) The central office
(3) The board of education

Each decision was analyzed from the perspective of each level where the decision could take place and, finally, coded with these responsibilities:

(1) RR = review

(2) R = recommendation
(3) A = approval
(4) D = decision

Further, those decisions that were established through federal and/or state law were explicated as such and were not thrown into the mix.

Out of this exercise, there evolved some 256 specific decisions that were recognized as important enough for special consideration, and these were made the topic of an extended summer workshop on the matrix. As a result of the committee's work, the workshop, and the ongoing dialogue, this district is able to work through the issues and difficulties that arise during the implementation of the SBM concept.

The goal of a definitive list of decisions and where the responsibility is located is not yet forthcoming, but the understanding of the process and the flexibility required to make the SBM concept work effectively is strong and will enhance the work of the district as it strives to meet the educational needs of its students.

The work of the committee has served to strengthen the understanding of the concept and made it possible for the staff and the community to work together to meet the issues and problems of the district. The board has come to a better understanding of its role and responsibilities under the SBM approach, while the superintendent has become a staunch advocate of the students in the district. The atmosphere of collegiality and mutual respect and support is making the concept work in this district.

VIGNETTE #2

Pitfalls and Opportunities

In one of our southern states, where all school districts are dependent districts, which means that the school district is dependent on the city government for its budget and for related services, the role of the school board is difficult to identify and understand. Because the school's chief executive officer, who is often called the department head of the school, instead of the superintendent of schools, is part of the city command structure, the position requires a different relationship to the city officials, particularly the mayor and city council. The school board, while it does have the power to set policy and to make budgeting decisions after the amount of total budget is allocated through the city council process, really has little flexibility to adjust the income of the system to meet its need.

One such district, where the author has had the opportunity to observe and participate in the development of the SBM approach to school organization is the focus of this vignette.

The superintendent, newly appointed for the 1991–92 academic year, had been the superintendent of a middle-sized urban school system in one of our northern states, where he had established himself as a fine administrator and innovator. He was, in fact, recruited by the mayor of this urban center and accepted the appointment because he and the mayor were on the same wavelength as far as school system development was concerned. Because this superintendent had successfully implemented SBM in his prior assignment and because he strongly believed in the potential for SBM, particularly in the urban centers of the country, one of the first efforts he started in his new assignment was the introduction of the SBM concept. The mayor endorsed the concept and got the city council to support the concept as well. In fact, the city council approved an additional capital outlay budget of over $150 million for school construction and renovation. This amount was far in excess of what had ever been allocated before and showed the impact of the new school director and his ideas on the city power structure.

As the superintendent attempted to place into focus the necessary policies in order to start the implementation of SBM, he was amazed to find that the school board was reticent to approve and change the policies of the district to accommodate the flexibility needed for the SBM concept to operate. After several attempts to propose such changes to the board, the superintendent became discouraged and began the slow process of educating the board. In order to provide the education needed for the board to understand the SBM concept, the superintendent enlisted the various community groups that were already anxious to have the flexibility promised through the use of the SBM concept. These community groups had a far greater impact on the board than did the superintendent and his staff. The superintendent arranged for the board and representatives of the community groups to visit districts where the SBM process was in effect and working. In addition, he initiated a staff development program where the central staff, the principals, and the teachers, as well as the parents, began to define the concept as it would be initiated in this city. He invited several of us to participate in the exploratory meetings, during which the staff attempted to define the process for the city. We played the role of devil's advocate and forced the staff and parents to think through the process thoroughly regarding what it could do for the school system.

By the 1992–93 academic year, the board was convinced that the SBM process was a fine innovation for the city schools (actually, the school district encompasses the entire county) and began to introduce and accept the modification of policies so the SBM process could be implemented. During the 1991–92 academic year, the school system developed its strategic plan and the subsequent work plan that flowed from the strategic plan. Early in the 1992–93 year, the district modified the strategic plan and set the process of developing school strategic and work plans into motion. These were to be negotiated with the central office in time for 1993–94 implementation.

The central staff were an important part of the staff development process because a complete restructuring and refocusing of the central staff was required. The superintendent developed a position on the functions of the school system patterned after the author's definitions developed in the book, *School System Administration: A Strategic Plan for Site-Based Management,* published by Technomic Publishing Co., Inc. in 1991. In this book, the following crucial functions of every school district were identified as

(1) Planning
(2) Delivery
(3) Evaluation
(4) Communications
(5) Non-instructional support services
(6) Instructional support services
(7) Personnel services

The reorganization was accomplished through the application of the functions, as identified in the book, and those personnel who did not meet the functional definitions were reassigned and/or retrained to become planners and/or evaluators. The resulting central office staff, while not enamored of the new role, were aware and accepting of the need to change the approach to the clients of the central office: the schools. The bulk of the time was spent in changing the attitude of the staff from a directing mode to a supporting mode. This required a great deal of time and effort because the central staff was so used to acting in a directing mode and issuing orders to the school. While not accepting the new organizational pattern in toto, the central staff, nonetheless, understood what the requirements and expectations for their performance were. As time went by, the staff seemed to better accept and understand the changed requirements for performance.

As of this writing, the city (actually county) council and the mayor are pleased by the developments in the school district. The school board is slowly getting a feel for the changed organizational structure and is starting to enjoy the expanded role of the board in the setting and changing of existing policies. The superintendent is forging ahead with drawing the various schools out as far as innovations and improvements are concerned. The various schools are working hard to develop programs based on the district's strategic plan and the students needs as defined locally, and the parents are gaining confidence in the inclusion process and are volunteering to serve on the various committees and task forces. It appears that the SBM process is taking hold in this particular city and will become an important part of the solution to the pressing problems facing the educational system.

Chapter 4

A PLANNING/EVALUATION/ DECISION-MAKING MODEL FOR SITE-BASED MANAGEMENT

Good education depends upon the good planning and delivery of programs. Good planning derives from good needs assessment and an understanding of the way the delivery system works. Good planning must have a fine evaluation system operating in concert with the planning effort in order to develop corrective mechanisms for keeping the programs on track and effective. Educators must always have the benefit of a good planning/evaluation system in order to make the best possible decisions about the implementation of programs.

When committing to the initiation of a Site-Based Management (SBM) approach to the delivery of educational services, the district needs a common language to use as it plans and evaluates the effort. Decisions must be made with institutional goals uppermost in mind. There are many planning/evaluation models from which to chose when searching for a model to use in the implementation of SBM. Rather than creating another model for use in this development, the author recommends the use of an existing model, one that has proven itself over the years as an appropriate model for educators to utilize in their efforts to improve the delivery of educational services.

A district that commits itself to the implementation of the SBM organizational approach must develop a consistent mode for making decisions, for planning operations, and for evaluating the effort. After some forty-five years in education as a teacher, professor, superintendent, and state commissioner of education, the author has come to the conclusion that the Context, Input, Process, Product (CIPP) model for planning/evaluation/decision making is the best model ever posed for this type of activity. First, the Context, Input, Process, and Product acronyms provide for the discovery of all pertinent aspects of the issue that might arise. Second, the terminology and application of definitions are consistent across the board. Third, CIPP focuses on the reality of the situation and sorts out the minutia. Fourth, CIPP, when applied consistently, provides data upon which to base decisions. Finally, CIPP is easy to learn and to adapt to changing conditions. The beauty of CIPP is in its simplicity and ease of application for every situation and need.

From CIPP, a variety of other evaluation designs and efforts are spawned. Using CIPP as the base for the development of all data, program, school, and district evaluations are readily available and usable. Personnel evaluations are also generated through the application of the CIPP model, augmented with the special duties and outcomes implied by a particular position. Good decisions are made through the use of good data. CIPP demands that the data developed in the context analysis be the best data available and that the data be changed as new and improved data become available.

Through the use of available data and through the development of programs that meet the high priority needs of students and that are based on the data about the students, school districts can provide for a variety of efforts to meet the students' educational needs. The SBM organization is a means of providing the avenue for meeting the students' needs on a more realistic and timely basis without the bureaucratic pitfalls that are always present in large organizations.

THE CIPP (CONTEXT, INPUT, PROCESS, PRODUCT) MODEL

Evaluations were first given priority by the Elementary and Secondary Education Act of 1965, which recognized the need for systematic and rigorous evaluation efforts to provide information needed to judge the effects of certain programs and efforts on the students receiving them. The Phi Delta Kappa board of directors named a study committee on evaluation in the spring of 1966. This committee, headed by Dr. Daniel Stufflebeam, published the results of its research in the spring of 1971. The ensuing book *Educational Evaluation and Decision Making* was published by Phi Delta Kappa. The book developed the CIPP model and explained its uses for the practitioner.

Stufflebeam developed a new definition: "Evaluation is the process of delineating, obtaining, and providing useful information for judging decision alternatives."[1] Stufflebeam further explains, "Of particular importance is the fact that the evaluation process is a continuing activity rather than as terminal or as having a discrete beginning and ending.[2]

The concept of educational improvement is the result of the identification of unmet needs, and action to mitigate these needs is taken by the educator. This requires that correct data and information be acquired for use by the educator in the development of programs to meet the students' needs—of information, Stufflebeam says, "Descriptive or interpretive data about entities (tangible or intangible) and their relationships, in terms of some purpose."[3] Stufflebeam stresses that information must be more than a collection of facts and data. These data must be organized to serve some purpose to be intelligible. Information serves to differentiate the alternatives involved in the decision situation and supplies data for prioritizing the alternatives.

If evaluation is a process that furnishes information useful in guiding decision making, the first operational step is identifying the most useful information. Thus, the CIPP model becomes most helpful as a planning tool, as well as an evaluation design. Actually, the CIPP acronym identifies the four basic types of evaluation that correspond to the four basic types of decisions that are made: planning decisions, structuring decisions, implementing decisions, and recycling decisions.[4] Context evaluation serves planning decisions to determine objectives; input evaluation serves restructuring decisions to determine project designs; process evaluation serves implementing decisions to control project operations; and product evaluation serves recycling decisions to judge and react to project attainments.[5]

SBM must base its program formulation on the kinds of data and information developed as a result of the use of the CIPP evaluations. It should be remembered that the context evaluation is general and systemic, provides information on needed changes, and serves to monitor the situation. The other three types of evaluation are specific and ad hoc; they come into play only after a planning decision has been reached to affect some sort of system change, and specific evaluation designs for each vary according to the setting for the change. Generally speaking, the greater the change and the lower the information grasp (the decision maker's knowledge of how to affect the change), the more formal, structured, and comprehensive is the evaluation required.

Context Evaluation

Context evaluation is the most basic type of evaluation. Its purpose is to provide a rationale for determination of objectives. Specifically, it defines the relevant environment, describes the desired and actual conditions pertaining to that environment, identifies unmet needs and unused opportunities, and diagnoses the problems that prevent needs from being met and opportunities from being used. Diagnosis of problems provides an essential basis for developing objectives whose achievement results in program improvement.

Context evaluation is macro-analytic; it sets the boundaries of the system to be evaluated and then describes and analyzes it. Through its focus on variables known to be important for achieving given goals, it is a reflection of theoretical and empirical knowledge in a field. In this respect, it determines whether practice is consistent with the validated principles of a relevant theory. Context evaluation provides a basis for starting change objectives through diagnosing and ranking problems in meeting needs or using opportunities, and it analyzes change objectives to determine the amount of change to be affected and the amount of information grasp available for support.

Through its dynamic baseline of information regarding the operations and accomplishments of the total system, context evaluation provides a basis for widespread communication, including a factual basis for public information services. It also poses new problems for theory development and empirical research (pertaining to the substance of the program being evaluated) and provides a repository of information with potential utility for testing research hypotheses. Overall, context evaluation is systematic; it monitors the system to maintain a current baseline of information about it yet is ad hoc when centered on diagnosing problems that block meeting needs or using opportunities.

The methodology of context evaluation is of two modes: contingency and congruence. In the contingency mode, the context evaluation searches for opportunities and pressures outside of the immediate system to promote improvement within it. This involves exploratory probing within loosely defined boundaries—study visits to other systems; exploration of the research and development literature; brainstorming retreats; assessments of community values, attitudes, and priorities; and so forth. This mode of context evaluation also probes the future, including social needs and values, technological advances, political trends, economic developments, and population statistics.

The contingency mode of context evaluation asks the "if-then" type of questions and is really the basis for much of the long-range planning done by the school system. Questions are addressed such as, "If a new major industry moves into town, then how must the present educational system be changed to meet the needs of the increased student population?" or, "If the teachers in the school system go on strike, then what can be done to provide uninterrupted educational services to the student population?" or, "If the school budget is increased 30%, how would it be used and what would result?" or, "If it becomes possible to totally computerize the instructional program, then what will be the educational and economic benefits, and for what purposes will teachers be needed?" Such deliberate questions must be served by strong contingency context evaluation mechanisms that are exemplified by policy research centers that probe into the future for information to be used as a basis to project national education policies. This is now known as strategic planning and is carried out at every level of education.

The second mode of context evaluation, congruence, compares actual and intended system performance. An essential element of this mode of context evaluation is a specified data base for the system, which is used to monitor all vital aspects of the system and to maintain a dynamic baseline of data about performance. Given an appropriate data base, information can be collected and stored systematically for retrieval whenever there is a need to test conformity of system performance. Discrepancy information then can be reported to system administrators so they can determine what unmet needs exist and how they should be taken care of. Among the discrepancies that might require attention are a lack of acceptable standardized test performance in specified subject matter areas at given age or grade levels; a lack of equal educational opportunities for children of differing socioeconomic, racial, and cultural backgrounds; an excessively high rate of failure in college; a preponderance of negative student attitudes towards a particular subject area; evidence of narcotics use; evidence of malnutrition; and a high dropout rate. In most school systems, conditions such as these are cause for concern and action; however, remediation cannot be undertaken until needs have been identified and problems have been diagnosed.

Operationally, educational institutions should maintain context evaluation mechanisms that provide both congruence and contingency data. Given the goals and values of a system, it is important to continually investigate whether, and how well, those goals and values are being served (congruence evaluation). In a rapidly changing society, the needs of persons and localities are subject to constant change, as is our ability to meet those needs. Consequently, systems should continually ask the "if-then" questions (contingency evaluation) to determine whether goals and policies should be changed.

An example of a school context evaluation under the SBM organizational pattern would look much like the following: context evaluation would provide information on system and student needs, system and school problems, opportunities that the school might use to improve programs and other aspects of the school, and assessments of district and school goals and objectives. This information is useful for determining job and school targets early in the school year, for examining the significant accomplishments near the end of the school year, for placing the year-end assessment of effectiveness within the proper context of constraints that may have impeded achievement, and for examining opportunities that did or could have enhanced accomplishments.

For both early target setting and later examination of the significance of the accomplishments, the school should review available district and school data, which might include any or all of the following:

- student achievement data disaggregated by grade, content area, gender, and race and contrasted to previous years and to results from similar districts and schools (Data about the district as a whole and for the particular campus must be analyzed.)
- student attendance for the district and the school (This should be disaggregated by race, age, grade level, gender, and, if possible, socioeconomic level.)
- student graduation rates, if applicable, for the school
- incidents of crime at the school and district
- records of student immunization
- up-to-date data on diversity and extent of integration of the student body and school staff
- survey results on school climate from every school
- report on the dispersion of ratings of effectiveness of teachers and other categories of school staff

- records of complaints about the district and school received in previous years
- difficulties, as indicated in the most recent school principal reports
- student mobility rate at the school and for the district for each of the past three years
- percent of district and school families below the poverty line
- percent of free and reduced fee lunches provided at the school (This data should be disaggregated.)
- the district's per pupil expenditure compared to that of similar districts in the region
- crime rate statistics for the district and the school
- data/editorials on school attitudes toward the district
- the district's record in passing school funding issues over the past five years
- data on teen pregnancies for each of the past three years (Data should be gathered from the school and for the district.)
- percentage of single-parent families for the school and for the district
- test data for the district and for the school disaggregated by race, gender, grade level, and socioeconomic levels
- data about the percent of students from the school who attend institutions of higher education
- community data and statistics to provide a community needs assessment
- staff data and statistics providing a base of knowledge about the staff
- projections about the enrollment at the school for the next five years (This should be by race, gender, and socioeconomic levels.)
- other pertinent data about the area and district

Obviously, school districts and schools vary widely on the environmental factors listed above. Depending on their status on these and related factors, some districts and schools have a much easier time than others in raising achievement levels. It is fair and reasonable for schools to at least consider what environmental conditions affected the performance of the students and staff.

The provision of such data on a school by school basis is essential under the SBM approach to school system organization. Each school must understand its own situation and plan with the needs of the school and its students uppermost in mind. The central staff is available to act as planning/evaluation consultants and to perform the advocacy role between the school and the district.

Input Evaluation

The purpose of input evaluation is to provide information for determining how to utilize resources to meet program goals. This is accomplished by identifying and assessing (a) relevant capabilities of the responsible agency, (b) strategies for achieving program goals, and (c) designs for implementing a selected strategy. This information is essential for structuring specific designs to accomplish program objectives.

According to Stufflebeam, "The end product of input evaluation is an analysis of one or more procedural designs in terms of potential costs and benefits. Specifically, alternative designs are assessed concerning staffing, time, and budget requirements; potential procedural barriers, the consequences of not overcoming these barriers, and the possibilities and costs of overcoming them; relevance of the designs to program objectives; and overall potential of the design to meet the objectives."[6]

Essentially, input evaluation provides information to decide if outside assistance is required to meet objectives, how the objectives should be stated operationally, what general strategy should be employed (for example, the adoption of available solutions or the development of new ones), and what design or procedural plan should be employed to implement the selected strategy. Project proposals exemplify the results of decisions based upon input evaluation.

While context evaluation is mainly systematic and macro-analytic, input evaluation is essentially ad hoc and micro-analytic. Its emphasis is on the objectives for change established due to needs, opportunities, and problems in the context. Its function is to determine how best to meet newly stated objectives.

This type of evaluation asks many questions. Among them are: Are the given objectives stated operationally, and is their accomplishment feasible? What strategies already exist with potential relevance for meeting the established objectives? How can alternative strategies be generated? What are the potential costs and benefits of each competing strategy? What are the operating characteristics and effects of competing strategies under pilot conditions? Is it logical to believe that a given strategy can accomplish the stated objectives? Has this kind of plan worked in the past? In the particular strategy based on valid theoretical principles? Is it legal?

How much training will the staff require before they can implement the strategy or plan? What specific calendar and schedule of events and activities will be needed to implement the strategy? How can existing staff and facilities best be utilized in the implementation of the new strategy? What side effects might a particular strategy produce? What are the attitudes of students, parents, teachers, etc., toward this particular strategy? Do they understand and know about the strategy? How should a particular strategy be administered, evaluated, and reviewed at various levels of the organization? What process and product evaluation designs are required for efficient and effective strategy implementation? Following a pilot test, how feasible is strategy institutionalization?

These and similar questions indicate the importance of input evaluation data: if program objectives are to be achieved, it is essential to select and structure strategies with the promise of satisfactorily meeting the objectives at a reasonable level of expenditure. Input evaluation is intended to assist program personnel to answer questions that are important in the selection and structuring of project designs.

Such questions indicate the many and varied considerations of input evaluation. As it aids in the selection of overall strategies, it is general. As it looks at the theoretical relationship between strategies and objectives, it is logical, but as it collects performance data about competing strategies under pilot considerations, it is empirical. In projecting costs and benefits, input evaluation is future-oriented, but in obtaining data about the previous use of a strategy, it is past-oriented.

Techniques for input evaluations are lacking in the educational arena but can be modified from other fields. The use of the Delphi technique, for example, has great promise for education as does the programming and budgeting system. Program evaluation and review techniques (PERT) also can be easily modified for use in input evaluation.

Decisions based on input evaluation usually result in the specification of procedures, materials, facilities, equipment, schedule, organizational schemes, staff requirements, and budgets in proposals to funding sources. This is especially important under the SBM approach because the school can identify every type of resource needed to make the program operational and the funding agency (in this case, the central office) has ample information for completing ongoing evaluations.

In their definitive study, *Superintendent's Performance Evaluation: The State of the Art,* Candoli, Cullen, and Stufflebeam write that, "Input evaluations provide information and judgments concerning district budgets, strategic plans, personnel assignments, calendar of events, and staff work plans, as well as information on potentially relevant educational and administrative strategies used elsewhere or recommended in the literature."[7]

Specific information needed for input evaluations (remember that input evaluation drives the planning process) include

1. Plans from previous years
    1.1 District strategic plans
    1.2 School strategic plans
        1.2a. School improvement plans
    1.3 School and district work plans
    1.4 Board and superintendent assessments of implementation and results from previous years
2. Financial information from previous years
    2.1 District budgets
    2.2 School budgets
    2.3 Audited financial reports
    2.4 Board and superintendent assessment of adequacy of budgets in previous years
    2.5 School staff and principal assessment of adequacy of school budget in previous years
3. Plan for the present year (district)
    3.1 School plan for the present year
    3.2 Overall district plan
    3.3 Specific plans keyed to priority needs and problems
    3.4 District and school calendar for the year
    3.5 Work plan for the year (district and school)
    3.6 Independent evaluations of the planning documents
4. Reports on effective practices in other districts and schools
    4.1 Example strategic district and school plans, budgets, and year-long calendars from similar districts and schools with reputations for excellence

4.2 Evaluation reports from projects that address problems being faced in the present district and/or school
   4.3 Reviews of the literature on educational and administrative strategies that might be adopted by the school and/or district
5. Approach to planning in the district and school
   5.1 Description of the district's approach to strategic planning
   5.2 Decription of the school approach to strategic planning
   5.3 Description of the school work plan development and implementation
   5.4 Records of involvement of stakeholders in the planning process
   5.5 Evaluation reports on the district's and the school's planning process

All units should regularly review plans, budgets, accounting reports from previous years, work plans, and calendars. They should do so in the interest that plans appropriately address unmet student needs. The school, as the key unit in an SBM approach to managing the system, must become familiar with the various plans and opportunities available for the school to utilize in meeting their objectives.

Input evolves around the allocation of resources, monetary as well as human, to meeting the highest priority needs of the students at the school. Under SBM, the school has great flexibility in the utilization of those resources allocated to it and can, with careful planning and creative application, realize increased resources for the specific needs of the students at that school.

Context and input evaluations are essential for providing the data for good planning. These data will offer the basis for the development of a strategic plan that is based on the perceived needs of the students and citizens of the district. The data will also provide the limitations as far as budget is concerned. The materials generated by the performance of the context and input evaluations will become the basis for district and school planning for the year ahead.

Process Evaluation

Once a designed course of action has begun, process evaluation is necessary to provide periodic feedback to persons responsible for implementing plans and procedures. Process evaluation has three main objectives. The first is to detect or predict defects in the procedural design or its implementation during the implementation stages, the second is to provide information for programming decisions, and the third is to maintain a record of the procedure as it occurs.

There are three strategies to be followed in process evaluation. The first of these is to identify and monitor continuously the potential sources of failure in a project. These include, but are not limited to, interpersonal relationships among staff and students, communications channels, logistics, understandings of and agreement with the intent of the program by persons involved in and affected by it, and adequacy of the resources, physical facilities, staff, and time schedule.

The second strategy involves projecting and servicing preprogrammed decisions to be made by project managers during the implementation of a project. An example of these preprogrammed decisions is found in test development projects where it is necessary to choose a specific sample of schools for participation in trying out newly written test items. Such a decision can be projected well in advance of the actual time when the choice is to be made, but the choice cannot be made until a mailing list of schools has been developed, these schools have been contacted, and determinations have been made concerning those schools that are willing to participate in the tryout administration. Then the test developer must select those schools that, in combination, best meet the requirements of the sampling design (a previous structuring decision), and he/she must schedule the specifics pertaining to the administration of tryout test forms. If the input evaluation and structuring decisions have been implemented effectively, the evaluator should have little difficulty in delineating preprogrammed decisions and their associated information requirements. Such delineation will form a major basis for the original process evaluation design.

The third process evaluation strategy is to note the main features of the project design, such as concepts to be taught and the amount of discussion to take place, and, in these terms, to describe what actually takes place. This information will be especially useful later in determining why objectives were or were not achieved, i.e., that certain concepts were not learned might or might not be the fault of the design or the procedure.

Two points are worth noting about the relation of process evaluation to the other kinds of evaluation. First, process evaluation is a function of the extent to which context and input evaluations have been performed adequately—the more adequate the context and input evaluation, the more certain the project director can be of how well his/her design will operate, and the less critical is the need for process evaluation. When the rationale for the given objectives and project design is vague, the project probably is headed for trouble and, perhaps, for failure. To identify and remedy problems early during the process, it is essential to have continuous feedback about how the project is functioning. Thus, in this instance, process evaluation can perform a vital function.

Under SBM, what kinds of information could be assembled to permit adequate process evaluations? The following is a listing of the kinds of data that might be appropriate for school process evaluations:

- progress reports on special projects, staffing, product development (programs being developed), delivery of instruction, delivery of student services, and stakeholder involvement
- accounting reports on the school budget—results of resource procurement efforts and plans/suggestions for raising funds for projects
- exception reports, e.g., modifications in plans, assignments, schedules, and budgets
- independent assessments of operations

These data are then used to keep the board, community advisory committee, and the community informed about the affairs of the school and the implementation of plans at the school. The data are also useful for maintaining fiscal accountability, as well as providing an early warning system for identifying and addressing potential problems about the implementation effort. The information is also used to maintain a record of implementation for use in interpreting outcomes during the product evaluation stage.

Process evaluation is crucial to the decision makers for providing data on which to base corrective measures and for providing product evaluation data. Process evaluation should be the basis for continuing, changing, and/or discarding a project. The school staff and community must learn to value the process evaluations because they will make the school much more efficient and focused on the priorities of the school.

Product Evaluation

The fourth type of evaluation is product evaluation. Its purpose is to measure and interpret attainments not only at the end of a project cycle, but as often as necessary during the project term. It is mainly used to evaluate the project at the end of the project cycle and to make a determination of the worth and value of the project. The general method of product evaluation includes devising operational definitions of objectives, measuring criteria associated with the objectives of the activity, comparing these measurements with predetermined absolute or relative standards, and making rational interpretations of the outcomes using the recorded context, input, and process information.

While all four types of evaluations are important to the SBM organizational pattern, the product evaluation is usually the summative evaluation effort that focuses on whether or not the program has met its objectives and, if not, why not. The decision makers then must ask the tough questions about whether or not the program can or should be continued. These issues can be explored by considering all of the data provided by other evaluations. For example, context evaluation provides the data for assessing the extent to which ends are being attained; context evaluation develops data from the systemic standpoint and product evaluation from the change and project standpoint. Thus, context evaluation provides the specifications in terms of which product evaluation is later carried out. Product evaluation is an evaluation of certain aspects of the total system and is usually performed on an ad hoc basis.

Input and product evaluations are easily distinguishable, because input evaluation occurs prior to the operationalization of a change project, and product evaluation occurs during and after the project. Whereas context evaluation determines the specifications for product evaluation, input evaluation provides the specifications for process evaluation. A major step within the input evaluation phase is assessing the appropriateness of alternative process and product designs that could be implemented as part of a designed procedure.

Product evaluation investigates the extent to which objectives have been or are being attained; process evaluation assesses the extent to which procedures are operating as intended. Both types of evaluation provide feedback for controlling and evolving change procedures in process. Process evaluation makes it possible to determine if actual procedure shows discrepency from design, and product evaluation assists in determining whether objectives are being attained. Together, both kinds of information provide a stronger rationale than either one alone to judge whether a procedure should be continued as is, modified, or completely revamped.

Product evaluation reports that objectives were or were not achieved; process evaluation provides a basis for interpreting the reason for the outcome. If the objectives were not achieved, it would be important to know whether the intended procedure was actually implemented, and process evaluation provides information for this determination. If objectives were achieved, it would be important to have a description of the actual procedure that produced the outcome.

Product evaluation data needed include the following:

- comprehensive identification of outcomes
- comparison of outcomes to assessed needs, assigned duties, previous trends, achievement in similar campuses, and pertinent norms
- judgments of outcomes in consideration of needs, opportunities, problems, constraints, and costs

Much of the needed data are available through use of the district's data banks, through school climate surveys, through the school portfolio of accomplishments, through a survey of stakeholders, through use of board/superintendent reports of progress, and through independent ratings of the school by community and staff.

Product evaluation data is used to determine the feasibility of a particular project, to assist in developing a list of educational priorities for the school, to justify the continuation or recycling of a project, and to evaluate the staff of the project in terms of its effectiveness. Product evaluation is usually summative in nature and provides the data for a "go-no go" decision about a particular effort or program. An example of product evaluation indicators would be if improvement were seen in the following areas:

(*1*) Teacher attendance
(*2*) Involvement of stakeholders in the school planning process
(*3*) Racial balance of staff across the schools of the district
(*4*) Maintenance of school buildings
(*5*) Constructive coverage of school programs by the media

(6) Improvement in the dropout rate
(7) Percentage of students having needed immunizations
(8) Achievement test scores of all students, for the district and school, disaggregated by sex, race, and socioeconomic status
(9) Measures of school climate for the district and the school
(10) Student attendance, for the district and school, disaggregated by sex, race, age, and socioeconomic status
(11) Physical fitness of students at the school and for the district

The preceding list is only illustrative. It is suggested that, in any given year, the expected outcomes be agreed to at the school level and used to provide data for product evaluations.

The foregoing discussion of context, input, process, and product is summarized in Figure 4.1. As was stated earlier, continuous and stringent evaluation must be an ongoing activity under the SBM form of organization. Data are needed to justify the activities and priorities developed by the school, especially if these are different from the priorities of the district and other schools.

The CIPP model can serve as a mechanism for planning, for evaluation, and for decision making. It uses a common language that most educators can quickly grasp and is extremely useful in focusing only on that which can be accomplished. For decades, educators have evaluated solely on inputs, assuming that, if the inputs were there, the outcomes would automatically take care of themselves. Now, there is a mechanism for evaluating both the inputs and the outcomes, which should make practicing educators much more willing to attempt change. The CIPP model permits the school and its staff to evaluate every program and every activity to determine whether or not that program and/or activity assists the school in meeting its goals and objectives. Further, the CIPP model assists the school in recognizing the changes needed in the processes to make the programs viable and acceptable.

SCHOOL/DISTRICT/PROGRAM EVALUATIONS

Using the CIPP model as a base, the author would like to prepare the reader for planning/evaluation/decision-making situations found in the school system, particularly those who have committed to the SBM approach to organization. The CIPP evaluations will provide enough

	CONTEXT EVALUATION	INPUT EVALUATION	PROCESS EVALUATION	PRODUCT EVALUATION
INFORMATION	1. Multiyear district data: • test results • student attendance • graduation • dropouts • student characteristics • staff characteristics • staff evaluations • school environment • school programs • student services • district finances • district facilities • complaints 2. Data from comparable districts 3. Pertinent national and state norms 4. Conclusions about needs, problems, opportunities	1. District strategic plan 2. Staff assignments 3. District calendar 4. Budget 5. Accounting reports from prior plans 6. Superintendent duties 7. Superintendent salary 8. Superintendent work plan 9. Parent and community involvement 10. Promising new strategies and associated evaluations 11. Independent assessment of the district's plans, strategies, assignments, and budgets	1. Progress reports on • special projects • staffing • product development • delivery of instruction • delivery of student services • stakeholder involvement 2. Accounting reports 3. Exception reports, e.g., modifications in • plans • assignments • schedules • budgets 4. Independent assessment of operations	1. Comprehensive identification of outcomes 2. Comparison of outcomes to • assessed needs • assigned duties • previous trends • achievements in similar districts • pertinent norms 3. Judgments of outcomes in consideration of • needs • opportunities • problems • constraints • costs

Figure 4.1 Four types of evaluation.

	CONTEXT EVALUATION	INPUT EVALUATION	PROCESS EVALUATION	PRODUCT EVALUATION
METHOD	1. District data banks 2. Stakeholder panel 3. School climate surveys 4. Annual principal reports 5. Clippings file 6. Hearings 7. Quantitative and qualitative analysis	1. Strategic planning process 2. Budget planning process 3. Records of stakeholder involvement in planning 4. Site visits to other districts 5. External evaluators	1. Staff/superintendent progress reports 2. Accounting reports 3. Superintendent portfolio of activities 4. Records of stakeholder involvement in programs	1. District data bank 2. School climate surveys 3. Superintendent portfolio of accomplishments 4. Survey of stakeholders 5. Independent ratings by board members 6. Synthesis report by board president/committee
USE	1. Set district priorities 2. Set superintendent job targets 3. Provide basis for judging significance of accomplishments 4. Consider district constraints in judging superintendent performance 5. Target pertinent opportunites for use in school improvement	1. Clarify board/superintendent understanding of plans, assignments, budgets 2. Improve plans, assignments, budgets 3. Involve stakeholders in planning 4. Provide clear guidance for superintendent performance	1. Keep board and community informed about implementation of plans 2. Maintain fiscal accountability 3. Provide early warning system for identifying and addressing implementation problems 4. Maintain record of implementation for use in interpreting outcomes	1. Help board assess merit and/or worth of superintendent's accomplishments 2. Help board develop outcome-based decisions on superintendent's • salary • continuation • professional development plan 3. Help board be accountable to community for oversight of superintendent's accomplishments

Figure 4.1 (*continued*).

data on which to base every planning decision required to make the school responsive to the needs of the students. The context analysis will generate what data now exist for the school and school district and will provide the information necessary to accomplish good strategic planning. Once the school district and school personnel get adjusted to the CIPP model and its application, they can apply the model to every program and project being implemented at the school. It becomes good practice to think in CIPP terms and to extrapolate all activities in those terms as a mechanism for getting everyone used to the terminology and application of the model.

As was said earlier, "Evaluation is the process of delineating, obtaining, and providing useful information for judging decision alternatives." Data or information make every decision much easier if the information is focused on the task at hand and if the needs of the persons being served are defined and prioritized. It must be remembered that the school exists to serve the students and not the staff or the adult community; therefore, the student educational needs must first be recognized and prioritized. CIPP will permit this to be done as efficiently and effectively as possible. Using the recommended context materials as a base, the school personnel can assemble and prioritize a needs assessment for the school. Actually, most districts have the information available as a part of their strategic planning process, so starting with what is available and adding information unique to the school will be a relatively easy task. This is really a part of getting the school's strategic plan ready for completion and initiating a work plan.

The strategic plan based, as it should be, on the district's strategic plan, should identify those areas where the school achievement levels are not to the staff's and community's expectations and must be addressed as priority items. Context evaluation basically lists what the realities of the school and district are at the moment and, when viewed in the context of what the students need, provides a listing of the priorities for the coming period of time. Because evaluation is an ongoing activity, the school always makes corrections in the context analysis so that they are always current and can change their applications to meet the students' emerging needs quickly and effectively.

The CIPP model can be thought of as a cyclical model (Figure 4.2) with each letter of the acronym a discrete set of applications and activities. The context should be followed by the input evaluation so that the application of scarce resources can be predicated on the needs as

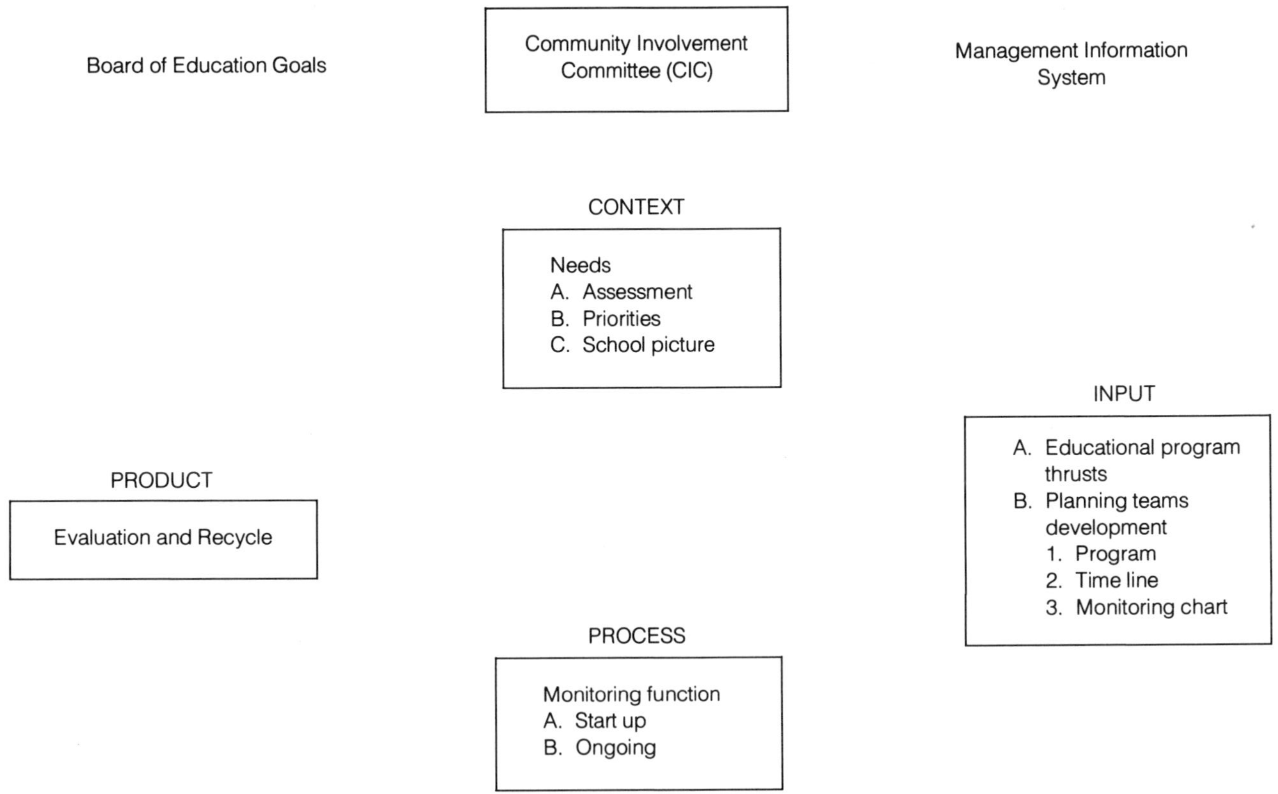

Management Information System

Community Involvement Committee (CIC)

Board of Education Goals

INPUT

A. Educational program thrusts
B. Planning teams development
  1. Program
  2. Time line
  3. Monitoring chart

CONTEXT

Needs
A. Assessment
B. Priorities
C. School picture

PROCESS

Monitoring function
A. Start up
B. Ongoing

PRODUCT

Evaluation and Recycle

Figure 4.2 Educational planning: a development process model.

explicated by the context evaluation. Input can always be adjusted and modified to meet particular needs and to resolve particular situations.

As Figure 4.2 shows, the application of the CIPP model at the school starts with the school community involvement committee (CIC) (actually, there are a number of terms such as the governance committee or strategic planning committee given to this committee) initiating the context evaluation to provide information for the planning process to proceed. After establishing the context, the input evaluation stage is started. This provides an understanding of the resources and conditions inherent to the school, which must be utilized and maximized for the programs to be successful. The actual planning takes place during the input evaluation stage, and it is there that the processes are analyzed and prioritized so the decision makers can select those options that make the most sense and provide the best programs within the resource limitations of the school. Process evaluation is ongoing and makes it possible for the unit to make adjustments during the implementation stage in order to make the program meet the requirements and the objectives of the school. Product evaluation is mostly summative and provides the data that tells whether or not the objectives were met and whether or not the program was in the best interest of the students. Product evaluation provides the data on which to base "go-no go" decisions. It provides information on what and how to restructure and whether or not the program is worth saving or is best discarded with the resources going to meet another high-priority need. CIPP is a method for producing available data and using it to address the priority needs of the district/school.

A primary use for the CIPP evaluations is to conduct evaluations of the various programs and the schools themselves. CIPP can also be useful in the evaluation of school districts for accreditation purposes and for judging the effectiveness of the school district in addressing the student needs and priority program delivery. Many accreditation agencies utilize the CIPP, or similar model, for making the information about the district available in a standard format; thus, every person working on the district evaluation understands the comparative analysis of school district traits and strengths, as well as weaknesses.

District context analysis is usually accomplished through required submission of district data to the state education agency so that every district in the state has similar data on file with the state agency for use in these evaluations. Information such as test data, socioeconomic data, racial data, attendance data, staff data, dropout data, school climate data, and other school district data are included in the information requested by the state agency from member districts. Also included is the financial information, often accompanied by the annual audit of the district's books by an outside accounting firm, as required by law in most states. This provides information as to the resources available, the amount of local effort made by the local community, per pupil expenditures for the district, amount of school dollars allocated to the various functions performed by the school system, and other pertinent financial data.

From these data, similar to the data listed in the context and input analysis section, a school district profile is engendered. This is used to conduct the preliminary review of the district's accreditation. The data are then compared to the actual facts discovered when a site visit takes place and when the accrediting officials attempt to match the profile with the actual site information as observed while at the site.

Most accreditation visits take into consideration data about the member schools of the district while the observations are being made. District data is also available on a school by school basis. Indeed, many states require that the information be submitted on a classroom by classroom basis to provide information on every classroom in the state. The accreditation teams also take into consideration the school strategic and work plans so that the school is evaluated on how well it recognizes the priorities and how well it plans to meet the high-priority student needs. Basically, the school staff develops the approach to meeting the needs of the students enrolled at the school and then are expected to provide what they say they will provide. In this way, no school is expected to produce more than they say they are capable of performing, and the expectations are not inflated above the normal expectations for the student body.

The responses to the list of input indicators as presented also provide for an accurate description of the input at the school and district levels. The product expectations are developed as a result of an examination of the input and context evaluations, which suggest what the strategic plan for the school and district should focus on. Process is evaluated after the programs are implemented to see if the results are what the staff wishes them to be and if the results are in line with the student needs analysis done during the context and input stages. Process evaluation also engenders information about how well, or even if, the staff is using the agreed-upon processes in the delivery of programs. If the staff is not using the processes agreed upon, corrections are quickly possible as a result of the process analysis.

Another way of looking at the procedure is to allocate the various steps to the various actors in the educational arena. For example, product evaluation and product expectations are the purview of the policy-setting body of the district. That is, the board should set the product expectations for the schools in the system and hold the staff responsible for meeting those product expectations. This is accomplished through the adoption of the strategic and work plans for the district. These plans become the parameters under which the schools develop their own strategic and work plans for implementation. The final school work plan is arrived at through negotiations between the board (superintendent) and the school so that the board is assured that the plan is in sync with the district plan and yet has the flexibility to focus on unique school needs and priorities.

The processes are the responsibility of the staff because they are largely pedagogical strategies and mechanisms developed by the local staff to meet particular student needs. The context and input evaluations are mainly an enumeration of conditions as they currently are at the various sites, and they provide information on which to base plans and programs. Both context and input must involve the community because they are the prime ingredients on these evaluations. Thus, we see that the context and input phases are all-inclusive, with the staff, board, and community all having a part to play in them, while the process evaluation is mainly the responsibility of the staff because it is a pedagogical or professional responsibility, and, finally, the product evaluation is summative and the setting of product expectations is the responsibility of the policy board of the district.

URBAN ELEMENTARY SCHOOL SIMULATION

In the following vignette, the author will take the reader through a simulated application of the CIPP model to realize the planning, evaluation, and decision-making capacities of the model. The simulated school is an urban elementary school housing 600 students. Urban Elementary has, under the authorized staff strength as negotiated by the teachers' union, the following staff: twenty-four classroom teachers, two music teachers, two art teachers, two physical education teachers, two curriculum coordinators who perform as helping teachers, four special education teachers who teach those students who are in need of special instructional assistance (forty-eight students), an assistant principal, and a principal. In addition, the professional staff includes a guidance counselor and a part-time psychologist who is available to the school for three half days a week. Nonprofessional staff includes five secretaries (two for the office and three allocated to the rest of the staff). There also are eight paraprofessional educators on the staff, one for each grade level and one for the special education staff. In addition, there are three custodians (one on days, the others on nights) and four kitchen personnel who prepare food and feed the students at the school. The budget amounts to approximately $1,427,600 for professional salaries and $288,000 for nonprofessional salaries. Other budgets items include the following:

Teaching supplies ($60/pupil)	$36,000.00
Capital outlay ($40/pupil)	24,000.00
Teachers' personal supply ($100/teacher)	3,730.00
Staff development	10,000.00
Textbook allowance ($50/pupil)	30,000.00
Office expense	5,000.00
Telephone expense	6,000.00
Substitute teachers (6 days/teacher) $50/day/substitute	8,400.00
Vandalism budget (previous experience)	3,000.00
Utilities	35,000.00
Miscellaneous expense	4,000.00
sub-total	$165,130.00

Adding the salary amounts to this total provides a total budget for Urban Elementary School of $1,880,730.00 for a per pupil expenditure of $3,134.55 when considering only school costs. However, when all costs are factored in, the per pupil costs for the district rise to $5,224.25. This figure indicates that approximately 40% of the total budget is expended on nondirect student-related expenditures. This figure is quite high, and the district has made it a high priority to cut this expenditure by at least 25% during the next three years through restructuring and the initiation of an SBM organizational effort. This will make several central office positions obsolete and no longer needed.

Data assembled while performing the context evaluation show that the student population of Urban Elementary is 40% Black, 30% Hispanic, 10% Asian, and 20% Anglo. The school is located in a middle-class housing neighborhood, with a majority of the students coming from middle-class homes. A single housing project produces almost half of the Black and Hispanic children for the school who are all on the free and/or reduced fee lunch program. These students are bused in to Urban Elementary School from the project, which is located some three miles from the school. This amounts to approximately 240 students who are below the poverty line at Urban Elementary School.

Of 39.3 professional staff members at the school, there are thirteen Blacks, seven Hispanics, and two Asians, with 17.3 members of the staff being Anglo. Both the principal, a Black, and the assistant principal, a Hispanic, are minorities.

Urban Elementary School has been performing fairly well on most standardized measures. As an example, the following scores and statistics apply to the school:

(1) *ITBS scores:* forty-third percentile. This has not changed in years. The poor children are at the 30th percentile, while the middle class children are at the 49th percentile.
(2) *Attendance:* 93% average daily attendance
(3) *Teacher attendance:* Teachers average eight days annual sick leave.
(4) *Parent involvement:* PTA average attendance is about 100 parents.
(5) *School climate:* generally positive and supportive of teachers.
(6) *Neighborhood climate:* Positive about the school, worried about crime, want to become involved with the school.
(7) *Programs offered at the school:* Traditional range of programs, mostly self-contained efforts on a classroom by classroom basis. Special education is self-contained as well. Special teachers teach to give the classroom teacher a planning period. Guidance person is largely a clerk, keeping track of students. Curriculum specialists are also clerical and do "turn teaching" to relieve classroom teachers for short breaks.
(8) *Principal:* Mr. Tom White is just finishing his first year on the job. He has gotten to know the staff and community and is now ready to make some adjustments aimed at improving the achievement rate at the school. He has the following objectives in mind and shares them with the newly organized community involvement committee:
  • to develop improved test scores for every student

- to provide opportunity for staff to develop more innovative program efforts
- to open the school to the parents and seek their involvement
- to involve the staff and community in the decision process
- to reduce the student/teacher ratio to 20/1
- to reduce the use of sick leave below the district average (six days/teacher)
- to work toward individualizing instruction
- to mainstream all special education students (The district provides special classes for those who are severely handicapped.)
- to reduce expenditures for such things as vandalism, utilities, and other nonstudent-directed expenditures

At the organization meeting of the community involvement committee (eleven members appointed by the staff and the PTA—five educators, six community members—and the principal), Tom suggests that they might want to consider his priority objectives and, also, that they might want to apply for Site-Based Management status since the district is getting ready to embark on a pilot program of SBM and are requesting volunteers for the program. To his surprise and delight, the CIC overwhelmingly approves the objectives and indicates their desire to become a pilot SBM school. Because it is now February, and all plans must be completed by June, Mr. White appoints a staff/community strategic planning committee and initiates the first meeting the very next day. This group, which ultimately becomes the CIC for the school, has the expertise to develop the plans called for in the Request for Proposal (RFP). The school is accepted as a pilot school for the SBM organizational effort and readies the objectives for submittal to the central office.

Mr. White has all of the data ready for the planning group, and, after they have digested the information, they become excited over the potential the school could realize. They, to a person, are aware of the high potential the students bring to the school and feel that, through some changed procedures and programs, the results will show that potential. The staff committee, along with the CIC, participate in the development of the strategic and work plans for the Urban Elementary School. Among the basic considerations for improved student performance are the following:

(1) Reduce the class size to a maximum of twenty students to each classroom teacher.

(2) Integrate all special education students into regular classrooms. Reduce the number of special education personnel from four to two, and use them as consultants to the regular teachers.

(3) Reduce the number of special teachers from six to three, and have the three provide for the teaching of music, art, and physical education for all classes.

(4) Do away with the guidance position. It is not providing any real benefit to students and is extraneous.

(5) Reduce the number of curriculum specialists from two to one. Make this person the planning/evaluation assistance specialist, and charge him/her with causing all of the planning and evaluation to take place at the school.

(6) Use the six positions gained to raise the number of classroom teachers from twenty-four to thirty, thereby gaining the desired 20/1 student/teacher ratio.

(7) Take the funds gained from the eliminated seventh position (the guidance counselor—$40,000) and allocate the resources to the provision of sufficient computers to permit every student to spend at least thirty minutes a day at a computer. (The provision of twenty-five computers each for K−2, for 3−4, for 5−6 will provide this resource capably). (Since the school already has thirty-five computers, the purchase of forty additional computers will make the desired ratio possible.)

(8) Use the resources gained from trading the special positions for classroom positions to permit the purchase of computer software for computer-assisted instruction. This will generate $10,000 to use for this purpose.

(9) Use the staff development budget to provide the staff with expertise in the individualization of instruction. This, along with the computerized instruction, will permit educational improvement, particularly in the basic skills.

(10) Move toward a nongraded school to permit the grouping of students along needs, rather than age. Assign staff to provide the total educational experience to a group of students for a three-year

period in order to provide continuity. The assignment of four staff to eighty students would permit the greater individualization of the instructional program.
(*11*) Involve the parents as teacher aide volunteers so the parents are more effectively involved in the educational process.
(*12*) Agree to meet with the CIC on a monthly basis, with special meetings to be called when necessary. The CIC shall be the policy-setting group for the school and shall establish all product expectations for the school. The CIC shall be made up of not more than eleven people: four teachers, one support person, six parents or community members, and the principal. They shall approve all expenditures made at the school level and shall adjust line item budgets when necessary. They shall also provide the basis for an expansion of resources and shall develop proposals for consideration by funding agencies. The planning specialist shall work directly with the CIC to develop proposals.
(*13*) The CIC shall evaluate every program at the school level annually to determine how the program may be improved or whether elements should be discarded. The planning specialist shall have this as a primary responsibility.
(*14*) The CIC shall develop goals and objectives to enable the school to evaluate itself annually.

Specific objectives against which the school will be judged include

(*1*) The student ITBS scores will improve at least four percentile points over the current year. The average scores of the high needs students shall improve at least five percentile points, while the scores of the rest of the student body will improve at least three percentile points.
(*2*) Average daily attendance will improve from 93% to 95%.
(*3*) Teacher absenteeism will decrease from eight days per teacher per year to four days per teacher per year.
(*4*) Parental and community participation will increase from attendance of roughly 100 at every called PTA meeting to an average of 300 per meeting.
(*5*) The staff shall develop an individual IEP for every student.
(*6*) The staff shall take responsibility for student growth and hold themselves accountable for meeting the objectives.

(7) The staff shall develop a program to assist in the teaching of higher order thinking skills for implementation the following year.
(8) Each teacher shall visit every student's home during the academic year.
(9) Computer literacy shall be the objective of every staff member in order to be of assistance to the students as they participate in the computer-assisted instruction program.
(10) Vandalism damage at school shall decrease by 50% during the school year.
(11) Energy costs shall be reduced by at least 15% through the energy conservation program initiated by Mr. White. This will provide an additional $4,350.00 for student awards and staff development.
(12) Urban Elementary School shall become known as an exemplary school and be so recognized by the local media.

The new academic year is an exciting and rewarding one for the staff, students, and community. The community becomes excited about the potential of the school and is totally committed to the partnership arrangement that the staff has proposed to the community. They, the community, are willing participants in the SBM process and have already provided much in the way of extra resources and volunteer assistance to the school. They are as committed to change as the staff and Mr. White are. All are anxiously awaiting the summative and formative evaluations that are to be shared by the conclusion of the academic year. They are also awaiting work plans for the ensuing year, which will be a subject of community approval and discussion. The CIC has completed these plans and is getting them ready for staff and community examination and approval.

Finally, the summative evaluations are ready for perusal and action. The staff is delighted over the preliminary evaluations of the various programs and projects. ITBS scores have jumped almost seven points to the 50th percentile for the school, while the scores of the poor children increased to the 44th percentile.

Average daily attendance has increased to 96.5%. This is even better than expected and is worthy of mention.

The staff was able to meet the teacher absenteeism objective by cutting the average teacher use of sick leave from eight days per teacher to six days per teacher. This was in spite of several major illnesses and accidents that caused extended sick leave on the part of several staff members.

Approximately $6,000.00 was saved from the energy budget because of the conservation program and because of the interest of the total staff in affecting a savings in this budget category.

The staff development program is proving to be very popular with the staff, and there is evidence that the individualization effort is progressing very well. The individualization thrust has been accompanied by a peer instruction program, which fully complements the individualization effort and provides active instructional assistance to the students in need of such assistance. Also, the computerized instruction program is being embraced by the students, and the rise in basic skills proficiency is evidenced in the rise of the ITBS scores. All told, the evaluation of the programs and projects at Urban Elementary School have been most positive. This, then, is the basis for developing the work plan for the subsequent year.

The CIC adopts the following objectives for inclusion in the work plan for the coming year. First, the objective for student growth shall be that the school shall achieve the 55th percentile in the ITBS, with the poor children reaching the 47th percentile. Second, the school shall average 97% in daily attendance. Third, the school staff shall average less than five days per person in sick leave for the year. Fourth, the school shall continue to pursue the individualized instructional program with IEPs to initiate the inclusion of student objectives in the higher order thinking skills this year. Fifth, parental involvement will continue to increase with a goal of an average attendance of 400 at all community and PTA meetings. Sixth, the movement toward a nongraded school will accelerate this year, with the development of a plan for submittal to the CIC and the community during the academic year. Seventh, the staff development program will continue to emphasize individualized instruction and the development of instructional teams across the school. This is in preparation for the nongraded move in the next year. Eighth, vandalism shall continue to decrease, with a savings of $4,000 expected. Ninth, the salary of the discontinued guidance position shall be allocated toward upgrading and extending the software and hardware needed to improve the computer instructional program. As the staff and community gather to approve the work plan and to bask in the glow of a very successful year, they pause to give thanks to a dedicated and supportive community and a hardworking and capable staff who have made the Urban Elementary School the model for the district.

PERSONNEL EVALUATIONS AS A DERIVATIVE

The evaluation of educational personnel is always a touchy issue because of the difficulty in measuring the impact of the staff on the learning rate of the students. Consequently, many models for teacher evaluation are based on teacher duties and their accomplishment or teacher behavior while being observed or on the teacher certification, which assumes that the teacher, once certified, is automatically a capable teacher. For principals, superintendents, and other educational personnel, the same difficulty applies. There, evaluations are largely based on the recognized duties of the position and measure how well the incumbent performs those duties associated with the position.

In 1990, with the emergence of CREATE as an arm of the National Evaluation Center located at Western Michigan University in Kalamazoo, Michigan, a formal approach to the evaluation of educational personnel was undertaken. CREATE is an acronym for a national center called Center for Research on Educational Accountability and Teacher Evaluation. This Center, funded through a federal grant, has been developing approaches to the evaluation of programs, schools, districts, and the various personnel employed by the school systems of the country.

Researchers for CREATE, including this author, have concluded that any personnel evaluation system must include a component recognizing the student growth as a result of the educational staff members' efforts. Such inclusion must also reflect the position being evaluated and its relative contribution to the teaching/learning process. Thus, the teacher evaluation should have a more encompassing inclusion of the student growth factor than, say, the superintendent's evaluation. However, every position must recognize that the ultimate objective of the school system is the education of students, and all should be held accountable for that objective.

The research conducted by the CREATE staff has led to several discrete models being tested across the country, with some of the more promising including a "portfolio" as part of the total evaluation of the professional. The teacher evaluation effort is being headed by Dr.

Michael Scrivan and primarily focuses on the development and verification of a suggested listing of teacher duties. These, in concert with student outcomes, will be the basis for the instrument being developed.

There is a strong opinion, now being verified, that all personnel in a building are part and parcel of the evaluative results done at that school and should share in the evaluation. This, then, proposes that all evaluations start with the evaluation of the building and that all staff share in that evaluation result. This results in the direct link between CIPP and personnel evaluations with the school evaluations being the basis for the staff evaluations. It is probable that, eventually, all staff evaluations will initiate with the school or district evaluation and have special notations or indicators for the particular position or service performed by the employee.

In the development of an evaluation instrument for the evaluation of the chief administrators of the system and/or school, the CREATE staff have started with the diagram shown as Figure 4.3 as the basis for constructing the instrument. This diagram conceptualizes the closeness between the evaluation of the district (school) and the evaluation of the administrative head of that unit.

As can be seen by examining Figure 4.3, the evaluation of educational personnel is a complex and difficult task. The process as shown here starts with the assessment of the district, using the context and input evaluation to determine the state of the district (school).

As was mentioned earlier, any adequate evaluation requires the delineation of accountabilities and obtaining the necessary information to perform the evaluation. As the figure shows, delineating accountabilities includes such items as indicators, weights, and standards, as well as an identification of the users and uses of the evaluation and the various data sources providing the information.

The obtained information leads to evaluation of the person, as well as the product evaluation, which is summative in nature. The implementation evaluation is used to provide formative feedback, while the product evaluation leads to the summative evaluation of the individual. The final step in the evaluative process is to apply the findings to improve the situation, to reward the evaluatee, and to make the needed personnel decisions for the school or district.

It is essential that any acceptable evaluation system be grounded in sound communications. CREATE suggests that a district and school accountability commission be appointed to oversee the development and

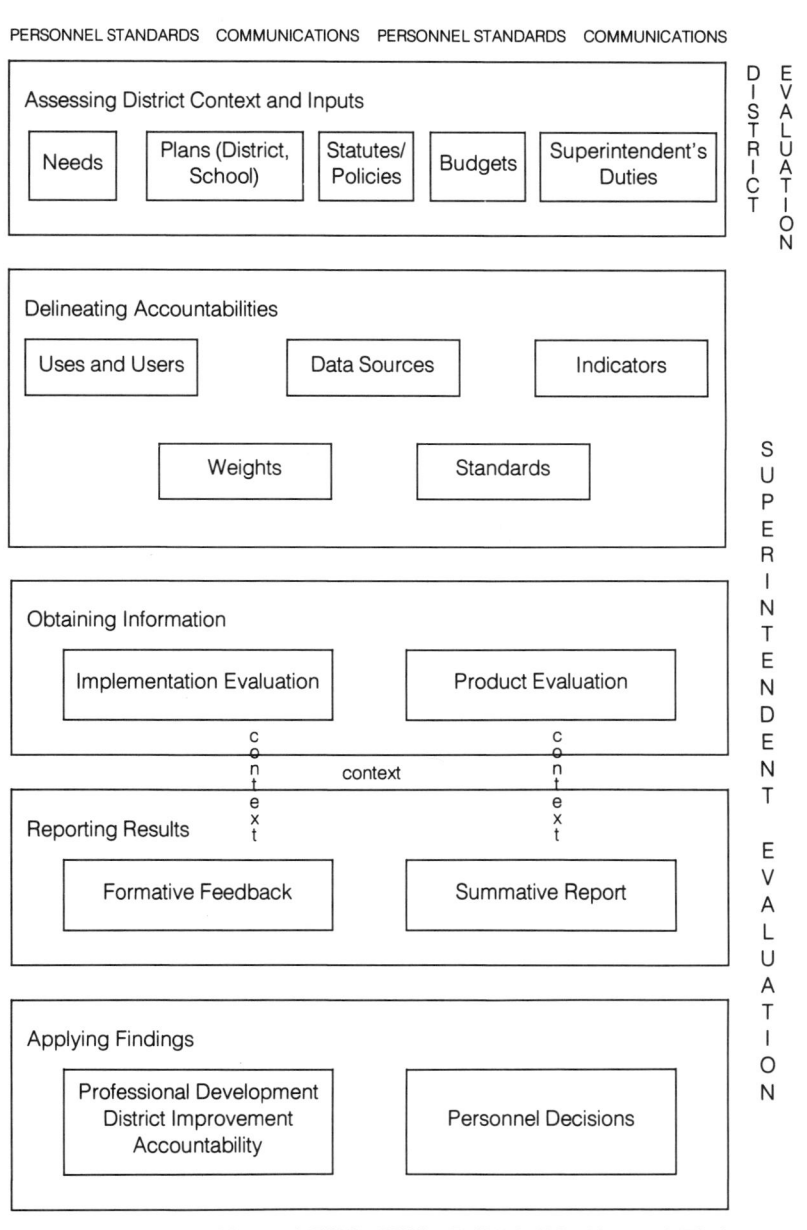

Figure 4.3 Superintendent evaluation model.

to perform periodic review and improvement of the personnel evaluation system. Also, the district must provide school personnel and the public with clear and up-to-date information on the structure, implementation, and results of the evaluation system. Channels should be defined and kept open so that the stakeholders can have input into the improvement of the personnel evaluation system.

One final note: the scheduling and assigning responsibilities for the personnel evaluation tasks entail developing a work schedule that corresponds to the annual agenda of the board and meets the legal requirements for personnel evaluations. Many states set a deadline for completing the personnel evaluation during the school year and provide that, if the evaluation is not completed by a certain date, the contract of the employee is automatically extended for the next year.

Using the superintendent evaluation as an example, certain evaluation tasks can be assigned various time sequences so that the legal aspects of such evaluation are observed. When approaching the evaluation of the superintendent, a district can develop the tasks required in the evaluation on a quarter by quarter basis as follows:

(1) Quarter #1
- Review prior years' activities and results (especially student performance data, performance evaluations of school staff, and system needs).
- Set preliminary strategic plan.
- Set general priorities; review duties.
- Set preliminary superintendent objectives and work plans/duties.

(2) Quarter #2
- Accept school improvement plans.
- Set priorities for the year; update duties.
- Adjust strategic plan.
- Adjust superintendent work plan as needed.
- Establish superintendent evaluation design (including intended uses and users, performance indicators and weights, performance standards, data sources and procedures, and reporting schedule).

(3) Quarter #3
- Report progress on implementation of strategic plan and assigned duties.

- Have formative evaluation exchanges between board and superintendent.
- Adjust superintendent priorities and tasks.
- Set improvement targets.

(4) Quarter #4
- Get accountability report from the superintendent.
- Gather data from students, schools, and community.
- Evaluate summatively the superintendent.
- Develop a professional improvement plan, if needed.
- Obtain pertinent personnel decisions.
- Give summary report to the community.
- Recycle the strategic plan.

While similar time lines can and should be developed for every professional employee at the district and school level, care must be taken to involve each employee in his/her own evaluation. Each professional should be given the chance to develop his/her own work plan. These plans must be consistent with the district and school work plans and be structured around the objectives of the school and district. It is important that each professional know and appreciate the main thrust of the school and district and become a part of the total delivery mechanism of the district. It must be remembered that evaluation is intended to *improve* and not to *prove*.

Figure 4.4 suggests the main evaluation emphasis for each quarter of the year. This is stated in CIPP terms to indicate the compatibility and close relationship between CIPP and the various personnel evaluation models as they are developed. As shown in Figure 4.4, the first quarter emphasis relating to personnel evaluations is on Context Evaluation. The board and superintendent review the prior year's activities and results, especially to identify unmet needs in both student accomplishments and district offerings. Such review is useful in assisting the board in defining the superintendent's main responsibilities for the year.

During the second quarter, the emphasis is more on Input Evaluation. The board and superintendent review and adjust the strategic plan and evaluate the school plans to provide feedback for their improvement. A time line for formal evaluation is established and initiated for all staff members.

The third quarter of personnel evaluation emphasizes Process Evaluation. The professional educator maintains a portfolio of information of

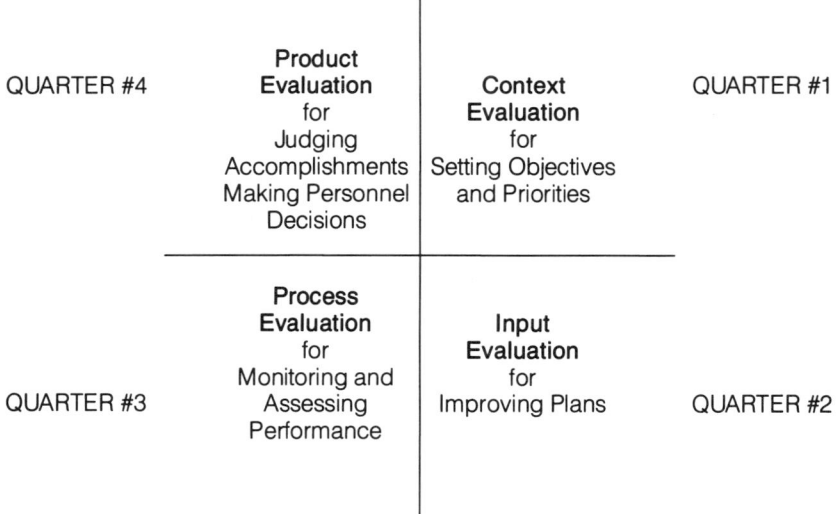

Figure 4.4 Main evaluation emphases in each quarter.

implementation of specific plans and provides progress reports on the implementation. The evaluator provides formative feedback to the evaluatee.

During the fourth quarter, personnel evaluation emphasizes Product Evaluation. The employee provides an accountability report to the evaluator through the use of a portfolio maintained during the year. The evaluator may gather additional data, e.g., judgments from the community and students. The evaluator then compiles a summary evaluation of the performance. This information may be used to make decisions on continuation/termination, set salaries for the next year, establish an improvement plan for the employee, report to the community on the status of the district's employees, and initiate revision of the district and school strategic plans.

Finally, context, input, process, and product evaluations are keyed to

(*1*) Helping boards and educators focus district and school efforts on meeting student needs
(2) Assigning professional responsibilities in order to best address district, school, and student needs

(*3*) Monitoring progress to help assure that responsibilities are being implemented professionally and effectively
(*4*) Assessing outcomes and taking actions focused on improving performance in meeting student, school, and district needs

It is important to recognize that each school and district should develop their own approach to the total evaluation of programs and personnel. The foregoing has been an effort to provide the theoretical framework for such a development. As the school and district struggle to create their own plan for evaluation, their objectives and particular nuances and needs will become obvious and will dictate the approach taken.

QUESTIONS ARISING FROM THE USE OF THE CIPP MODEL FOR EVALUATION

Q-1: Is the CIPP model the only model applicable for use under Site-Based Management?

A-1: Of course not. It was submitted as a means to the desired end of total evaluation and easier decision making. There are other models of evaluation available for use, but all of them contain the same basic need for appropriate information and data.

Q-2: The CIPP model does not permit us to use our personal knowledge and feelings about a program or project. Is this good?

A-2: If you are committed to fair, unbiased evaluation, the CIPP model provides the basis for such an evaluation. Besides, CIPP is perfectly applicable as a planning model as well.

Q-3: Our school does not have the luxury of having personnel to allocate to the planning/evaluation process. How can we implement the CIPP model without the necessary personnel to gather and interpret data?

A-3: A fine question. If you are committed to providing the staff and community with good objective information as the basis for good planning and evaluation leading to appropriate decision making, you must find the human resource to gather and interpret information. Many school districts have a planning office that gathers the data on a school by school basis and makes the data available to each school. Take the data and use it as the baseline information for your school and supplement it with what you can derive from the community and the school.

Q-4: Our school planner is providing so much data that we are overcome with facts and cannot make any sense from these disjointed facts. How can we develop an appropriate data base from which to plan and evaluate?

A-4: This happens often when overzealous planners develop the data base for the planning effort. Remember that the planner is there to serve you and the staff of your school. You ask for the information you need to adequately plan an activity or program. Discard all data that are not germane to the issues at hand.

Q-5: Our context and input evaluations show that certain programs are not meeting expectations. Because these programs are the pets of certain staff, they are not being modified or changed to meet the needs of the students. What can we, as parents, do about this?

A-5: This protection of turf sometimes happens and is very disabling to the program. Raise the issue at a CIC meeting and keep after the issue until you have a satisfactory answer. If necessary, go to the next level of the district to appeal the decision.

Q-6: In evaluating personnel, our principal sometimes allows his personal feelings to interfere with an objective evaluation of a person. He has kept an inferior teacher around for several years because he likes the person and will not hear of providing the negative evaluation needed to change the person's assignment. What can we, as a staff, do about this?

A-6: Use the data you have at your disposal to make the case – data such as peer evaluations, community evaluations, student evaluations, student gains resulting from the person's classroom, anecdotal records about the person, and other information available. Present this data to the principal and demand action be taken. If this is not successful, take the appeal to the district's human resources office for action.

Q-7: Planning, evaluation, decision making, CIPP, all of this is getting to many of us who are classroom teachers. What we want to do is teach our students and provide a safe haven for these children without all of the activity that is now taking time away from our teaching. How can we recapture our independence and be permitted to teach our classes with dignity?

A-7: This is another crucial question arising from the changes occurring in the educational enterprise. I'm sure that you agree that the system must change in order to better serve today's students. A changed system calls for increased capacity to make appropriate decisions based on good information and data. CIPP is a mechanism for generating this data. Give yourself a chance to understand the terminology and the application of CIPP. With understanding will come an appreciation for the time that CIPP can save you and your colleagues, time that you can spend with your students.

Q-8: I am firmly committed to centralization and disagree with claims that decentralization of the educational system is good for the students. How can I generate data that will affirm my position?

A-8: You can try to use the current performance data to support your claim that decentralizing is not a good idea. However, if you use data derived from those districts that are truly decentralized and operate from a position of providing information for use at the point of student contact, the data will not support your claim. SBM, using such methods as CIPP for planning and evaluation, permits the school to better serve the students and allows the staff to utilize their professional capacities to better serve the students. After all, we are in the business of serving students in the best possible manner, and SBM is proving to be that method of providing better service to students.

VIGNETTE #1

Planning, Evaluation of SBM

The school district showing the most promise and having the finest results after using the SBM concept is the capital city of one of the mid-western farm states. This district is a 30,000–35,000 student district located in a city of approximately 200,000 population. Its student body is diverse, particularly when considered in the light of the population of the city and state in general. The city, as the state capital, feels the impact of being under the nose of state officials.

The superintendent, when invited to assume the position some five years earlier, followed a fine superintendent who had introduced many educational innovations and had the schools performing very well, with scores on such instruments as the ITBS (Iowa Test of Basic Skills) at a level far beyond the expectations for an urban center.

As the new superintendent settled into the position, he initiated a planning process based on the CIPP (Context, Input, Process, Product) model of planning/evaluation. During the context evaluation and analysis phase, he noted that the test scores and other measures, when disaggregated by race and socioeconomic levels, were much at variance from the mainstream results. He concluded that, while the district served the majority youth very well, it did little to accommodate the needs of the minority and poor youngsters. As the data garnered from the CIPP analysis provided the information needed for the development of the strategic plan, it became clear that some attention was to be accorded the needs of the youngsters not presently being served very well.

One of the major surprises for the new superintendent was the readiness of the staff to change and the cooperative posture of the staff in thinking through a new and different structure and changing roles for their behavior. Part of this was due to the excellent leadership provided by the former superintendent, and part of it was due to a recognition of the need to better serve all students of the city. At any rate, this posture was a breath of fresh air to the new superintendent, and he set out to explore, with his staff and board, the mechanism for change in the school system.

Starting with the application of CIPP in the planning mode, the board, staff, and superintendent all noted the vast differences between the city's schools and how the clientele of each of the schools was markedly different from the others. Because the superintendent had been involved with the development of the SBM concept in another state where he had served as a high school principal and had spearheaded the drive toward the establishment of the SBM organizational pattern, he was favorably disposed when the board and staff suggested that a move toward SBM might assist those schools in meeting the needs of the students whose needs were so vastly different from the mainstream student needs.

The better part of three years was spent in developing the definitions of SBM for the district. In addition, the evaluation system was established during that time with every program, every project, every school doing a self-evaluation study using the CIPP model. Also established was a process of reporting results of evaluations to the board in terms of the CIPP acronym. Thus, every report to the board was couched in CIPP terms, and every staff member became familiar with the CIPP model and what it could do for the district.

As the SBM concept expanded and as the city's schools began to explore the flexibility inherent in the SBM concept, the need for a more formal evaluation system, with experts in evaluation available to the schools, became evident. These evaluation experts, along with planning experts, came from the existing staff of the district. The original staff was already lean and overworked so it became important to examine what they were doing and what they could forgo in order to assume the planning/evaluation responsibility.

Because of the work ethic of the staff and because of their readiness to change from longstanding, traditional roles to newly emerging support roles, the staff of the district quickly embraced the new concept. Again, the retiring superintendent had prepared the staff well for emerging changes, by making sure that all staff were generalists, rather than specialists, in their particular assignments. As generalists, they quickly accepted the emerging requirements for their operation.

The principals, too, were quick to approve and test the new arrangement by developing new and flexible approaches to serving students and by involving their staffs and parents in these developments. The principals quickly accepted the CIPP data and used it to develop programs aimed at solving the high-priority needs of the school. As a result, the schools of the city, while remaining within the boundaries set by the district strategic and work plans, have extended the horizons and scope of the educational program so that all students are served on an ongoing basis. Through use of the CIPP evaluation design, the schools can and do make changes in programs as soon as the data indicate such changes are needed to keep the program serving the student's needs.

As an added and important piece of the puzzle, the system is now developing a personnel evaluation system using CIPP as the base, but incorporating the personnel evaluation standards as defined by the National Committee on Personnel Evaluation. This is being initiated through the development of the superintendent's evaluation design and will expand to encompass the evaluation of every staff member and board member of the district.

It is striking to note the continued improvement in test scores and in other measures made in the district over the past five years. Innovative programs dot the curriculum, and staffs are encouraged to experiment and produce programs best-suited for their students. There have been a number of innovations developed, tried, evaluated, and found ineffective and dropped. The climate is one of risk taking, and developmental efforts are applauded by the entire city. The schools are important to the citizens of the city, and they want them to be the best they can.

Many organizations have become involved through the school adoption programs and have made major contributions to the betterment of the educational program offered students of the city. The major employers of the city have banded together to provide employment counseling to the students of the high schools. They also provide advice and council to the high schools as far as preemployment course offerings are concerned. It is rewarding to observe the reaction of the general citizen when asked his opinion of the school system and its effectiveness. The schools are generally accorded a very high mark from the citizens of the city, and most are comfortable participating in the decisions made at the school level. It appears as though this school system will become ever more responsive to its students and their needs.

Proof of the citizen's acceptance of the school's efforts are best explained by the manner in which the citizens have supported the financial needs of the school system by approving referendums on increasing the operating resources by increasing local taxes on property in each of the past three years. Each year, the measure has passed with an increasing majority; the last was over 75% voting for the tax increase.

In addition, the voters approved a bond issue for renovation of existing facilities and for new schools in the amount of $125,000,000. This was the result of all of the city's architects volunteering to serve as consultant to each school to get the community of each school to develop a plan for making the local school an appropriate facility for the 21st century. The superintendent was successful in having the local American Institute of Architects (AIA) chapter commit their personnel and members to conducting this activity at no cost to the district. This is but one example of how well the schools are able to tap into the resources found in the community. It is also an indication of how well the system is responding to the needs of all of its citizens and of how much they, the citizens, appreciate it. This school system can be identified as a model for urban education in the country.

VIGNETTE #2

Planning and Evaluation

Lest the reader think that every move toward the SBM type of organization is positive and leads to vast improvement in the performance of the educational system, permit the examination of a major school district in one of our southern states.

After the state legislature passed legislation requiring the development of the SBM concept in every district in the state by the end of the 1990−91 academic year, this district set out to meet the requirements of the law by informing every school community that it would be responsible for every activity conducted at the school starting in the 1991−92 academic year. The district placed no restrictions or parameters on the activities of the schools and did little to require evaluation of the efforts initiated at the various schools.

While the district had developed a strategic plan during the 1990−91 school year, it had done little to make the strategic plan the foundation for the development of school strategic plans and subsequent school improvement plans.

As the various schools developed their own strategic and work plans, it became obvious that there was no thread to hold the schools together in a common mission and no set of common priorities for each school to accept as priority objectives. Thus, each school set about the development of its own set of objectives and priorities and, then, began to operationalize the plan as accepted for the school by the local leadership team.

The district was very successful in decentralizing the decision-making process to the school level. In fact, the district now resembles an amalgamation of 120 separate school districts (the number of schools) bound together by geography. Each school has developed its own set of personnel standards and has started to effectively trade positions as set in the budget for other positions required in the school plan, with little regard for where these persons will be employed when the school changes its mind and requires a different set of skills under their educational plan. The district's personnel department is virtually a nightmare to operate for they have no idea of where the school is going and where its personnel needs are being defined. Similarly, the budgeting process is causing severe trauma because some of the schools have not yet learned that it is necessary to balance the budget and that they do not have a free hand at increasing expenditures at the site.

In an effort to corral the runaway schools, the district developed a four-area decentralization concept and placed an assistant superintendent in charge of each geographic area. However, these persons were not allocated any support staff and were given little authority and power with which to bring some order out of the chaos that exists. In the meantime, the huge curriculum and instructional staff continues on its merry way, developing programs that will never be used because that authority is now in the hands of the schools. This very large staff does not have any contact with the schools and is of little use to the district, but it remains intact because the staff has so many political allies among the board members that any move towards changing and reducing this staff would be inviting disaster.

A study of the use of resources in the district revealed that the infrastructure of the district was taking almost 50% of the budget, while the average for the state was approximately 35% for the same purpose. Thus, the district expends much more than the average district to support such unnecessary activities, while the average teacher's salary is below the state average.

The district is starting its search for its third superintendent in three years because the situation is so muddled that no person can resolve the issues separating the board and the superintendent. The board is starting to realize that they have allowed a situation to develop that could destroy the system but, as of this date, are not willing to take the bull by the horns and resolve the major issue: that of permitting each school to operate with little or no evaluation of its performance.

For the schools, an easy answer is that the district cannot meddle in their affairs because they are in compliance with the state requirement for an SBM system of organization and that it is the schools' right to make every decision that comes down the pike. This, of course, is not the case, and it is the responsibility of the board to attempt to straighten this misinformation out. In the meantime, the students are not being well served because they are being neglected while adults fight for power and territorial rights.

While there are many schools who are providing excellent programs for their students because the staff and community have the capacity to plan and implement appropriate programs, other schools that do not have the capacity to accommodate the needs of their students without assistance from the district office are sinking into oblivion. The central staff is not serving the schools because they are still operating under the old, traditional organizational pattern where they were empowered to make changes at their will. As they attempt to order the school to operate under such dictates, they find that the school tells them to go fly a kite, and they are ignored.

As the board completes its search for a new superintendent, it is hoped that the board will invite a person to assume the superintendency who is well versed in the SBM mode of operation and who can begin to pull the disparate parts of the system together again. The incoming superintendent must develop an accountability system that will evaluate every program, every project, every person in the district in order to make the system responsive to the needs of the students.

One final note: this district has an excellent teaching/administrative staff and operates in a fine community. While the board is guilty of playing politics with the education of its children, the quality of the system is such that, with proper leadership, it can recover and again take its place among the finest urban districts in the country. The electorate has started the change process by electing four new board members at the last election and have given the board a strong message.

ENDNOTES

1. Stufflebeam, Daniel (chair). 1971. *Education Evaluation and Decision Making*. Itasca, IL: F. E. Peacock Publishers, Inc., p. xxv.
2. Stufflebeam, Daniel (chair). 1971. *Education Evaluation and Decision Making*. Itasca, IL: F. E. Peacock Publishers, Inc., p. 40.
3. Stufflebeam, Daniel (chair). 1971. *Education Evaluation and Decision Making*. Itasca, IL: F. E. Peacock Publishers, Inc., p. 41.
4. Stufflebeam, Daniel (chair). 1971. *Education Evaluation and Decision Making*. Itasca, IL: F. E. Peacock Publishers, Inc., p. 80.
5. Stufflebeam, Daniel (chair). 1971. *Education Evaluation and Decision Making*. Itasca, IL: F. E. Peacock Publishers, Inc., p. 218.
6. Stufflebeam, Daniel (chair). 1971. *Education Evaluation and Decision Making*. Itasca, IL: F. E. Peacock Publishers, Inc., p. 223.
7. Candoli, Cullin, and Stufflebeam. 1994. *Superintendent's Performance Evaluation: the State of the Art*. Kalamazoo, MI: CREATE, p. 201.

Glossary

Accountabilities The areas of performance that are to be given priority in the evaluation and for which the evaluatee will be held accountable.

Accountability The responsibility for implementing a process or procedures, for justifying decisions and expenditures made and for the results or outcomes of professional activities.

Accounting The procedure of maintaining systematic records of events relating to persons, objects, or money and summarizing, analyzing, and interpreting the results thereof.

Accreditation The awarding of credentials to a school or school district by an external accrediting body.

Accrual Basis The basis of accounting under which revenues are recorded when earned or when levies are made, and expenditures are recorded as soon as they result in liabilities, regardless of when the revenue is actually received or the payment is actually made.

Accuracy The extent to which an evaluation conveys technically adequate information about the performance of an evaluatee.

Administration Management of an organization through such actions as planning, staffing, motivating, directing, controlling, communicating, and evaluating.

Administration-Dominated Budget A budgeting processing that is monopolized by management and, more specifically, the central office.

Administrative Processes Sequences of behaviors or activities that are part of the job of administrator, e.g., planning, leading, and communicating.

Administrative Unit, Intermediate A unit smaller than the state that exists primarily to provide consultative, advisory, or statistical services to local basic administrative units or to exercise certain regulatory and inspection functions over local basic administrative units.

Affirmative Action Practices Require an employer to increase the employment and promotion of certain protected classes of people.

Appropriation An authorization granted by a legislative body to make expenditures and to incur obligations for specific purposes.

Appropriation, School Money received out of funds set aside periodically by the appropriating body (school district, city council, or other governmental body) for school purposes; these funds have not been specifically collected as school taxes.

Arbitration Mandatory settlement of a dispute between groups by an agent specified as a part of the negotiated agreement.

Assessment The act of rating or describing an individual on some variable of interest.

Assessment Center A process (not necessarily a location) employing techniques to identify and measure a wide variety of administrative job skills. Most centers are designed to identify or select individuals for advancement into or within school administration. The participants engage in a number of activities that simulate behaviors typically found in management or administrative positions.

Audit The examination of records and documents and the securing of other evidence for one or more of the following purposes: (a) determining the propriety of proposed or completed transactions, (b) ascertaining whether all transaction have been recorded, and (c) determining whether transactions are accurately recorded in the accounts and in the statement drawn from the accounts.

Behavior Specific, observable actions of an individual in response to internal and external stimuli.

Benefit-Cost Analysis An analytical approach to solving problems of choice that requires the definition of objectives and the identification of alternatives and that yields the greatest benefits for any given costs or yields a required or determined amount of benefits for the least cost.

Bias Any constant error; any systemic influence on measures or on statistical results irrelevant to the purpose of measurement.

Board of Education The group of local citizens, usually (but not always) elected, who are empowered by state law to administer a public school system.

Budget A plan of financial operation incorporating an estimate of proposed expenditures for a given period or purpose and the proposed means of financing them.

Budgeting Pertains to budget planning, formulation, administration, analysis, and evaluation.

Capital Outlay An expenditure that requests the acquisition of fixed assets or additions to fixed assets that are presumed to have benefits for more than one year. It is an expenditure fund for land or existing buildings.

Categorical Aid Educational support funds provided from higher governmental levels and specifically limited to a given purpose.

Centralized Budget A budgeting process that treats all schools in a system alike. Though efficient in a sense, little consideration is permitted for differing needs among the various communities served under this type of process.

Checklist A printed form consisting of a series of statements for marking the presence or not of specific indicators or performance, such as traits, processes, or outcomes.

Competency A skill, knowledge, or experience that is suitable or sufficient for some purpose.

Comprehensive Planning Planning usually done through a comprehensive survey that reveals future goals, needs, and resources.

Constituents The groups, such as parents and the community, on whose behalf administrators act.

Content Domain A body of knowledge and/or a set of tasks or other behaviors defined (usually for a specific job or function) so that given facts or behaviors may be classified as included or excluded.

Context The set of circumstances or acts that surround and may effect a particular job situation.

Contextual Variables Indicators or dimensions that are useful in describing the facts or circumstances that surround a particular job situation and influence a person's performance of that job.

Credibility Worthy of belief or confidence by virtue of being trustworthy and possessing pertinent knowledge, skills, and experience.

Criteria (Evaluation) The dimensions of performance on which educators are judged, e.g., traits, processes, and outcomes.

Data Material gathered during the course of an evaluation that serves as the basis for information, discussion, and inference.

Data Base A comprehensive collection of data composed of files relating to specific areas of information such as pupils, staff, property, finance, instructional programs, and the community.

Data Collection Methods Any technique or set of steps used to obtain information about the performance of a program or an individual.

Decentralized Budget A budgetary process that especially applies to large school systems. Each school in a system establishes individual budgets and establishes its own educational priorities within the parameters of the total system. The process fosters a high degree of participation by a wide variety of persons.

Design (Evaluation) A representation of the set of decisions that determine how an evaluation is to be conducted, e.g., data collection schedule, report schedules, questions to be addressed, analysis plans, management plan, etc. Designs may be either preordinate or emergent.

Diagnoses The determination of strengths and weaknesses, usually in response to an identified need for improvement and as a basis for preparing a professional development plan.

Dimension An aspect or element of educator performance or of an evaluation system.

Duties The obligatory tasks, conduct, service, or functions enjoined by order, ethical code, or usage according to rank, occupation, or profession.

Duties-Based Evaluation An evaluation model based on what the educator can be legally and professionally required to do as the position holder.

Dynamic Programming A technique used for solving multistaged problems in which the output of one stage becomes the input for another stage.

Educational Budget The translation of educational needs into a financial plan that is interpreted to the public in such a way that, when formally adopted, it expresses the kind of educational program the community is willing to support for the budget period.

Employee Benefits Compensation, in addition to regular salary, provided to an employee. This may include such benefits as health insurance, life insurance, annual leave, sick leave, retirement, and social security.

Encumbrances Purchase orders, contracts, and salary or other commitments that are chargeable to an appropriation and for which a part of the appropriation is reserved. They cease to be encumbrances when paid or when actual liability is set up.

Evaluatee The person whose performance is evaluated.

Evaluation Systematic investigation of the merit or worth of something, e.g., a person's qualifications or performance in a given role or a program's success and/or failure in meeting objectives.

Evaluation Model A distinctive and comprehensive conception, approach, system, or method for producing data and judgments relating to the performance of a school, program, or educator.

Evaluation System A regularized structure and set of procedures by which an institution initiates, designs, implements, and uses evaluations or its personnel and/or programs.

Evaluator Anyone who accepts and executes responsibility for planning, conducting, and reporting evaluations.

External Evaluation Evaluation conducted by an evaluator from outside the organization in which the evaluation is occurring.

Feasibility The extent to which an evaluation is appropriate and practical for implementation.

Feedback The information and recommendations given to an educator based on the results of an evaluation, which are designed to help improve performance.

Formal Evaluation Evaluation conducted in accordance with a prescribed plan or structure.

Formative Evaluation Evaluation designed and used to promote growth and improvement in a person's performance or in a program's effectiveness.

Fund Balance The excess of the assets of a fund over its liabilities and reserves, except in the case of funds subject to budgetary accounting where, prior to the end of a fiscal period, it represents the excess of the fund's assets and estimated revenues for the period over its liabilities, reserves, and appropriations for the period; also called equity.

Goal An intended outcome that an individual or group works to achieve. Usually general in nature and in contrast to *objectives,* which are more specifically defined. Goals may differ among stakeholder groups, and they may change over time.

Grants-in-Aid Contributions made by a government unit and/or other philanthropic organization and not related to specific revenue sources of the respective government or organization, that is, a general or specific grant of resources to be used for specific or general purposes.

Informal Evaluation Evaluation conducted without a prescribed plan or structure.

Input-Output Analysis A method for analyzing the consequences of alternate spending plans throughout a governmental unit. Educators can use it to help determine optimum levels of school financing within a city or community.

Instrument An assessment device adopted, adapted, or constructed for the purpose of evaluation.

Interview A process in which a series of verbally delivered questions are posed to elicit information about the qualifications, competencies, and/or job performance of an educator.

Job Description A summary of the qualifications, role, responsibilities, duties, and working conditions associated with a specific position.

Joint Committee on Standards for Educational Evaluation A group representing the major professional educational organizations, which convene to develop a series of standards for use in assessing educational evaluation systems.

Legal Opinion The opinion of an official authorized to render it, such as an attorney, as to legality.

Local Education Agency Educational agency created by the state to carry out state policies and operate schools.

Management by Objectives (MBO) Process wherein management provides a structure of individuals and subsystems of the organization to relate their objectives to those of the larger system in a cooperative mode and to be evaluated on the achievement of the results.

Management by Objectives-Based Evaluation An evaluation model based on predetermined objectives set for and usually agreed upon by the educator.

Merit Evaluatee excellence as assessed by intrinsic qualities or performance, in contrast to extrinsic value or worth to the organization.

Needs Assessment A basic procedure for determining the quantitative and/or qualitative extent of the discrepancies between what is and what is required.

Objectives (Performance) A specific description (often written) of intended outcomes that an individual or group works to achieve. Objectives are specified so that they are observable and measurable.

Objective Evaluation Evaluation carried out in a way that minimizes error or bias due to the predilections of the evaluator.

Observation The recording of notes and evidence about performance while watching the educator on the job. This may involve direct observation or the use of videotapes.

Observer The person who makes notes about performance while watching the educator on the job. This individual is not necessarily the evaluator.

Outcomes The result of the educator's professional activities, e.g., student achievement scores, new delivery modes, teacher morale, etc. Outcomes are the products of both educator traits and processes.

Participatory Budget A budgetary process that attempts to involve school staff and lay public in the various levels of budget making. This process uses a combination of formal and informal methods to get persons involved.

Participatory Governance A governance structure that involves school staff and community in the decision-making process. This is a common trait of the Site-Based Management mode of operations.

Glossary

Performance The execution of the job of educator. Performance is a function of educator competency, as well as the specific content of the job.

Performance Contract An agreement, usually written, between the board and the superintendent stipulating the results or outcomes that the superintendent is expected to achieve and the consequences of success and/or failure in doing so.

Performance Standard A formal specification of the expected level of achievement in fulfilling a performance objective or job function.

Personnel Evaluation The systematic assessment of a person's performance and/or qualifications in relation to a role and some specified, defensible institutional purpose.

Planning The selection or identification of the overall, long-range goals, priorities, and objectives of the organization and the formulation of various courses of action to be followed in working toward achieving those goals, priorities, and objectives.

Portfolio A collection of documents or artifacts gathered to show aspects of the educator's performance, such as surveys of stakeholder groups, descriptions of professional activities, a videotape of the educator at work, letters from parents, and awards from professional organizations.

Principal The chief executive officer of a school. This person is charged with the responsibility for all operating activities at the school, including the delivery of the instructional programs, the welfare of the students and staff, and the community activities that are a part of the school's mission.

Propriety The extent to which an evaluation is conducted legally, ethically, and with due regard for the welfare of those involved in the evaluation, as well as those affected by its results.

Questionnaire A printed form consisting of a series of queries or statements that are designed to produce information about aspects of educator performance, including traits, processes, and outcomes.

Random Sampling Drawing a number of items or individuals from a larger group or population so that every item or individual has the same (and independent) chance of being chosen.

Rating Scale A printed form designed to elicit judgments on a graduated scale (usually of three to nine points) about aspects of educator performance. The scale may be numerical or descriptive.

Reliability The extent to which an evaluation provides consistent information about the performance being assessed.

Responsibilities The areas of activity that define what an educator is expected or obliged to do as the position holder. More specific and localized than duties.

Sample A part of a defined population of items or individuals.

School District A legally constituted collection of institutions, within defined geographic boundaries, that collaborate in teaching persons under college age.

School System All the schools and supporting services operated by the board of education, by a specific administrative unit, or by another organization that operates one or more schools.

Self-Evaluation The process of reviewing one's own performance.

Site-Based Decision Making The planned decentralization of certain decisions to the school site. Typically, the decisions that affect students directly are those that are decentralized.

Site-Based Committees A variety of committees appointed at the site to provide for a number of activities that are required under the SBM type of organization. These committees are representative of the parents and the staff of the school.

Site-Based Leadership Team The site-based committee that assumes the responsibility for those leadership decisions required of it.

Site-Based Management Managerial decisions and processes carried out at the local school site, rather than at a higher organizational level.

Stakeholders Those individuals who have a vested interest in the results of activities at the school. This usually includes the students, parents, community, and staff of the school. These are individuals and/or group representatives who share common interests in the educational process directed by a school or district.

Standard A principle commonly agreed upon by experts in the conduct or use of evaluation, by which to measure the value or quality of an evaluation.

Strategic Plan A total long-range plan for the conduct of school district's programs for a specific period of time. The strategic plan provides projections of all activities of the district, including finance, personnel, program delivery, and all other aspects of the conduct of the affairs of the district.

Student Outcomes Measures of the results of professional activities on students, e.g., test scores, attendance rates, and college entrance, etc.

Subjective Evaluation An evaluation not open to verification by others, not using public or communicable standards.

Summative Evaluation Evaluation designed to present conclusions about the merit and/or worth of a person's performance.

Superintendent The chief executive officer of a school system. This position is usually filled by appointment by the board of education and reports to the board of education on all matters concerning the operation of the school district.

Traits Characteristics or competencies seen as possessed by an individual, e.g., attitudes, training, experience, knowledge, and skills.

Utility The extent to which an evaluation serves the relevant information needs of evaluatees and other users.

Validity The degree to which an evaluation supports the inferences that are drawn from an evaluation.

Work Plan The specific operational plan drawn from the strategic plan of the district. The work or school improvement plan is usually a short-range plan developed annually to guide the activities of the district and schools. It is used in the evaluation of the activities of the schools and the district.

Worth The extrinsic value of the evaluatee to the organization or in relation to a purpose or need. Merit is a necessary, but not a sufficient, condition for worth.